POLICING
WHITE
SUPREMACY

ALSO BY MICHAEL GERMAN

Thinking Like a Terrorist

Disrupt, Discredit, Divide

ALSO BY BETH ZASLOFF

Hold Fast to Dreams

POLICING
WHITE
SUPREMACY

Michael German

with Beth Zasloff

THE
NEW
PRESS

NEW YORK
LONDON

Requests for permission to reproduce selections from this book should be made through our website: https://thenewpress.com/contact.

Published in the United States by The New Press, New York, 2025

Distributed by Two Rivers Distribution

ISBN 978-1-62097-706-4 (hc)
ISBN 978-1-62097-707-1 (ebook)

CIP data is available

The New Press publishes books that promote and enrich public discussion and understanding of the issues vital to our democracy and to a more equitable world. These books are made possible by the enthusiasm of our readers; the support of a committed group of donors, large and small; the collaboration of our many partners in the independent media and the not-for-profit sector; booksellers, who often hand-sell New Press books; librarians; and above all by our authors.

www.thenewpress.com

Composition by Dix Digital Prepress and Design

This book was set in Minion Pro Regular

Printed in the United States of America

10 9 8 7 6 5 4 3 2 1

CONTENTS

POLICING
WHITE
SUPREMACY

INTRODUCTION: DEMOCRACY IN DANGER

When a horde of Donald Trump supporters breached the outer perimeter of the U.S. Capitol grounds on January 6, 2021, I started receiving panicked emails from colleagues and friends in the civil rights community. One alarmed colleague forwarded a video showing Capitol Police officers abandoning their posts and removing the bike-rack-style metal barricades that rioters were pushing aside as they marched toward the Capitol. My colleague's shock was not that a violent crowd of white supremacists and far-right militants was trying to prevent Congress from certifying the election of President Joe Biden. After all, Trump had promoted the January 6 Stop the Steal rally with a tweet that said, "Be there, will be wild!"[1] We all knew that far-right militants had instigated violence at rallies across the country for years and had previously attacked state legislatures with increasing frequency. What stunned us was that law enforcement wasn't stopping them.

The concern was shared across political lines. Steve Schmidt, the former Republican operative and McCain for President campaign manager turned Never Trumper, tweeted that video clip with this comment: "It appears to me on the basis of video evidence that the US Capitol Police have been infiltrated and compromised. There is a fifth column within their ranks. They have surrendered the US Capitol to insurrectionists without a shot fired."[2]

My first reaction was to seek evidence that could defend the police response. I knew from my sixteen-year career in the FBI that a small snippet of a video can often distort what's happening, rather than depict it. After looking at the video more closely, I noted to my colleagues that, while the camera was focused on the officers pulling the barricades aside and seemingly letting the insurgents rush through, several other rioters could be seen in the background jumping over an unmanned vehicle barrier. The perimeter had already been lost, so there was no reasonable option for the officers at the barricades except to fall back to a more defensible position.

In fact, I had seen the Capitol Police deploy a similar tactic during a large, peaceful anti-war rally in 2007. At that protest, I watched from a short distance as a small splinter group of anarchists marched toward a phalanx of police officers decked out in riot gear. I expected the police to respond to the provocation with indiscriminate force, which had become a common sight as law enforcement adopted a more militant approach to protests after 9/11. Instead, the police picked up the barricades, moved back about twenty-five yards, and set up a new, more defensible perimeter closer to the Capitol. The tactical retreat took the steam out of the anarchists' approach and served the Capitol Police's mandate to protect the building and its occupants rather than the grounds. No violence occurred, and there were no injuries to police or protesters.[3]

My hope that the Capitol Police were similarly prepared and employing this same tactic on January 6, 2021, was quickly thwarted. Cable news channels broadcast images of woefully outnumbered police officers, many without helmets or protective gear, being beaten and overwhelmed. The mob breached the Capitol building too easily, and members of Congress and the vice president fled for their lives as the rioters marched through the halls of Congress shouting, "Hang Pence" and "Where's Nancy?," with a scaffold built outside to make the threat appear more than rhetorical.

I was dumbfounded by law enforcement's clear lack of preparation. The attack on the Capitol had been planned in public and was carried out by groups that had become infamous for their violence and threatening misbehavior at far-right rallies, including at two post-election protests in Washington, D.C., over the previous two months. There were the Proud Boys, a "Western chauvinist" gang that had committed violence against their perceived enemies at public rallies all across the country since Trump was elected; the Oath Keepers, a far-right militia group whose members had previously participated in armed standoffs against federal law enforcement in Nevada and Oregon; and the Three Percenters, a decentralized paramilitary movement whose adherents had committed murders, bombed mosques, and plotted to kill police, among other crimes. Though some of the far-right militants belonging to these groups would deny they were white supremacists, they had often appeared at Trump rallies side by side with avowed racist groups, where they committed violence in common cause. January 6 was no different.

My familiarity with these groups doesn't come from following them on the obscure social media platforms they favor for imaginary protection from government monitoring. I got a bellyful of their hateful rhetoric when I worked undercover in white supremacist and militia groups in the 1990s. Instead, I study the government's response—or lack of response—to far-right violence. In doing so, I follow academic researchers, reporters, and anti-racism activists who study, cover, and oppose far-right militants, which made it easy for me to identify the modern "alt-right" white nationalist and far-right militant symbols in the images broadcast on January 6. While over the years white supremacists have adopted new branding and catchphrases to fool the uninitiated, the ideas they promote today are very similar to what they've pushed in the past.

Representatives of obscure white nationalist, nativist, and alt-right groups that started as online communities and internet memes, like the fictional nation Kekistan, VDARE, and the Groyper Army, flew their flags alongside historical American Revolution–era banners co-opted by more traditional far-right militants to symbolize their desire to overthrow the government.[4] Many in the crowd flashed the "OK" hand signal, which had become a favorite means for white nationalists to troll and confuse onlookers since Trump was elected in 2016. Others were more obvious about their beliefs, including the rioter who wore a "Camp Auschwitz" sweatshirt.[5] It was deeply troubling for me to see hateful symbols that once operated under the radar so openly flaunted. One of the modern-day insurrectionists carried the Confederate battle flag proudly through the Capitol, something the Confederate Army had never accomplished before it surrendered in 1865.

Many in the crowd were known to law enforcement, having previously been convicted of serious crimes. Some gained prominence and rose to leadership positions within the militant movement because they had been filmed engaging in violence at previous far-right rallies. The *Washington Post* reported that "dozens" of the white supremacists who came to Washington, D.C., for the January 6 rally had previously been placed on the U.S. government's terrorist watch lists.[6] Several rioters assaulting the Capitol carried firearms, knives, at least one spear, and one improvised explosive device.[7] Others used batons, clubs, bear spray, and stun guns and turned fire extinguishers into improvised weapons.[8] Some even attacked police officers with flagpoles sporting "Blue Lives Matter" banners.[9]

As the violence outside the Capitol escalated, I waited for reinforcements to arrive to quell the riot. Commenters on cable news asked why the National Guard wasn't there, but I wondered why there were so few police, especially in comparison to forces usually deployed in preparation for any large rally. The U.S. Capitol Police Department is relatively well staffed, with over 1,800 officers. The Washington, D.C., Metropolitan Police Department, which operates under federal authority, has more officers per capita than any medium-to-large city in the United States. State and local police departments in nearby Virginia and Maryland regularly train with them and deploy on joint law enforcement operations in the District.[10] And because it is the seat of the U.S. government, thousands of federal law enforcement officers from the FBI, Department of Homeland Security, and an array of other agencies work in the District of Columbia as well. I had seen the U.S. Park Police and Metropolitan Police Department put down a riotous protest before, so I know they are well equipped and more than capable. Why weren't they able to muster quick-reaction forces to the Capitol once the riot began or as it raged over several hours, putting Congress's ability to certify a presidential election increasingly at risk?

I knew that the lack of preparation could not be blamed on inadequate resources for intelligence. White supremacist and far-right militant violence is considered a domestic terrorism threat, which means guarding against it falls under the purview of federal law enforcement. Since the September 11, 2001, al Qaeda terrorist attacks on the United States, Congress lavished federal, state, and local law enforcement agencies with resources and broad new authorities to increase their intelligence collection and information-sharing capabilities. The FBI's Joint Terrorism Task Forces, which incorporate other federal, state, and local law enforcement entities, expanded significantly. Congress established the Department of Homeland Security and funded a national network of state and local law enforcement intelligence fusion centers, which were given access to federal counterterrorism intelligence systems. How had these powerful networks failed so spectacularly once again?

If their own intelligence networks hadn't warned them of the gathering storm, FBI, DHS, and Capitol Police officials could simply have read a front-page article in the *Washington Post* on January 5, 2021. The headline read, "Pro-Trump Forums Erupt with Violent Threats Ahead of Wednesday's Rally Against the 2020 Election."[11] The warning signs for serious violence were so clear that the Hotel Harrington and its locally (in)famous bar, which had become a favorite haunt of Proud Boys during earlier Trump rallies, closed down from January 4 through 6. The owners decided to forgo three nights' revenue rather than host the far-right militants again and subject their employees to potential harassment and injury. This decision was likewise prominently reported in the Washington press.[12] It was impossible that none of these warnings circulated through the intelligence networks, yet neither the FBI nor the DHS produced a threat assessment for the rally, a common practice for any large gathering, from sporting events to music festivals as well as protests.[13]

I also knew, however, that far-right violence was a blind spot for federal, state, and local law enforcement. I left the FBI in 2004 after blowing the whistle on the FBI's continuing mismanagement of terrorism investigations. In my subsequent work at the American Civil Liberties Union and the Brennan Center for Justice, I documented how the FBI's post-9/11 counterterrorism programs deprioritized investigations of white supremacist violence, preferring instead to focus on perceived threats from Muslim, Black, Native American, and immigrant activists, environmentalists, and progressive protest groups. It should not have surprised me when this failure to acknowledge and defend against white supremacist violence threatened the very core of American democracy on January 6.

After 9/11, white supremacist violence rarely made the national news, and certainly didn't receive the level of coverage that followed terror attacks by Muslims. But white supremacists and far-right militias continued their deadly ways. Examples include the shooting of three South Asian men by an Aryan Brotherhood member seeking revenge against Muslims (2001), a white supremacist's ambush murder of three Pittsburgh police officers (2009), a border militia's home invasion murders of a Latino American father and daughter in Arizona (2009), and a neo-Nazi's shooting rampage at a Sikh temple in Wisconsin (2012).[14] Many self-identified experts on the subject suggest that white supremacist activity increased after Barack Obama was elected president in 2008, but it had been happening all along, just outside the media spotlight. The Extremist Crime Database maintained by the University of Maryland documented 375 far-right homicide incidents from 1990 to 2010.[15] The Combating Terrorism Center at West Point counted 637 far-right fatalities over that period, and 194 from 2001 through 2007 alone.[16]

When Donald Trump started his 2015 campaign for the White House with explicitly racist remarks, he opened a door for white supremacist and far-right militants to support his candidacy. Groups that once operated in the shadows were emboldened to come out in the open in public displays of violence, most notably the 2017 Unite the Right rally in Charlottesville, Virginia. The violence persisted and became more flagrant thereafter. In a multitude of assaults, vehicular attacks, bombings, shootings, and stabbings, far-right militants killed 175 people from 2017, the year of the Unite the Right rally, through 2022, according to the Anti-Defamation League.[17]

Increased visibility brought increased government attention. In 2019, the U.S. House of Representatives started holding some of the first hearings since the post-9/11 "war on terror" began that focused on domestic terrorism, and specifically on white supremacist violence, its deadliest form. Yet law enforcement at the federal, state, and local levels continued practices that ignored or mismanaged the white supremacist threat, overpolicing overwhelmingly peaceful Black Lives Matter protesters, anti-fascists, and environmentalists while underpolicing white supremacist violence.

Why does law enforcement seem unable to assess and defend against white supremacist violence properly, especially when police officers are so often its victims? The root of this blindness lies at least in part in affinity for far-right ideals among law enforcement officials, if not outright bias in their favor. These biases undoubtedly came into play in law enforcement's failure to prepare for violence at the January 6 Stop the Steal rally. Law enforcement is traditionally a conservative profession that remains predominately white and male, a key demographic for supporting Donald Trump, and sympathy for pro-Trump rioters certainly played a role in how police misperceived their threat.[18] In addition, law enforcement bias often manifests as antipathy for the opponents of the far right—racial and social justice activists, environmentalists, and protesters opposing police violence. As just one example, weeks before the attack, a high-level Department of Homeland Security intelligence official publicly reported that his superiors at the top of the department had instructed him to downplay threats of white supremacist violence in his unit's intelligence reports, and to focus instead on highlighting anti-fascist violence.[19]

The January 6 attack also turned public attention to another alarming problem: actual affiliation with white supremacist and far-right militant groups by members of law enforcement. While most of the Capitol Police and Metropolitan Police Department officers at the Capitol that day fought valiantly to prevent the rioters from entering the Capitol or harming those inside, images of some officers appearing to fraternize with the insurrectionists, and even taking selfies with them, made me think Steve Schmidt might be right that law enforcement had been compromised. It quickly became clear that more than two dozen law enforcement officers from across the country attended the Stop the Steal rally alongside white nationalists and far-right militants. Several of these officers were later charged with crimes for their participation in the attempt to overthrow our democracy.

It is hard to overstate the danger that white supremacist police pose to people they are sworn to protect. Yet the FBI has shown stubborn resistance to acknowledging the problem. Just over three months before the attack on the Capitol, I testified in the House of Representatives regarding the unfortunate persistence of racism, white supremacy, and far-right militancy within law enforcement.[20] The subcommittee chairman who invited me, Rep. Jamie Raskin (D-MD), also asked FBI officials to testify at the hearing, but they refused. Raskin said the bureau managers disavowed previously released FBI intelligence reports that had warned about white supremacy in law enforcement and stated they did not currently consider it a significant concern. They were wrong, blinded by their biases and unwilling to let evidence rather than their personal and institutional prejudices dictate their counterterrorism policies. The January 6 attack made the threat posed by white supremacy and far-right militancy in law enforcement much harder to deny.

This book is a call to action. It underlines the urgent need for law enforcement at federal, state, and local levels to better protect the public from far-right violence and to root out overt racism and white supremacy within the ranks. It also addresses the complicated relationship between police and white supremacy writ large. Through U.S. history, police have been marshaled to enforce racist laws, starting from the American colonies' slave patrols. Today, white supremacy endures in the well-documented racial inequities in our political, economic, and social institutions, particularly the criminal justice system. Inaction by law enforcement in the face of white supremacist violence, including racist police violence, supports these discriminatory systems and sends a message about whose lives matter most in America.

The good news is that fixing deficiencies in policing violent forms of white supremacy is more straightforward than one might imagine. Congress has already provided sufficient authority and resources for law enforcement to investigate, prosecute, and punish white supremacist and far-right violence. When law enforcement employs these tools, they are very effective. As of this writing, the U.S. Justice Department has charged more than 1,200 people who attacked the Capitol on January 6, including members of well-known white supremacist and far-right militant groups who it successfully convicted of crimes of terrorism and sedition. Most of those charged have pleaded guilty or were convicted at trial.[21] Federal, state, and local prosecutors have also leveled dozens of charges against a defeated former president of the United States and his co-conspirators for attempting illegally to overturn the results of a free and fair election.

What has been lacking is the determination to prioritize the investigation and prosecution of far-right violence as a serious national security threat. Hundreds of rioters who attacked the Capitol on

January 6 have yet to be charged, despite being identified by volunteer "sedition hunters" who reported them to the FBI. And far-right militants continue to engage in public violence without a sufficient law enforcement response.[22] The Justice Department and FBI have so far resisted congressional demands to collect comprehensive national data on the violent acts perpetrated by white supremacist and far-right militants. Acknowledging that white supremacist violence is a serious problem is the first step, and gathering the data that proves it is the next. Once the problem is accurately scoped, enforcement efforts can be properly tailored, and the agencies responsible for addressing these crimes can be held publicly accountable.

To address white supremacist violence effectively, law enforcement needs approaches that are more strategic and more focused: more strategic by using data to evaluate the extent and nature of white supremacist violence, and by understanding militants' overarching goal of normalizing and legitimizing this violence as a political tool; and more focused because law enforcement must concentrate its efforts and resources on evidence of violent criminal activity, rather than policing political expression and associations, no matter how odious. Policing violence, not ideology, will guard against biased investigations and ensure that law enforcement resources are targeted toward real threats, not disfavored political groups.

Effectively policing white supremacy also means limiting the role of police. Instead of expanding law enforcement authorities and resources, our nation should invest in and empower the communities impacted by white supremacist and far-right militant violence. Responses must include restorative approaches to hate crimes and far-right violence, which can help rebuild the social cohesion that white supremacists are trying to destroy.

As the title suggests, *Policing White Supremacy* offers concrete proposals for reforms needed in a national strategy to address far-right violence. The book will also demonstrate the ways reactionary state and nonstate actors use violence to maintain white-dominated, racially discriminatory systems and turn back progress in our pluralistic democracy.

The first part of this book describes the nature of the white supremacist threat by tracing the growing alignment between law enforcement, far-right militant groups, and the far-right establishment from the 2015 Trump campaign launch through the January 6, 2021, attack on the Capitol. Part 2 describes the obstacles that impede effective enforcement, including the Justice Department's deferral of hate crime investigations to state and local law enforcement and its resistance to collecting complete and objective data about white supremacist and far-right violence. It sets forth proposals for a focused and strategic approach that narrows police powers, ends tolerance of explicit racism and white supremacist affiliation within federal, state, and local governments, and mitigates the harm that racist law enforcement violence inflicts on vulnerable communities.

On January 6, 2021, white supremacist violence revealed itself as the menace it always was: a mortal threat to our democracy. Yet as the shock of that attack has worn off, just as it did with thousands of white supremacist outrages that came before it, the complacency with which our government views racist violence has returned.

Thousands of Americans across the country poured into the streets in 2020 to protest the police killings of George Floyd Jr., Breonna Taylor, and too many other unarmed Black people. They demanded accountability for police brutality, an end to police racism, and a new, less violent, more supportive, and accountable vision of public safety in their communities. Though the protests were overwhelmingly peaceful, they were met with violence from white supremacists and far-right militants and, even more often, from riot police, National Guard, and federal agents. Politicians and law enforcement leaders acknowledged that the status quo was untenable, but the reforms they implemented were illusory. Police killings reached a record high in 2022, then again in 2023, and Black people remain disproportionately represented as victims.[23]

Better policing won't solve white supremacy or cure racism. It will take a much broader whole-of-society effort to correct the persistent racial disparities and discrimination that infect all our government institutions, particularly the criminal justice system. But law enforcement has an essential role to play, as it did on January 6, when the police officers who chose to uphold the law protected democracy from a mob determined to destroy it.

Reactionary forces have not rested, and white supremacist conspiracies are increasingly part of mainstream political discourse. Our democracy remains in peril. If it is to survive, we must end tolerance for racist policing and prioritize far-right violence as a risk to the safety and security of all Americans.

I know that many in law enforcement, along with prosecutors, judges, politicians, community leaders, and activists, recognize the harm that racist violence inflicts on the communities they serve and want to be part of a solution. This book is dedicated to the officers, agents, and analysts at the street level doing the day-to-day work to keep their communities safe and hold their profession accountable.

A NOTE ON TERMINOLOGY

The broader white supremacist movement includes reactionary groups that operate in the same ecosystems, share a common lexicon—particularly in identifying and describing their enemies—and use violence and the threat of violence to recruit, organize, and accomplish their political goals. Within these groups, terminology is varied and highly contested. Some, like neo-Nazis, fully embrace the term "white supremacist," while others prefer "white nationalist," "white separatist," "racialist," or the newer "identitarian." Others claim to reject white supremacy and even recruit nonwhite members but express specific forms of bigotry such as anti-Semitism, Islamophobia, homophobia, or nativism. Some groups are animated by mainstream right-wing or conservative issues, such as anti-tax, anti-immigration, anti-abortion, or anti-gun-control, but take their advocacy to an extreme position that justifies using violence against their political opposition, and often organize alongside white supremacists. Many individuals mobilize for violence in common cause with these groups but don't formally join one. Some of these individuals live on the fringes of society, but others, in the military, law enforcement, and public office, have the power to employ state violence in pursuit of their white supremacist agendas.

The leaders of these violent groups often use debates about the proper terminology regarding their beliefs as a recruiting tool, knowing that public discussions about the finer details of their ideology and political goals will spark interest among some listeners, no matter how odious they sound to the average person. They also use these discussions about their ideology to divert the conversation away from the criminal violence they perpetrate. For the purposes of this book, to be as comprehensive as possible while avoiding distracting arguments about complex beliefs, and to make clear that I am focusing on the violent elements within the movement, I use the phrase "white supremacist and far-right militants" to describe the parts of the movement that law enforcement needs to address.

Part One

FROM THE SHADOWS TO THE SPOTLIGHT

1

UNITING THE RIGHT

On the evening of August 11, 2017, hundreds of torch-bearing white supremacists chanting "Jews will not replace us" and "Blood and soil" marched across the University of Virginia campus, and then descended upon a small group of students and community members who had gathered at the Rotunda in protest. The torch-bearers surrounded the anti-racist protesters, cutting off any escape, then attacked them with fists, sticks, pepper spray, lighter fluid, and flaming torches, as campus police watched passively from an elevated position.[1] The University Police Department had been alerted about the unpermitted torch march well before it began. But they rebuffed offers of support from the Virginia State Police and local police in Charlottesville and Albemarle County, who, according to mutual assistance agreements, required a request from university police before they could respond to on-campus events.[2] Still, some of these state and local officers began to draw nearer in anticipation of trouble. It was only after the brawling ended that university police called them in to help disperse the remaining crowd. Additional skirmishes broke out as some of the departing white supremacists crossed paths with worshippers leaving a nearby prayer vigil.

Despite the violence happening right in front of them, police made just one arrest that evening. The failure to police the torch march properly was just the latest in a long line of opportunities to avert a tragedy that law enforcement simply forfeited. It wouldn't be the last.

Police inaction that Friday emboldened the racist militants and set the stage for even greater violence the following day, when hundreds of heavily armed white supremacists and far-right militants from across the country converged in Charlottesville for the long-planned and well-publicized Unite the Right rally.[3] In preparation for the Saturday rally, the official operations plans issued by the Charlottesville Police and the Virginia State Police authorized normal use-of-force policies, including arrests for any observed unlawful conduct. The morning of the event, however, police leaders ordered officers not to go into the crowds if they felt their own safety was compromised. They told the officers "not to break up fights" or interrupt "mutual combat," according to an independent review conducted by former U.S. attorney Timothy J. Heaphy, which was commissioned by the Charlottesville City Council after the rally to evaluate the law enforcement response.[4] Despite the violence at the previous evening's torch march and many other clear indications that the white supremacists could and would commit violence at the rally, law enforcement officials—at the federal, state, local, and university levels—remained passive in their response. The result was that the police officers on the ground stood down and watched as heavily armed white supremacists rampaged through Charlottesville. The police declared an unlawful assembly and pushed the white supremacists out of Emancipation Park, where the contested statue of Confederate general Robert E. Lee was to serve as the centerpiece for their rally. But this action only increased the violence by forcing the militants back into the streets, where anti-racist protesters, clergy members, journalists, and members of the public had gathered in opposition.

Police watched but did not intervene as Unite the Right militants assaulted people with flagpoles, shields, projectiles, and pepper spray. When residents sought police assistance or pointed out people who had attacked them, police standing behind barricades refused to respond.[5] A Klansman standing in the middle of the street drew, aimed, and fired a pistol at a Black protester, then retreated past a long line of police officers without being arrested.[6] The violence reached a crescendo when James Alex Fields, a white nationalist who had come from Ohio to march in the rally, accelerated his Dodge Challenger through an intersection the police had abandoned and into a group of anti-racist protesters, killing Heather Heyer and seriously injuring dozens of others.

Despite scores of violent acts taking place, police made just four arrests that Saturday. These included Fields, who was charged with murder and hate crimes, one other white supremacist charged with a misdemeanor firearms violation, and two anti-racist protesters charged with disorderly conduct and misdemeanor assault and battery.[7] By contrast, just months earlier, in Washington, D.C., police brought felony charges against more than two hundred people arrested at the 2017 anti-Trump Disrupt J20 protests because they happened to be on the same block when windows were broken.[8] In Charlottesville, dozens of assaults causing serious bodily harm were committed within clear view of police officers, who did not intervene.

It is reasonable to imagine that the deficient police response to the Unite the Right violence was the result of an intelligence failure. But the Heaphy report identified the intelligence operations before and during the two days of racist rioting as one of the few things that "went right."[9] Law enforcement officials planning and responding to the Unite the Right rally received "reliable, accurate, and timely information" from the Virginia Fusion Center (a state police intelligence center) and the FBI, along with rally organizers, their opponents, and Charlottesville residents. Law enforcement social media monitoring operations tracked the plans of those coming to the rally, as well as those coming to protest it. Police also coordinated directly with "security members" and a "security manager" designated by the Unite the Right organizers, though it does not appear these individuals were licensed to provide security services, as required by Virginia law.[10]

During the event, police officials in an on-site command post had access to the rally participants' real-time public social media postings. The command post also included live video feeds from a police helicopter and from cameras throughout the city, which together covered the entire area of operations and captured events as they occurred. At least one police department had deployed several undercover officers into the crowd.

As the Heaphy report states, law enforcement "could not have been reasonably surprised by what occurred on August 12."[11] Another evaluation of the Virginia State Police performance, conducted by the International Association of Chiefs of Police, likewise assessed that a "robust" and "focused" effort by the Virginia Fusion Center to gather and share protest-related intelligence before the rally "led seasoned and experienced analysts to believe that the parties scheduled to participate were planning to be aggressive and violent."[12] Both reviews also determined that law enforcement intelligence operations disseminated timely and relevant warnings to the proper authorities.

This conclusion, reached in two separate evaluations, begs a question that the reports don't adequately answer. If law enforcement leaders knew the white supremacist rally was likely to result in violence, why did they adopt and maintain a passive approach that allowed that violence to occur and the perpetrators to escape without identification or arrest? Timely and accurate intelligence is worthless if it doesn't compel law enforcement officials to take the actions necessary to mitigate the threat. Both reports could be faulted for giving too much credence to law enforcement excuses that simple training deficiencies caused the failure, especially given the deadly results of their inaction. Despite this shortcoming, the reviews do indicate how the intelligence had been analyzed through a biased prism.

BOTH-SIDES FRAMING UNDERMINES ANALYSIS

First, the reports suggest that law enforcement—and the reviewers themselves—perceived the violence at the rally as the result of two opposing groups converging in Charlottesville for "mutual combat." Both reviews show that law enforcement officials preparing for the Unite the

Right rally were as concerned about Black Lives Matter and anti-fascist counterprotesters as they were about the white supremacists and militias. When his report was released, Timothy Heaphy summarized his view of the deficiency in the police response to the *Daily Progress*: "It was treated like a free-speech event, not like an event in which people who hate each other would want to fight."[13] The International Association of Chiefs of Police contributed to this both-sides narrative, describing the difficulties in dealing with a "new era of protest" that involves white supremacists and counterprotesters bringing firearms and other weapons "with a stated intent to cause physical harm to others."[14] Law enforcement has long drawn this false equivalence, ignoring significant evidence indicating that only one side has regularly engaged in deadly violence.

As important from an intelligence and terrorism prevention perspective, the both-sides framing also ignored the tactical history of far-right militant mobilization. Staging public demonstrations as a method of instigating violence is a timeworn tactic for far-right militants, going back to the Nazi Party's storm troopers during the Weimar Republic. Then as now, fascist groups choose to hold public rallies and marches in communities where they know they have strong political opposition. They hope to draw their political opponents out to protest the rallies so that they can then attack them, disingenuously claiming self-defense or an infringement of their speech and association rights as justification.[15]

The far-right militants typically bring deadly weapons, often concealed, in anticipation of committing violence at these rallies, and are therefore able to inflict more serious wounds during clashes with those protesting them. Their strategy isn't necessarily to win these battles, but to use them for propaganda purposes. The spectacle of street violence gives the group broad media attention and increases its standing within the far-right movement for its willingness to take action to further the cause, risking bodily harm or potential legal consequences. If the group suffers injuries in the clashes, they become martyrs, all the better to present themselves as victims, a hallmark of fascist organizing. The public brawling also draws attention away from deadly far-right violence taking place outside of public view.[16]

So long as they avoid serious legal consequences, the perpetrators of street violence also expand their ability to recruit and gain support from authoritarian-minded politicians, government officials, and financiers. "Among the [Nazi Party's] tactics were low-level street violence, mass-media propaganda, and seeking patronage from respectable figures and organizations," wrote history professor Brian Crim, in a description that is just as applicable to today's far-right militants.[17] The danger increases when the would-be authoritarian elites in government and business take advantage of the public's concerns to exploit this street violence, either by conspiring directly with the militants or simply by exploiting their violence to seek additional powers.

The far-right tactic of staging rallies and marches to provoke street violence is also used to confuse the general public about which party—the fascists or their opponents—is the instigator of the violence. How the police, politicians, and the media respond to these provocations influences the public's interpretation as well. The militants often brand these events as political demonstrations and demand law enforcement protection of their "free speech" rights. When the police comply, it creates the appearance that the authorities side with the far right, which draws the ire and vitriol of their opponents toward law enforcement as well. This dynamic creates an opportunity for the far-right militants to bond with the police over their shared disdain for anti-fascist community organizers.

The far-right militants rely on this tactic because it often works. But the deception can be easily pierced by examining their statements, the weapons they bring to the "rallies," and, most importantly, their violent criminal histories.

ALIGNING INTERESTS

Law enforcement well understood this far-right tactic in the 1990s, when I worked undercover in far-right groups.[18] Police recognized that the fascist rallies were intended to provoke violence, and law enforcement did what they could to identify the most dangerous individuals beforehand, taking all possible lawful measures to prevent them from being able to do harm at the events, or to arrest them immediately after they did. But the following two decades saw a political polarization in the United States, in which many in law enforcement have found themselves more aligned politically with far-right militants on a host of issues.

Part of this aligning of interests was triggered by the horror of the al Qaeda terrorist attacks on September 11, 2001, and the subsequent wars in the Middle East and North Africa. Racist counterterrorism training materials produced by the Defense Department and FBI depicted Muslims and Arabs as backward and inherently violent, fueling anti-Muslim sentiment in the military and law enforcement.[19] News media platformed fringe anti-Muslim activists as counterterrorism experts, who mainstreamed Islamophobic and xenophobic sentiments into public discourse about public safety.[20] Security measures were enhanced, taking precedence over other values including equal protection and civil rights. The increased fear of foreigners extended to the border with Mexico: immigration issues, normally treated as a civil matter, transformed into the front lines of the counterterrorism fight for the newly created Department of Homeland Security.

Many white supremacists expressed early admiration for al Qaeda after the attacks on the World Trade Center and the Pentagon, which they saw as command structures of the "Zionist Occupied Government," and therefore legitimate targets. But as Islamophobia and xenophobia became more mainstream, they quickly pivoted to embrace anti-Muslim activism, often alongside conservative activist groups and first responders. At the same time, many far-right militia leaders sensed the increased patriotic sentiments toward the federal government as we became a nation at war and remodeled themselves as border militias—auxiliaries assisting U.S. Border Patrol and immigration agents rather than adversaries of the federal government. Their uniforms of choice began to match the U.S. special operations soldiers and sailors who were widely respected for carrying the burden of the heaviest combat rotations overseas. Law enforcement likewise adopted more militarized attire, equipment, and tactics as many veterans of "war on terror" operations were recruited into law enforcement. An affinity for military-styled firearms became another area of common interest. Firearms ranges, gun shows, and military expos have always been places where far-right militants can mingle with law enforcement.

When the Black Lives Matter movement started engaging in street demonstrations following the 2014 police killing of unarmed Black teenager Michael Brown in Ferguson, Missouri, white supremacists and far-right militants seized another opportunity to align with police and stoke the racial conflict, hoping to provoke a wider race war.[21] The Oath Keepers, a far-right militant organization, directly recruited from the ranks of law enforcement and the military—too often successfully despite their seditious rhetoric and criminal activities.[22] In 2014, the same year that Oath Keepers from across the country participated in an armed standoff with federal law enforcement officers in Nevada, a group of Missouri Oath Keepers took rooftop positions to overlook the Ferguson Black Lives Matter protest.[23] In response to public criticism, the St. Louis Police chief asked them to leave, threatening to arrest them for providing private security services without a license after they initially refused.[24] At anniversary demonstrations the following year, however, police reportedly allowed another group of heavily armed Oath Keepers to roam through the Ferguson protests, purportedly to provide security for Infowars journalist Joe

Biggs, who was later convicted for his role leading the Proud Boys' attack on the U.S. Capitol.[25]

Many far-right militias also started appearing at Blue Lives Matter demonstrations—a pro–law enforcement response in opposition to the Black Lives Matter movement. Far-right militants often carried thin blue line flags or wore them on their uniforms. The groups the FBI called "anti-government" militias in the 1990s now needed a new name as they adopted a pro-Trump, pro-police posture. But law enforcement officials should not have been fooled, as these far-right militants continued to kill police officers at a greater rate than any other extremist groups. The Southern Poverty Law Center documented forty police officers killed by far-right militants between 2005 and 2018. In 2020, far-right Boogaloo militants, so named for their goal of inciting a new civil war, exploited law enforcement's focus on the Black Lives Matter protesters to attack police. These incidents included a firebomb plot targeting police officers at a Black Lives Matter protest in Las Vegas, the firing of several AK-47 rounds at a Minneapolis police station that resulted in its evacuation, and the ambush murder of two federal officers at a U.S. Homeland Security facility in Oakland.[26] Yet research showed that, during this same time period, police used violence against leftist protesters three times more often than against far-right demonstrators.[27]

UNEQUAL PROTEST POLICING

Visible evidence of police favoritism at far-right public gatherings further entrenched the perception that protecting the free speech rights of violent white supremacists was more important to law enforcement than protecting the victims of racist violence. In 2016, police in Anaheim, California, charged seven anti-racism protesters with assault at a violent KKK rally in 2016, but not the Ku Klux Klansman who stabbed three people.[28] In Huntington Beach, California, state park police refused to investigate the battery of *OC Weekly* journalists by members of the Rise Above Movement, a white supremacist fight club, at a March 2017 pro-Trump march, citing a lack of resources.[29] The Orange County district attorney somehow found the resources to prosecute an anti-fascist protester who attempted to defend the journalists by slapping one of the white supremacist attackers, however.[30] Neo-Nazis stabbed eight anti-racist protesters and a Black journalist at a June 2017 white supremacist rally in Sacramento, but police treated the knife-wielding skinheads as victims, and sought their cooperation in charging several of the wounded protesters with crimes.[31] Journalists and activists captured video of white supremacists and far-right militants engaging in street battles with anti-racism protesters at several lightly policed rallies in Berkeley, California, and Portland, Oregon, throughout 2017. The militants used those widely viewed and publicly available videos to promote themselves to leadership positions within their organizations, yet law enforcement subsequently charged few of them with crimes.

The failure of federal, state, and local law enforcement to pursue more effectively the perpetrators of violence at events leading up to, during, and after the Unite the Right rally allowed these far-right groups to expand and intensify their campaign of political violence across the country. It conditioned far-right militants to believe they could commit violence at public demonstrations without consequences, and often with the express support of law enforcement and elected public officials.

Individuals and groups that participated in the Unite the Right rally later engaged in threats, violence, and other criminal activity at white supremacist rallies in Florida, Michigan, Pennsylvania, and Tennessee; at far-right events in New York, Oregon, Rhode Island, and Washington State; and at anti-vaccine rallies in California and LGBTQ+ Pride events in Idaho and elsewhere before coming to D.C. in 2020 and committing violence at two post-election pro-Trump rallies.[32] The weak law enforcement response to this nationwide surge of public violence allowed these groups to establish national support networks that included military officials, law enforcement officers, and elected government officials. Far-right groups used social media to promote their violence, recruit, and raise funds. The regular use of interstate travel to stage events, given the lack of federal law enforcement attention, enabled these groups to build the logistical capabilities necessary to bring thousands of people willing to commit violence to Washington, D.C., on January 6, 2021, to prevent the peaceful transition of executive power to a duly elected president of the United States.

The restrained protest policing methods employed at violent far-right demonstrations stood in stark contrast to an aggressive, militarized, and indiscriminately violent police reaction to protests staged by anti-racists, anti-capitalists, and environmentalists, particularly when led by people of color. Black Lives Matter protests across the country were met by excessive police violence at a scale not seen since the 1960s, featuring arbitrary kettling (where police officers form cordons to restrain a crowd), mass arrests, flash-bangs, tear gas and pepper spray, baton strikes, rubber bullets, and real bullets. At protests following the May 2020 police killing of George Floyd, police made roughly seventeen thousand arrests, mostly for nonviolent misdemeanors, though many of the charges were ultimately dismissed for lack of evidence.[33] The Justice Department also charged more than three hundred people for federal crimes "committed adjacent to or under the guise of peaceful demonstrations."[34]

Attorney Greg Doucette collected videos documenting 958 acts of police violence during the 2020 protests.[35] The investigative journalism group Bellingcat documented 147 acts of police violence specifically targeting journalists covering the protests.[36] Law-enforcement-involved shootings during BLM protests resulted in at least two deaths.[37] Eight people were blinded by police munitions.[38] *The Guardian* reported that lawsuits alleging illegal police violence during the 2020 Black Lives Matter protests cost taxpayers in cities across the United States over $80 million in legal settlements.[39]

These data are all the more astonishing because, despite the sensationalized reporting regarding these protests, a *Washington Post* study of 7,305 protest events during the summer of 2020 found they were "overwhelmingly peaceful," with fewer than 4 percent resulting in property damage, and only 2.7 percent resulting in injuries reported by protesters, police, or bystanders.[40] More than a dozen after-action reviews by police departments across the country found police mishandled the protests, but they blamed a lack of proper training, and specifically did not examine racial bias as a potential cause.[41] Other analyses show that some of the most serious violence occurring at or near Black Lives Matter protests either was not attributable to the protesters or was instigated by unnecessarily aggressive law enforcement tactics.[42]

A significant portion of the violence was committed by far-right militants. At protests following the police shooting of Jamar Clark in Minneapolis, masked white supremacists shot at a Black Lives Matter encampment outside a police station, wounding five.[43] A Ku Klux Klansman rammed his truck into Black Lives Matter protesters in Virginia.[44] A white Texan whose racist texts and social media comments included fantasizing about attacking Black Lives Matter activists intentionally drove his car into a protest, then shot and killed a protester who tried to stop him.[45]

One might assume that what drew a more aggressive police response was that the Black Lives Matter protests directly targeted law enforcement officials for criticism. But the disparity in responses was stark even when far-right militants directly confronted law enforcement. For example, in 2014, heavily armed far-right militants in Nevada physically assaulted and threatened U.S. Bureau of Land Management rangers who had seized cattle owned by rancher Cliven Bundy in order to recover over $1 million in fines for illegally grazing on public land without permits. An armed standoff ensued, and it ended only when the local sheriff brokered a deal that had the Bureau of Land Management rangers release the cattle, suspend the roundup, and withdraw.[46] Two years later in North Dakota, federal, state, and local law enforcement, assisted by private security companies and National Guard soldiers, responded to nonviolent Native American water protectors protesting the construction of an oil pipeline across tribal lands with riot police, tear gas, flash-bangs, rubber bullets, and armored water cannons.[47] The FBI employed an informant who smuggled a firearm *into* the encampment, making the situation more dangerous by arming one of the protesters.[48] Police arrested more than eight hundred Standing Rock water protectors during the protest.[49]

At times, the disparity in treatment was visible at the same events. Police in Portland, Oregon, repeatedly cooperated with far-right militants from out of state who came into the city for rallies where they often engaged in violence, with little law enforcement intervention. After letting the far-right militants leave, police responded to the anti-racist protesters who had gathered in protest with batons, tear gas, rubber bullets, kettling, and mass arrests.[50] And it wasn't just state and local police that appeared to see far-right militants as allies: at one Portland rally, U.S. Department of Homeland Security officers requested the assistance of a far-right militiaman and a Proud Boy in arresting anti-racism protesters.[51] At similar Black Lives Matter protests in Ferguson, Kenosha, Philadelphia, and elsewhere around the country, police allowed far-right militant groups to act as unsanctioned auxiliary security forces.[52]

The incongruence of police reactions to these demonstrations suggested that law enforcement was acting based on racial and ideological bias rather than objective evaluations of threats these different groups posed. Public concerns about law enforcement bias were substantiated when a Portland Police training presentation mocking anti-racist protesters as "dirty hippies" and celebrating police violence against them was discovered in litigation.[53] This kind of bias is not unique to a local department; on the contrary, it extends up to the premier federal law enforcement agency, the FBI.

CONJURED THREATS: BLACK IDENTITY EXTREMISTS AND ANTIFA

Law enforcement has long viewed Black protest movements as more threatening to the social order than white supremacist violence, despite the evidence that the latter is consistently more deadly. This is particularly true for the FBI, which has a history of using its national security powers to suppress Black activism going back to its infiltration of Marcus Garvey's Universal Negro Improvement Association in 1919 and wiretapping the Rev. Dr. Martin Luther King Jr. and other civil rights leaders in the 1960s.[54] The FBI remains a predominantly white, male organization, and accusations of systemic racial discrimination within the bureau persist to this day.[55]

As the predominant U.S. law enforcement agency and the host agency for two hundred Joint Terrorism Task Forces across the country, the FBI holds a leadership position with regard to counterterrorism strategy, intelligence, training, and analysis. So the targets it prioritizes and the tactics it adopts often filter down to state and local law enforcement. The FBI's post-9/11 counterterrorism programs prioritized "international" terrorism investigations that mainly targeted Muslim Americans. In its domestic terrorism program, its primary targets included what the FBI dubbed "ecoterrorists": environmental justice and animal rights activists. But in 2017, the FBI's domestic terrorism focus shifted as the Black Lives Matter movement developed, and Black activism became a new priority.

Shortly before the Unite the Right rally, the FBI produced an intelligence assessment warning that a new category of domestic terrorists it called "Black Identity Extremists" posed a deadly threat to law enforcement. The assessment identified six cases over three years in which Black men, who were not associated with one another and did not share a common political ideology, social goal, or religious belief, killed or attempted to kill police officers. While these attacks were heinous, they were individual crimes whose only common attribute was the Black identity of the perpetrators. The assessment was clearly manufacturing this new Black Identity Extremist category within the FBI's domestic terrorism program as a proxy for the Black Lives Matter protesters. It situated the birth of this new brand of extremism to coincide with the police killing of Michael Brown, and identified "the perception of police brutality against African Americans" as the organizing driver of the movement. The FBI's distribution of this flawed analysis throughout the law enforcement community shortly before the Unite the Right rally also may have contributed to the misperception of the threat in Charlottesville.

This trend would only accelerate as the federal government, under the leadership of President Trump and Attorney General Robert Barr, identified anti-fascists, rather than fascists, as the primary domestic terrorism threat. Trump and Barr cleverly used the shorthand "Antifa," a branding quickly adopted in right-wing media. Using this nickname helped them to avoid the self-identification as fascists that calling anti-fascists your enemy logically produces. It also helped avoid charges of racism that would have followed from calling the Black Lives Matter protesters terrorists.

The Antifa enemy that Trump and Barr conjured—a well-funded, organized, secretive, and violent movement that transported fighters across the country by the busload to turn protests into riots, and then blend back into the crowd and disappear—never existed. Certainly, anti-fascism exists, in many forms. One could say my FBI undercover operations against violent white supremacists and far-right militias were anti-fascist actions. Fascism has a sordid history, so, until recent years, most people in the United States opposed it. Many self-identified anti-fascists are staunchly nonviolent and do not engage in direct actions. They simply track the activities of far-right militants online or through activist networks and report them, either to law enforcement or publicly, warning their communities about them. Some anti-fascists come to protests to confront fascist militants who parade in public, and sometimes groups of individuals will engage in violence against the fascists. Anti-fascists justify this conduct as a necessary defensive measure to protect their communities from the spread of routine far-right violence that law enforcement and government leaders too often ignore, which typically follows the public rallies. Dr. Cornel West, who came under attack while marching with clergy in opposition to racism at the Unite the Right rally, credited anti-fascists and anarchists for saving his and the clergy members' lives after police failed to protect them.[56]

Anti-fascist violence exists, of course, but it is typically reactive to fascist mobilizing, is rarely deadly, and is vanishingly infrequent in comparison to white supremacist violence.[57] It would be quite rare to see a group of armed anti-fascists march through a conservative town randomly assaulting people and instigating fights. So if law enforcement really wanted to prevent anti-fascist violence, it would more aggressively confront fascist violence, solving two problems at once. It is also important to recognize that not everyone who opposes racists or confronts them at public events organizes with anti-fascist groups or would identify themselves with that label. So by blaming all violence or property destruction at or near a protest on Antifa, right-wing media and politicians made something small and nonthreatening to the general public appear to be large, omnipresent, and dangerous.

To a large extent, bias against "anarchists" and other leftist protesters already existed within law enforcement for decades, and intensified in the wake of the violent 1999 World Trade Organization protests in Seattle that descended into riot. Afterward, law enforcement trainings tended to sensationalize the anarchist violence at this event, often calling it the "Battle of Seattle," to justify preparing for a more aggressive and militarized response to later leftist protests. But Norm Stamper, the Seattle police chief at the time, cited the violent police overreaction to the protest, tear-gassing nonviolent demonstrators, as the primary instigator of the riot.[58] A Seattle City Council investigation "found troubling examples of seemingly gratuitous assaults on citizens, including use of less-lethal weapons like tear gas, pepper gas, rubber bullets, and 'beanbag guns,' by officers who seemed motivated more by anger or fear than professional law enforcement." [59]

Regardless, the Trump administration's propaganda exaggerating the Antifa threat fell on fertile soil. Law enforcement, whether because they believed the propaganda or simply because they felt they had to respond to the president and attorney general's demands, began producing and distributing sensationalized intelligence reports about dubious threats from Antifa, often sourced directly from far-right social media. FBI agents sought to prove the president's Antifa allegations by conducting jailhouse interviews of people arrested by local police at demonstrations, but no evidence supports Trump's claim that anti-fascists were a significant factor in the protest violence. [60]

A review of dozens of law enforcement intelligence reports leaked from a government contractor in 2020 revealed a multitude of poorly sourced and sensationalized threat warnings about potential Antifa violence over the previous years, such as reported plots to stage brick piles throughout the country to be thrown at police during protests. [61] After a fake Antifa Twitter account set up by a white supremacist group indicated that buses with thousands of anti-fascist soldiers were heading to a Chicago Black Lives Matter protest, police reportedly shut down highways and sent helicopters out to find them. [62] A report produced by the Regional Organized Crime Information Center shortly before the Unite the Right rally identified street violence between fascists and anti-fascists as clashes between Antifa and "anti-Antifa," mischaracterizing the fascists and inverting which party was the provocateur and which was acting in response. [63] But this inversion was critical to developing a public position against anti-fascism among establishment figures: it is much easier to publicly support "anti-Antifa" groups than fascists.

Intelligence from the federal government was no better. U.S. Homeland Security analysts tried to link U.S. anti-fascists to Kurdish terrorist groups in Turkey and Syria based on a perceived similarity in ideologies.[64] An FBI intelligence report, distributed to state and local fusion centers, cited information from a satirical website as evidence that Antifa was paying people in Bitcoin to commit violence at protests.[65] The International Association of Chiefs of Police report on the violence in Charlottesville appeared to have embraced this conspiracy theory, however, alleging the involvement of paid protesters who received funding to travel to demonstrations like Unite the Right to "deliberately agitate the crowd."[66] Law enforcement officials have regularly used this "paid protester" trope to discredit left-wing protest movements, because it insinuates a lack of local grassroots support for the cause.[67] In right-wing circles, the conspiracy theory is tinged with anti-Semitism, often implying that Jews are funding the disruptive activities. Tellingly, the International Association of Chiefs of Police report provided no actual evidence to support this theory with regard to the Unite the Right rally, but rather inexplicably cited an interview it conducted with a Florida Highway Patrol official.

Sensationalized Antifa threat intelligence in advance of the Unite the Right rally, some of it shared by the Virginia Fusion Center, reportedly influenced the police leaders' directives not to intervene to stop or prevent violence, out of fear for the safety of the officers. These dubious threats included what the Heaphy report called "credible" allegations that Antifa was planning to fill soda cans with cement to throw at police, and "rumors" that Antifa would attack police officers with fentanyl.[68]

IGNORING CRITICAL INTELLIGENCE: THE VALUE OF CRIMINAL HISTORIES

The International Association of Chiefs of Police report did cite one important failure by law enforcement officials that no doubt contributed to their inability to recognize that the Unite the Right rally was never intended to be a peaceful First Amendment demonstration. While law enforcement officials properly collected and shared intelligence regarding the potential for violence at the rally, the report acknowledged that, due to a flawed interpretation of their internal privacy policies, they did not evaluate or disseminate known participants' criminal histories. Not surprisingly, many of the white supremacist groups and individuals who were planning the rally had long histories of racist violence, as well as other crimes, which included recent arrests at previous racist rallies in Charlottesville.[69]

Jason Kessler, who applied for the permit to stage the Unite the Right rally, was a vocal white nationalist and Proud Boy member already well known to local police.[70] Kessler had been arrested twice in racially charged incidents in Charlottesville earlier that year. In January 2017, police charged Kessler with misdemeanor assault for punching a man who refused to sign Kessler's petition to recall a Black Charlottesville city councilman.[71] Kessler also filed charges against his victim, claiming the man punched him first, but video of the incident disproved this claim.[72] Kessler pleaded guilty to the assault and received a thirty-day suspended sentence and fifty hours of community service.

He was arrested again shortly after he entered his guilty plea, however, this time for disorderly conduct after pulling down anti-racist signs and using a bullhorn to disrupt a May 2017 candlelight vigil protesting an earlier white supremacist torch march through Charlottesville that had not gained national attention. A spokeswoman for the commonwealth attorney acknowledged that Kessler's actions did in fact incite violence at the vigil, but her office declined to prosecute, citing the First Amendment, apparently unaware that in 1969 the Supreme Court ruled that the First Amendment does not protect speech that imminently incites violence.[73]

It was also unclear why Kessler was not forced to serve the thirty-day suspended sentence for his previous assault after this second arrest.

And only after the August Unite the Right rally did prosecutors file a felony perjury charge against Kessler for falsely accusing his victim in the January attack of hitting him first. At trial, prosecutors inexplicably failed to establish that Kessler filed the false statement within the court's jurisdiction, leading the judge to dismiss the charge.[74]

The lenient handling of Kessler's crimes wasn't unusual. Local police also had the opportunity to arrest another Unite the Right organizer, white nationalist Christopher Cantwell, the morning before the UVA torch march. Albemarle County police officers answering a call about a man with a firearm at the local Walmart found Cantwell, a New Hampshire resident, and his supporters, who had been confronted by local activists. Cantwell admitted carrying a firearm, for which he held a concealed carry permit, but claimed he did not brandish it.[75] If the police had checked his record, however, they would have seen that Cantwell previously served jail time for weapons, theft, and drunk driving charges, and had once before pulled out a pistol during a confrontation in Keene, New Hampshire, according to his own accounts.[76] While Cantwell was not previously convicted of a felony, which would have made it illegal for him to possess a weapon, the earlier charges could lead a reasonable police officer to discount his denial that he brandished the weapon at the Walmart. Indeed, Cantwell went on to engage in violence during the torch rally later that evening, which included pepper-spraying counterprotesters. The assault was clearly captured in photographs and in a *Vice News* documentary, but police didn't arrest him that evening either.[77] It was only days later, after Charlottesville activist Emily Gorcenski went to the police station to press assault charges against him, that a warrant was issued for Cantwell's arrest.

Another Unite the Right organizer, Matthew Heimbach, led the Traditionalist Worker Party, a U.S. neo-Nazi group whose name was a play on Adolf Hitler's original National Socialist German Workers Party. The Traditionalist Worker Party was one of the racist groups involved in the Sacramento, California, skinhead rally in which eight anti-racist protesters were stabbed just a few months earlier. A Traditionalist Worker Party skinhead, the only neo-Nazi charged with committing an assault at the Sacramento rally, was later arrested after vandalizing a Colorado Springs synagogue.[78]

Heimbach had recently been found guilty of disorderly conduct for repeatedly pushing a Black woman protester at a 2016 Trump rally. During his July 2017 sentencing, the judge ordered a ninety-day jail sentence but suspended it on the condition that he not reoffend for two years.[79] Yet when the Charlottesville police asked the FBI for threat information regarding the Traditionalist Worker Party, the agent reportedly responded that the group was not a threat, but those coming out to oppose them might be.[80]

Still another Unite the Right organizer, Michael Tubbs, a leader of the League of the South, had a more serious criminal history. Tubbs, while serving as a U.S. Army Green Beret in 1987, committed thefts and armed robberies of military equipment as part of a Ku Klux Klan plot to start a race war, stealing weapons and enough "explosives to destroy a city block."[81] The FBI arrested him and two accomplices in 1991, and he served four years in federal prison. Two of Tubbs's League of the South colleagues who came to Charlottesville for the rally had been arrested for engaging in violence at white supremacist rallies earlier in the year.[82] Tubbs, whose long hair, white beard, and bearlike frame made him easy to spot in the crowd, was filmed leading his League of the South followers in several violent assaults on anti-racist protesters during the Unite the Right march, but he was not arrested.[83]

The rally organizers also included Nathan Damigo, the leader of Identity Evropa, a white supremacist group that had been distributing racist materials on college campuses across the country. Damigo earned the invitation to speak at Unite the Right by starring in a viral video sucker-punching a female anti-fascist protester in the face at a far-right rally in Berkeley, California, a few months earlier.[84] Damigo, a former U.S. Marine, previously served prison time in California for armed robbery after sticking up a cabdriver he thought looked like an Iraqi.[85]

Members of a white supremacist fight club called the Rise Above Movement came to the Unite the Right rally after engaging in video-taped public violence during far-right demonstrations in Huntington Beach, Berkeley (alongside Damigo), and San Bernardino, California. Their training and evidence of their violent and criminal exploits were posted openly on the Rise Above Movement's Instagram account. Two Rise Above Movement members who engaged in assaults during the Charlottesville rally, Tom Gillen and Ben Daley, had previous convictions for illegal possession of firearms.[86]

At least one white supremacist who traveled to Unite the Right from Texas was the subject of an active arrest warrant for assaulting his girlfriend. He had earlier been convicted of kidnapping a previous girlfriend, for which he served six years in prison.[87] Another rally participant who bludgeoned a Black counterprotester with a wooden board came to Charlottesville from Ohio, where he was known to local police as a white supremacist gang member who had menaced a Jewish classmate with a knife while still in middle school, according to an FBI affidavit.[88]

Law enforcement could and should have exploited these active arrest warrants, suspended sentences, and criminal histories—known in law enforcement terms as "criminal predicates." Focusing on criminal activity and those who commit it is the most relevant intelligence available to assist law enforcement in understanding the true nature of any planned event. As the International Association of Chiefs of Police report indicated, examining criminal histories would have enabled Charlottesville police to take appropriate actions to prevent the most likely suspects from being able to commit the most serious violence. It is absurd to suggest that First Amendment or internal privacy policies would allow law enforcement officials to monitor the social media accounts of people attending a rally and insert undercover agents among them, but prevent them from tracking the violent crimes the rally participants previously committed. Law enforcement is expected to trace criminal activities, and criminal histories are public records. By treating these violent criminals and the organized crime groups they operated as political activists rather than a persistent threat to public safety, law enforcement forfeited the opportunity to prevent the violence they later committed.

THE AFTERMATH: ANOTHER MISSED OPPORTUNITY

Even more perplexing to me, as a former FBI agent, was the relative inaction of law enforcement after the Unite the Right riot. Whatever misguided interpretation of the First Amendment or internal privacy policies may have convinced law enforcement officials to allow a group of violent criminals—who had publicly threatened to harm members of the community—to come into town and wreak havoc, there was certainly no bar to enforcing the law after the attacks. I assumed that the evidence of concerted assaults committed in public and recorded by participants and journalists, as well as the police, combined with the real-time social media monitoring during the event and the observations of undercover officers within the crowd, would trigger investigations of most if not all of the violent white supremacist groups that attended. I expected to see dozens of arrests of the people I had watched commit crimes on live video feeds over the following days and weeks.

While law enforcement's pre-crime intelligence collection powers were vastly expanded after 9/11, those efforts tend by nature to be poorly targeted and overbroad, making it easier to collect a lot of information but more difficult to separate signal from noise. This is especially true when bias misdirects the effort. But police powers of investigation after a crime has been committed are even more extensive, particularly with the development of electronic communications technology, and are often more effective because by their nature they are evidence-focused rather than predictive.

The development of the internet and social media have arguably made it easier for criminals to communicate, recruit, and plot, but these technologies also leave the criminals exposed to enormous vulnerabilities. Communications over email, text, and most social media platforms create a permanent electronic record that law enforcement or others can easily exploit. Once a crime has occurred, particularly in public, it becomes much easier for law enforcement to obtain subpoenas and warrants to conduct searches and seize electronic evidence that often reveals key associations and planning activities. Most importantly, this type of evidence helps document one of the elements of a crime that is most difficult to prove: the criminal intent. Once arrests are made, interrogations generate more leads to identify more subjects and locate more evidence. I expected the violence at the Unite the Right rally to jump-start what had been a moribund law enforcement effort to investigate the organized groups perpetuating far-right violence across the country. But that's not what happened.

Instead, it was left to civil society to identify the perpetrators and bring them to justice. Activist and journalist Shaun King used his Twitter account to crowdsource the identification of at least four white supremacists who attacked Charlottesville resident DeAndre Harris and left him bloodied and concussed.[89] ProPublica journalists didn't need to crowdsource identifications, as they had been tracking members of the Rise Above Movement for months, documenting the violence they perpetrated at far-right rallies in California, before coming to Charlottesville and doing the same.[90] ProPublica's detailed reporting, and the *Frontline* documentary that followed, appeared finally to have shamed the federal government into taking action a year after the Unite the Right rally, to prosecute the eight members of the Rise Above Movement featured in the stories (but no others).

These prosecutions of a relatively small number of individuals, sparked by the work of journalists, anti-fascists, and regular citizens, likewise did not lead to broader investigations of the Unite the Right instigators. It would take a civil lawsuit on behalf of survivors of the attacks to reveal the full scope of the conspiracy to bring racial violence and terror to the streets of Charlottesville and give a measure of justice to the survivors.

Two months after the Unite the Right rally, the legal advocacy group Integrity First for America filed a civil rights lawsuit on behalf of several injured survivors, seeking damages from the individuals and groups that organized the events. "That violence was no accident," Integrity First for America's executive director, Amy Spitalnick, later told Congress. "Rather, it was planned meticulously in advance—on social media sites like Discord, via text, and other channels—down to discussions of whether they could hit protesters with cars and claim self-defense."[91] The lawsuit alleged that the Unite the Right organizers

acted on the basis of racial, religious, and/or ethnic animus, and with the intention to deny Jewish people and people of color, as well as people advocating for the rights of Jewish people and people of color, equal protection and other rights that they are guaranteed under state and federal law. Defendant's conspiracy ultimately achieved its stated goals and did in fact repeatedly, systematically, and unmistakably violate the rights of religious and racial minorities in Charlottesville.[92]

The lawsuit benefited from the exposure of the organizers' Discord chats, composed during and after the rally, which were leaked by an anonymous source to Unicorn Riot, a news outlet that covers far-right militancy and the opposition to it.[93] Unicorn Riot published the leaked chats in a series of stories beginning on August 14, 2017, two days after the rally. The lawsuit, filed on October 12, 2017, quoted the organizers' own words as documented in the chats to demonstrate the conspiracy to instigate violence at the rally.[94]

It would be reasonable to assume, given the public attention to the racist violence at the Unite the Right rally, that the FBI would seek any evidence proving an illegal conspiracy to violate civil rights. But it wasn't until December 2018, sixteen months after the leaked chats had been published, that the FBI sought a search warrant for Jason Kessler's account information from Discord.[95] Ultimately, the Justice Department brought no federal charges against the Unite the Right organizers. In 2019, FBI agents filed additional search warrants, this time seeking the communications records of three *anti-fascists*, who they alleged committed an assault during the Charlottesville rally.[96] There is no public information to suggest the FBI remained interested in pursuing the fascists who committed violence at the Unite the Right rally.

Meanwhile, in 2022, it took the efforts of anti-fascist activists to identify an active-duty Woburn, Massachusetts, police officer who had participated in the Unite the Right rally and torch march, exposing another opportunity to prevent violence that law enforcement missed. The officer, John Donnelly, was found to be a member of the white supremacist group Identity Evropa and reportedly had a history of posting racist and anti-Semitic materials on social media and advocating violence against minority groups.[97] His social media posts indicated that he provided planning assistance and advice to people who were coming to the Unite the Right rally, as well as security services to the organizers at the event, including personal protection to perhaps the most media-friendly white nationalist personality speaking at the rally, Richard Spencer.[98] Officer Donnelly did not appear to have hidden his participation. He was filmed at the rally, wearing sunglasses but otherwise undisguised in coat and tie, and he even spoke on camera to videographers documenting the event. Yet he remained a police officer during the more than five years it took for activists—not law enforcement—to identify him.

This information was all the more alarming because Charlottesville police had coordinated directly with the Unite the Right rally security personnel, apparently without confirming whether the security personnel were licensed to provide personal protection services in Virginia. In fact, it appears the police did not even determine the true identity of the "security manager" they collaborated with, who they were told was affiliated with Spencer but was known to them only as "Jack Pierce."

Pierce (actually Identity Evropa member Allison Peirce IV) misled them regarding the true intentions of the organizers on the morning of the rally.[99] Pierce had negotiated a plan with the police to bring the speakers to a specific location so that police could escort them to Emancipation Park. Once the organizers failed to arrive as planned and Pierce's bad faith became clear, one officer muttered to a colleague, "They have no intention of this going well."[100]

Of course, they never did. The police could have leveraged the civil and criminal penalties associated with providing security services without a license, as the St. Louis County police chief had done with the Oath Keepers in Ferguson. This would at least have allowed them to determine the true identities of the "security personnel," and perhaps to uncover the active police officer among them. After the activists published the information about Officer Donnelly's participation in the rally, he resigned in the face of an internal investigation and was decertified as a police officer.[101] He was not charged with a crime.

In November 2021, more than four years after the rally, a jury hearing the Integrity First for America lawsuit found all of the Unite the Right organizers liable under Virginia laws against racial, religious, and ethnic harassment, assault, and battery, and imposed a judgment of $26 million in damages.[102] The jury deadlocked on the federal civil rights conspiracy claims, which, given the lower burden of proof required for civil judgments, might suggest that the Justice Department's decision not to bring criminal charges was prudent. But the FBI's criminal investigative authorities are much more powerful than civil discovery, and if federal agents and prosecutors had acted more aggressively immediately after the rally, they could have compelled the production of evidence in a more complete and timely manner and leveraged the potentially serious criminal penalties to coerce cooperation from co-conspirators. Federal law enforcement's continued passivity in the face of a national conspiracy to spread white supremacist violence all but ensured the attacks would escalate.

More dangerous for the survival of our democratic republic, the failure of law enforcement to respond appropriately to these violent street tactics allowed the fascists to fulfill their strategy of securing elite support for far-right militancy. In the aftermath of the Unite the Right rally, even with the horrific televised murder of a young woman dominating the airways, the white supremacists who organized it were about to receive an unimaginable boost from the highest authority in the land.

As a Republican candidate for president, Donald Trump opened his campaign with racist statements denigrating Mexican and Muslim immigrants as rapists and terrorists, which many saw as an appeal to gain the support of white nationalists. His rhetoric at rallies encouraged police violence and attacks on the media, and at times incited vigilante violence against protesters.[103] President Trump's first statement in response to the racist violence in Charlottesville, which he delivered from his New Jersey golf course where he was vacationing, didn't mention white supremacists, and instead blamed "many sides" for the violence.[104] For an audience attuned to dog-whistled support from politicians, the failure specifically to condemn white supremacy spoke volumes.

Trump modified his comments the following Monday in response to criticism, and denounced "the KKK, neo-Nazis, white supremacists and other hate groups."[105] But at his first press availability the following Tuesday, he made clear that his earlier hesitancy to criticize the white supremacists who planned and instigated the deadly riot was intentional. He defended the reputation of Confederate general Robert E. Lee, said that he thought the "alt-left" was as much to blame for the violence in Charlottesville as the racists, and added that there were "some very fine people on both sides."[106] The neo-Nazis thus achieved their goal of securing elite support for their militant activities, and the ability of law enforcement officials to curb the growth of this violence, if they had ever intended to, was lost for the foreseeable future. Policing white supremacy in the United States immediately became much more difficult.

2

THE RISE OF THE PROUD BOYS

White supremacist and far-right militant groups seek to legitimize themselves, their cause, and their violent methods by cultivating patronage within the right-wing establishment. Donald Trump explicitly voiced this form of support after Charlottesville and again when, during the first presidential debate in 2020, he responded to a question about whether he condemned white supremacists and right-wing militia groups by saying, "Proud Boys—stand back and stand by." [1]

When many people—including terrorism researchers, law enforcement officials, and policymakers—talk about the threat from white supremacists, they often talk about white supremacy as a form of "extremism," comparable to Islamic fundamentalism, anarchism, or Black nationalism. This "extremist" form of white supremacy, embodied by neo-Nazi skinheads, Aryan prison gangs, and hooded Klansmen burning crosses, certainly exists. Other parts of the broader white supremacist movement, however, are establishment figures: politicians, government officials, and business leaders. The force they wield—state violence—is far more potent because it is authorized and protected by law, supported politically, and resourced with a deep well of public funding. This is where white supremacy differs in kind from other ideologies labeled "extremism" in the United States: in its relationship with state power.

Historian Robert Paxton, who studies fascist governments, describes this dynamic in his definition of fascism.

Fascism may be defined as a form of political behavior . . . in which a mass-based party of committed nationalist militants, working in uneasy but effective collaboration with traditional elites, abandons democratic liberties and pursues with redemptive violence and without ethical or legal restraints goals of internal cleansing and external expansion.[2]

It is this relationship with state power that makes white supremacy the most dangerous threat, both because of the level of violence it can and does inflict on society, and because of the damage it does to America's hard-won progress as a pluralist democracy. Understanding the historical relationships among white supremacist groups, the state, and law enforcement is vital to addressing more effectively the white supremacist violence that menaces Americans today.

WHITE SUPREMACY AND STATE POWER

As an officially sanctioned ideology, white supremacy was enshrined in U.S. founding documents, with slavery protected in law for almost a century. Harsh racial subordination, inequality, and segregation authorized in law and enforced through state-sanctioned vigilante violence persisted for another hundred years. U.S. policy also expressed white supremacy through racist nativism, an exclusionary form of nationalism that imagines white Christians as the "true Americans" whose culture, beliefs, and bloodline needed to be defended against nonwhite, non-Christian immigration, racial integration, and miscegenation.

Policing in its earliest stages in the United States was often less about crime control than about maintaining the racial social order and protecting the property interests of the white privileged class. Slave patrols were among the first public policing organizations formed in the American colonies.[3] Even northern states that banned slavery, such as New York, Pennsylvania, Ohio, Indiana, and Illinois, enacted racist "Black laws," which restricted travel and denied civil rights regarding voting, education, employment, and even residency for free Black people.[4] The U.S. Congress passed the Fugitive Slave Act of 1850, which required law enforcement officials in free states to return escaped slaves to their enslavers in the South.[5] As the United States expanded westward, government agents enforced policies of violent ethnic cleansing against Native Americans and Mexican Americans. In the early twentieth century, Texas Rangers led lynching parties that targeted Mexican Americans residing in Texas border towns on specious allegations of banditry.[6]

Throughout U.S. history, every step toward racial equality has been met with violent resistance and political backlash. After the Civil War, when former Confederate soldiers unleashed the terror of Ku Klux Klan night riders to frustrate newly won Black voting rights, the new federal Department of Justice made its first task the dismantling of the Klan. But once Reconstruction efforts ended, de jure white supremacy was reimposed through Jim Crow laws, Black codes, and exclusion laws—legal limits on the rights of Black Americans even in states outside the defeated Confederacy.[7] To execute these racist laws, police routinely used force, often in concert with racist vigilante violence. Lynching was rarely prosecuted. Police officers, prosecutors, and judges were often openly sympathetic to, if not members of, the Ku Klux Klan and other violent racist groups.[8] By the 1920s, the Klan claimed 1 million members nationwide from New England to California and had fully infiltrated federal, state, and local governments to advance its exclusionist agenda.[9] Aspiring politicians regularly sought a public endorsement from the Klan, which was often necessary to win election to high office.[10]

The government also enforced explicit white supremacy through restrictive immigration laws. In 1882, the Chinese Exclusion Act halted Chinese immigration and denied naturalization to Chinese nationals already living in the United States.[11] The Immigration Act of 1924 was explicitly racist, codifying strict national origin quotas limiting nonwhite immigration in order to maintain the racial dominance of the "North-western European" racial stock.[12] The law barred all immigration from Japan and other Asian countries not already excluded by previous legislation.[13] It also included limits on Italian and Eastern European immigrants, many of whom were Jewish, highlighting how race is a social construct that shifts over time. Native Americans didn't receive U.S. citizenship until 1924, and their right to vote was withheld in some states until 1948.[14]

Once the civil rights movement of the 1950s and 1960s succeeded in mandating racial equality as a matter of law, explicit racism fell out of favor in polite society. Today, white supremacists know their overt racism and willingness to use violence to maintain the white racial hierarchy are odious to most Americans. Some embrace this social rejection and adopt the most abhorrent, costumed versions of white supremacy, such as neo-Nazi skinheads and robed Ku Klux Klansmen. They use well-known symbols of racial hatred to leverage the historical violence these groups have committed as a kind of shortcut to strike fear within racial and religious minority communities and exaggerate their power. But such tactics make it difficult to recruit anyone but the already most ardent racists to the cause.

The white supremacist groups seeking to recruit beyond committed racists, or to gain the support of establishment figures and influence government policy, have learned to be more coy. They often parry questions about their white supremacy by establishing a new lexicon. Groups organizing for the Unite the Right rally coined the term "alternative-right" or "alt-right." Some groups call themselves National Socialists, Identitarians, Groypers, or Kekistanis, terms meant to distinguish them from each other but also to confuse and mock the uninitiated "normies." Other far-right militant groups sharply deny that they are racists, much less white supremacists. But they often organize and mobilize with white supremacists and commit violence in common cause. Unfortunately, some journalists are taken in by these semantic games, and in attempting to expose these groups' abhorrent ideologies, they only assist in promoting them to a broader audience.

The militia movement of the mid-1990s was in some ways the culmination of a strategy advanced by white supremacist leaders earlier in that decade, when I was undercover in the neo-Nazi skinhead movement. Speakers at an Aryan youth conference I attended urged the skinheads to grow their hair and put away overtly racist symbols so that they could more effectively infiltrate mainstream conservative protest movements. Leaders advised us to avoid Nazi and Klan imagery in favor of the American flag, and to talk about the Founding Fathers and the American Revolution rather than Hitler and the Third Reich. They said to join anti-tax, anti-gun-control, and anti-immigration groups and find the militants within them to recruit into the movement and grow its ranks. The racist indoctrination could come after they were assembled into an effective action group.

As I looked around at the bored skinheads I was with, this strategy seemed far-fetched. But when the FBI asked me to go back undercover against what were then called anti-government militia groups after the 1995 Oklahoma bombing, I saw it in action. Far-right militants, who called themselves "patriots" and "constitutionalists" (though their interpretation of the national charter was that it protected only the rights of white men), welcomed me as a disaffected former racist skinhead seeking to join a group that could more effectively start a revolution. Though they publicly professed that the group was non-racist, many of them were openly bigoted in private and trafficked in the same racist conspiracy theories I had heard while undercover with Nazis.

Of course, there had always been a significant overlap between white supremacist groups and militias, going back to the original Ku Klux Klan, made up of former Confederate soldiers. Louis Beam, a Texas Klan leader in the 1970s and champion of the leaderless resistance strategy most white supremacist groups followed, also led a militia group he called the Texas Emergency Reserve.[15] The leaderless resistance strategy sought to frustrate law enforcement surveillance and infiltration tactics by dismantling formal hierarchal organizational structures in favor of small, autonomous cells of militants acting independently. There weren't rigid organizational rules that would prevent someone from being a member of a white supremacist group and a member of a militia at the same time.

Within the current far-right militia movement, many groups adopt white supremacist ideologies or other racist conspiracy theories, but not all. Some of these far-right militant groups threaten to sue journalists who describe them as white supremacists, even though they routinely make racist, anti-Semitic, Islamophobic, or xenophobic public statements and cooperate with white supremacist groups. They often point to their nonwhite members as proof of their racial tolerance, without acknowledging that there have always been examples of Jewish and nonwhite individuals joining white supremacist groups.[16] A wide variety of people are attracted to the image of power that white supremacy projects, or join for the protection or benefits it may provide them, however temporary. Moreover, white supremacist and far-right militant groups, despite their menace, are actually small in number. So they often welcome any support they can get, even if the person offering assistance doesn't fit neatly into a strict interpretation of their ideology.

The relationship between the various entities within the white supremacist movement—from the most extreme on one end of the spectrum to the most established on the other—is often uneasy, fraught with internal conflict, mutually exploitative, and masked from public view. An examination into the way the Proud Boys navigated its role as a conduit connecting violent white supremacists to the most powerful office in the land can help illuminate law enforcement's crucial role in aiding such collaboration.

PLANTING ESTABLISHMENT ROOTS

The evolution of the Proud Boys serves as an illustrative through line from the 2016 Trump campaign, through the violence at the 2017 Unite the Right rally, and to the January 6, 2021, attack, where they took a leadership role in the seditious conspiracy to prevent the peaceful transition of presidential power. As such, the group's history provides a window into the symbiotic relationship the militant far right seeks to develop with the more mainstream right-wing establishment.

The Proud Boys were never subtle about their violent intentions. When they burst onto the political scene during Donald Trump's 2016 presidential campaign, they openly promoted themselves as a violent gang of "Western chauvinists" operating across the country to menace their shared political enemies. The Proud Boys embraced political violence from their origin, promoted their national and even international scope, and established a defined organizational structure. All of these actions represented a radical departure from the leaderless resistance tactics that white supremacists and far-right militant groups had used for decades to avoid liability for the violence committed by their members.

Breaking these well-reasoned rules made the Proud Boys' successful rise, acceptance among political elites, and persistence as the vanguard of right-wing vigilantism in the United States all the more perplexing. Their history reveals law enforcement's blind spot to—if not sympathy for—a new generation of far-right, reactionary militants.

Proud Boys founder Gavin McInnes is a Canadian national who had made a small fortune as a gonzo journalist and co-founder of *Vice* magazine before leaving the outfit in 2008 as his bigoted and misogynistic rhetoric increasingly stoked controversy.[17] He announced his creation of a new militant group in *Taki's Magazine*, in a September 2016 piece titled "Introducing: The Proud Boys."[18] The piece began with a description of the group's meetings, which "usually consist of drinking, fighting, and reading aloud from Pat Buchanan's *Death of the West*."[19]

McInnes went on to describe the initiation process, and three ascending levels or "degrees" that a Proud Boy could attain by meeting certain criteria, the intentional absurdity of which forwards a misleading narrative that they are just a zany fraternity.[20]

McInnes also openly promoted political violence on his internet television show, stating, "Fighting solves everything—we need more violence from the Trump people."[21] In a February 2017 appearance on Joe Rogan's podcast, McInnes stated bluntly that he "started this gang called the Proud Boys."[22] He went on to describe a fourth level of Proud Boy membership, which required getting arrested or becoming involved in a serious violent fight or major altercation. Even Joe Rogan saw the liability inherent in this statement, advising McInnes to "erase that part." Typically, the federal government takes gang violence very seriously. When I heard McInnes's public acknowledgment of the violent nature of his new group, its interstate activities, and its clear organizational structure and hierarchy, I thought his admissions would make the Proud Boys an easy target for intervention by federal violent crimes, organized crime, and counterterrorism task forces. But even as McInnes's promotion of violence turned into real attacks on people at rallies all across the country—in Portland; New York City; Los Angeles; Miami; and Providence, Rhode Island, to name a few—federal intervention never materialized.[23]

McInnes's reference to Buchanan in his introduction of the Proud Boys was a wink to the far-right establishment and a clue to his strategy. Buchanan had been a White House adviser to Presidents Richard Nixon and Ronald Reagan, and later was a presidential candidate himself. His combative brand of right-wing populism kept him in the public eye for decades as a columnist and television personality, employed by supposedly liberal news outlets like CNN and MSNBC. Buchanan enjoyed this long public career despite a well-documented history of racist, nativist, homophobic, and anti-Semitic provocations and commentary.[24]

Buchanan was one of the architects of Nixon's southern strategy—a racist, fearmongering campaign to convince white working- and middle-class people, particularly in the South but across the country, to support Republicans as a bulwark against the racial justice gains won by the civil rights movement.[25] As such, Buchanan was on the leading edge of an era of dog-whistle politics, in which Republican politicians began speaking indirectly to white racists and far-right militants through coded language. Another former Reagan staffer, Lee Atwater, summarized this strategy in an epithet-filled interview recorded in 1981: "By 1968 you can't say [N-word]—that hurts you, backfires. So you say stuff like, uh, forced busing, states' rights, and all that stuff . . . cutting taxes, and all these things you're talking about are totally economic things and a byproduct of them is, blacks get hurt worse than whites."[26] Even Democrats would end up embracing these "economic things," such as welfare reform and tax cuts, to attract white voters.[27]

Throughout his career, Buchanan kept pushing his party closer to overt white Christian nationalism, declaring in his 1992 speech at the Republican National Convention that a religious culture war was under way for the "soul of America."[28] Conservative commentator Jonah Goldberg once said of Buchanan:

> He offers red meat to the extremists while at the same giving himself the wiggle room to deny he said anything controversial in the first place. This is no mean feat. To be able to say something that wins applause from racists and bigots without technically saying anything racist or bigoted is a great gift, for want of a better word.[29]

There was a fine line that separated dog-whistle politics from overt racism, and Buchanan often pushed against it. He defended accused Nazi war criminals, dabbled in Holocaust denial conspiracies, and called the Rev. Dr. Martin Luther King Jr. "one of the most divisive men in contemporary history."[30] During his independent campaign for the presidency, Buchanan had to dismiss two campaign staffers when their ties to white supremacist groups were uncovered in the press.[31]

Buchanan's books, particularly the one McInnes cited, *Death of the West*, promoted a white supremacist conspiracy theory that later became known as "white genocide" or the "great replacement" theory. Buchanan claimed that secularists, Marxists, socialists, and globalists—coded terms the far right often used to denote Jews—were conspiring to destroy Western culture by flooding the United States and Europe with nonwhite, non-Christian immigrants and dismantling white political control through racial and social justice initiatives. An authority figure's validation of conspiratorial myths of victimhood is a key element of fascist organizing, because the irrational fear it generates justifies preemptive violence against scapegoated out-groups.[32] During the Trump administration, white supremacist mass shooters in New York, Pennsylvania, and Texas would reference the great replacement theory to justify their attacks on Black people, Jews, and Latinos.

"JUST JOKING" AND OTHER WHITE SUPREMACIST DENIALS

Lacking the government-insider experience that Buchanan used to cloak his embrace of white supremacy, McInnes relied on his command of a subversive internet-savvy media counterculture, where the use of outrageous rhetoric could serve two purposes: both to promote odious viewpoints and to provoke liberal outrage in reaction, which could then be mocked. This allowed McInnes and his supporters to respond that he was a comedian who was "just joking" anytime anyone called out the awful statements and ideas that he platformed. It served as a method of desensitizing the audience to racist and sexist content while allowing them to denounce his critics as humorless scolds.

Like Buchanan, McInnes promoted a belief in the superiority of western European culture—which he defined as "Western chauvinism"—while simultaneously denying that he or his organization were white supremacist. McInnes often pointed to nonwhite Proud Boy members, claiming that the group wasn't racist but "anti-SJW," shorthand for "social justice warrior," an epithet meant to denigrate advocates for racial equality and economic fairness.[33] He insisted that he is an avowed opponent of racial discrimination and white supremacy, and went so far as to sue the Southern Poverty Law Center for defaming him by labeling the Proud Boys as a hate group.[34] But when the Proud Boys were fighting in the streets, it was often side by side with white supremacist groups, including at the Unite the Right rally, organized by a Proud Boy who was an unabashed racist and anti-Semite.[35]

Jason Kessler, one of the primary organizers and the permit holder for the Unite the Right rally, was a second-degree Proud Boy. McInnes let Jason Kessler come onto his show to promote the rally, but as it approached, McInnes seemed to balk at the direct association with an overtly white supremacist event.[36] McInnes denied that the Proud Boys shared the "alt-right" views promoted by the white supremacists who organized the Unite the Right rally, saying instead his group was "alt-light."[37] He publicly banned Proud Boys from attending, but several did anyway, including Enrique Tarrio, an Afro-Cuban American who later rose to a leadership position in the organization and was one of the Proud Boys later found guilty of seditious conspiracy in the January 6 attack.

McInnes's denials of the group's violent white supremacist nature were belied by his actions from the beginning. A white nationalist named Kyle "Based Stickman" Chapman had previously served thirty months in prison in Texas for armed robbery and evading police, almost three more years in California for grand larceny, and another five years in federal prison for illegally possessing a firearm as a convicted felon before he made a name for himself by being videotaped beating a leftist protester over the head with a leaded wood pole during a far-right rally in Berkeley, California, in 2017.[38] McInnes apparently liked what he saw and recruited Chapman as a Proud Boy leader, despite new felony charges added to his record after the Berkeley riot.

Chapman formed the Fraternal Order of the Alt-Knights, a group-within-the-group that would operate as the Proud Boys' "tactical defense arm." McInnes announced Chapman as the leader of "the military division of the #Proud Boys."[39] Despite the Berkeley arrest, Chapman was able to travel around the country as a speaker at far-right rallies, where he often instigated more violence. He picked up another felony assault charge for hitting a man with a barstool in Texas, another weapons arrest in Oakland, and a misdemeanor charge in San Francisco.[40] Despite his record, however, he received only probation and deferred sentences on these charges, leaving him free to continue menacing people across the country.

Chapman ultimately had a falling-out with McInnes, and later unsuccessfully attempted to wrest control of the Proud Boys and make it an overtly white supremacist group. "We will no longer cuck to the left by appointing token negroes as our leaders," Chapman announced, with similar slurs against LGBTQ+ communities and Jews. "We recognize that the West was built by the White Race alone and we owe nothing to any other race."[41] He was later charged with another felony for assaulting a health care worker when he was in a Boise, Idaho, hospital with pneumonia in 2021, for which he received a three-month sentence.[42]

McInnes's insistence that the Proud Boys weren't a white supremacist group highlights the delicate balance that far-right militant groups must keep in order to secure and maintain the support of establishment figures. Of course, no one knows what is in McInnes's heart. His racist, Islamophobic, anti-Semitic, and misogynistic commentary might all be a joke, and the Proud Boys' proximity to white supremacists at rallies and riots might all be coincidence. But McInnes likely recognized that masking the Proud Boys' affiliation with white supremacists was necessary to develop open relationships with establishment Republicans, ensure his group could continue to act with impunity, and enjoy the positive attention it received from the president of the United States.

In another indication that McInnes recognized the fine line he was treading, he formally resigned from the Proud Boys in November 2018, "disassociating" himself from the group "in all capacities, forever," via a video posted on YouTube.[43] His resignation came shortly after the New York Police Department arrested several Proud Boys for assaulting anti-fascist protesters at a Metropolitan Republican Club event that McInnes headlined, one of the first significant law enforcement responses to Proud Boy violence.[44] In the video, McInnes claimed he was never the leader of the Proud Boys, and that it wasn't a "gang." He again disavowed any ties to white nationalists, which he said "don't exist," and stated that his resignation was an effort reduce the potential sentences the arrested Proud Boys might face.[45] McInnes was not charged with any crimes related to his activities with the Proud Boys, though he reportedly continued associating with the group after his formal resignation.[46]

THE PROUD BOYS AND DONALD TRUMP

While most white supremacist and far-right militant groups were initially skeptical of the Israel-supporting New York City billionaire with a Jewish daughter, McInnes had been an early and vocal supporter of candidate Donald Trump. When McInnes introduced his gang to the world, he made clear they supported Trump for president, saying, "How could you not if you're a Proud Boy?"[47] Perhaps because of this early, vocal support, the Proud Boys attained extraordinary access to high-level members of Trump's inner circle and Republican elected officials across the country, no mean feat for a group of violent militants with many felony convictions among them.

One of their highest-level contacts was Roger Stone, another former Nixon staffer and Republican dirty trickster who was an old friend of and unofficial adviser to President Trump. Stone hired Proud Boys for security at his speaking events, defended them from media criticism, and reportedly provided personal and professional advice to its leaders Enrique Tarrio and Gavin McInnes.[48] The House Committee investigating the January 6 attack on the Capitol revealed video of Stone reciting the Proud Boys' fraternal creed, identifying himself as a Western chauvinist.[49] Reciting the creed was the requirement to become a first-degree Proud Boy, but Stone denied he had become a member. When Stone was on trial in federal court for obstruction of justice, witness tampering, and lying to Congress about his role in the release of hacked emails from the Democratic National Committee during the 2016 election, it was revealed that Tarrio and another Proud Boy had been assisting Stone in managing his social media accounts.[50] One of those posts triggered a federal investigation when it depicted the judge overseeing the case against Stone in what appeared to be rifle crosshairs. No one was charged.

Tarrio also ran an unofficial campaign support organization called Latinos for Trump. In this role, Tarrio, who previously had served time in federal prison for selling repackaged stolen medical equipment, was photographed in 2019 at a campaign event with the president's son Donald Trump Jr. Tarrio later sat in the gallery behind President Trump during a campaign speech wearing a "Roger Stone Did Nothing Wrong" T-shirt, in direct view of the press cameras covering Trump's remarks.[51]

In December 2020, Tarrio toured the White House. It was later dismissed as "just a public holiday tour," but such access still required an application to a member of Congress and vetting by the Secret Service. It is unclear how he obtained Secret Service clearance to attend these events despite his felony record. More importantly, it is hard to understand why the Secret Service missed or disregarded Tarrio's leadership position in a militant group that had instigated violence at a pro-Trump rally in Washington, D.C., just a month prior.[52]

After the White House visit, Tarrio and the Proud Boys again rampaged through the city, at one point tearing a Black Lives Matter banner from a historic Black church and burning it in the street.[53] Tarrio was the only Proud Boy charged in the incident, and the charge was a misdemeanor for destruction of property, not a hate crime.[54]

Elsewhere around the country, Proud Boys made inroads with state and local government officials. In Oregon, the Multnomah County Republican Party hired Proud Boys to provide security for an event. The Proud Boys, who were reportedly drinking and displaying weapons, patrolled the neighborhood, threatening and harassing people in the community. Responding police said they saw no criminal activity.[55] In Washington State, a Proud Boy who was jailed for assault in Oregon was asked to serve as sergeant-at-arms during a Clark County Republican Party meeting.[56] In Florida, five Proud Boys were named to the Miami-Dade Republican Executive Committee.[57]

PROUD BOYS AND POLICE

The most important relationships the Proud Boys developed, which allowed them to escape legal consequences for many of their violent acts, were with law enforcement officials. The Trump campaign became fertile ground for the Proud Boys and other violent white supremacists to solicit police support and recruit members from among their ranks.

When Donald Trump made overtly bigoted remarks about Mexicans and Muslims to kick off his campaign in 2015, many mainstream journalists began reaching out to prominent white supremacists for their opinions on the race for the White House. Some of these leaders had been out of the public spotlight for years. Though skeptical initially, they quickly realized the opportunity these media outlets were giving them to raise their profiles and bring their racist messages to mainstream audiences.[58] Not only did they promote Trump within the movement, they often showed up to provide a menacing presence at his rallies.

Trump was simultaneously cultivating another audience within law enforcement. He did this by appealing to perceptions that critics of police violence and racism were unfair, and that reform efforts were an obstacle to police effectiveness.[59] A *Police Magazine* survey of police officers who planned to vote in the 2016 election indicated that 84 percent supported Donald Trump and only 8 percent supported Hillary Clinton.[60]

Though he claimed to be the law-and-order candidate, President Trump actively promoted a "rough" form of policing, urging police officers not to be "too nice" when arresting suspected criminals.[61] At rallies, he described his political opponents and the news media as enemies seeking to destroy the United States. He urged and at times even incited his followers to commit violence against anti-Trump protesters.[62] This created an environment where white supremacists, far-right militants, and "rough" law enforcement officials could find common ground in supporting him and his administration's policies. Trump also provided them a set of common enemies: anti-Trump protesters and anti-fascists.

The Proud Boys were well positioned within this milieu to recruit support within law enforcement. They were a new group, so they didn't have a long criminal history associated with their name. They had a powerful media platform, where they presented themselves as a rowdy conservative drinking club that attended rallies to defend pro-Trump activists from anti-fascist violence. This was a facade, of course, which was belied by leaked chats and their public actions.[63] But the ambiguity about the nature of the group gave law enforcement license to treat them as friendlies.

The Proud Boys' cozy relationship with police was often on display during the pro-Trump rallies in Portland, Oregon. Throughout the Trump administration, Proud Boys and other white supremacist and far-right militant groups repeatedly traveled to Portland to commit violence, many of them from out of state.[64] Yet law enforcement rarely intervened, and at times appeared to assist them, leading to public accusations of police bias favoring the militants. During an official city inquiry into police behavior during a June 2017 rally, one Portland Police Bureau lieutenant explained law enforcement's apparent affinity for the far-right militants by stating they were "much more mainstream than the left-wing protesters."[65]

Allegations of law enforcement bias surfaced again when *Willamette Week*, Portland's alternative weekly newspaper, published friendly text messages between a Portland Police Bureau lieutenant and the out-of-state leader of a far-right group whose members had engaged in violence at these rallies. The lieutenant's texts included a message regarding Tusitala "Tiny" Toese, a Proud Boys brawler from Washington State who regularly instigated fights at rallies and was the subject of an active arrest warrant for a previous assault against a Portland resident. The texts advised the militant leader that Portland police had ignored the warrant when Toese came into town for an earlier protest, and that they wouldn't arrest him at an upcoming rally so long as he didn't commit a new crime.[66] The Portland police later claimed the texts were intended to gather intelligence and cooperation from the far-right groups in order to prevent violence at the rallies.[67] It wasn't clear how letting a repeat violent offender know that he could come to Portland without fear of arrest, despite an active warrant, could possibly reduce the likelihood of violence.

On the other side of the country, in 2019, civil rights advocates discovered that an East Hampton, Connecticut, police officer was a "dues-paying" member of the Proud Boys for eight months and demanded an investigation. The police chief determined that being a member of the Proud Boys did not violate department policy. The officer later retired, after claiming that the civil rights activists who had reported his affiliation to the department were trying to "silence conservative voices" and were attacking the group for "their 'love' of President Donald Trump."[68]

In 2019, in Washington, D.C., a group of Proud Boys disrupted a permitted flag burning by members of a communist group in front of the White House by initiating a scuffle.[69] D.C. police arrested two of the communists but escorted the Proud Boys away, fist-bumping them as they walked into a bar. An investigation determined the officers violated no police department policies.[70] In Philadelphia, police officers stood by and failed to intervene when mostly white mobs armed with bats, clubs, and long guns attacked journalists and protesters at a 2020 rally.[71] The district attorney vowed to investigate the matter. The following month, however, Philadelphia police officers openly socialized with several men wearing Proud Boys regalia and carrying a Proud Boys flag at a "Back the Blue" party at the Fraternal Order of Police Lodge.[72]

A Chicago police officer reportedly gave inconsistent statements when he was interviewed by FBI agents regarding his involvement with the Proud Boys in 2022, and then again by Chicago police internal affairs. Evidence showed he had communicated with them online for longer than he originally admitted and met them in person at bars and social events. He also reportedly helped a Proud Boy abscond from the scene after a bar fight, without reporting the incident. The department recommended a five-day suspension. The City of Chicago inspector general objected, and after a new investigation determined the officer had made false and "contradicting statements" regarding his association with the Proud Boys, violations that typically result in dismissal.[73] Through mediation, the police department and the officer agreed to a 120-day suspension, rather than termination.

Not all police departments saw the Proud Boys in the same light. Several prominent members of the Proud Boys were arrested by local police for engaging in violence at public events in Berkeley, California, in 2017; New York City in 2018; Portland, Oregon, in 2018, 2019, and 2020; Seattle, Washington, in 2020; and Washington, D.C., in both November and December 2020.[74] A Plaquemines Parish, Louisiana, sheriff's deputy was fired for violating the department's social media policies by posting about his Proud Boys membership while in uniform, which was determined to be "contradictory to the values and vision" of the sheriff's department.[75] Likewise, when photos were discovered in 2018 of a Clark County, Washington, sheriff's deputy modeling a Proud Boys sweatshirt, featuring a bloody switchblade, as part of an online marketing campaign, she was quickly fired.[76]

THE PROUD BOYS AND THE FBI

The Clark County deputy's firing followed an internal investigation that exposed the FBI's conflicted perspective on the Proud Boys. The investigation's report, obtained by *The Guardian*, revealed that during a southwest Washington State law enforcement briefing, an FBI analyst labeled the Proud Boys as "an extremist group with ties to white nationalism." The report included an FBI warning that "Proud Boys members have contributed to the recent escalation of violence at political rallies held on college campuses, and in cities like Charlottesville, Virginia, Portland, Oregon, and Seattle, Washington" and were recruiting locally.[77]

The *Guardian* article seemed to clarify the confusion regarding the nature of the Proud Boys and provided some comfort that the FBI was tracking their interstate crime spree. Hopes were dashed and confusion reintroduced, however, when the Oregon FBI special agent in charge, Renn Cannon, said during a subsequent press conference that the FBI "[does] not intend and did not intend to designate the group as extremist." According to the *Oregonian*, he went on to explain, "We will not open a case if someone belongs to antifa or even the Proud Boys. There has to be a credible allegation or a threat of violence before someone opens a case."[78]

It is true that the FBI has no legal authority to designate domestic groups as terrorists or "extremists." Nor should it. But Cannon's claim misstates other aspects of the FBI's authorities, which were expanded significantly after 9/11 and again in 2008, over the objections of civil libertarian groups. These changes to the FBI's rules, known as the Attorney General's Guidelines, allow agents to conduct more intrusive investigations of people and organizations even when there is no allegation or evidence indicating they are engaged in wrongdoing.[79] This expansion of authority was unnecessary, prone to abuse, and ultimately useless in stemming white supremacist and far-right violence.

Cannon also seems to disregard the well-documented violence the Proud Boys had perpetrated in Oregon and beyond, instead invoking the both-sides line of thinking that permeates the FBI's approach to far-right violence. The Proud Boys' violence, and evidence of interstate travel to commit it, should have provided ample justification for investigating the group. Yet there were no FBI arrests or federal prosecutions of Proud Boys for acts of violence taking place in Oregon.

Despite ample "credible allegations," actual charges laid by local officials, and the interstate nature of the crimes, the FBI didn't bring a single case against Proud Boys for violence committed at rallies until after the January 6, 2021, attack. These trials uncovered more information about what the FBI did and did not know about the Proud Boys. The seditious conspiracy trial against several Proud Boys who led the assault on the Capitol on January 6, 2021, revealed that over the years the FBI had multiple informants within the organization.[80] But rather than using these informants and other informal contacts to seek evidence of Proud Boys' crimes, the FBI had asked them to report only *on their anti-fascist enemies.*[81] It appears the FBI viewed the Proud Boys not as a threat but rather an ally in a shared effort to target anti-fascists.

Proud Boy leaders had long bragged that they had contacts within law enforcement and coordinated their events before they occurred.[82] In the course of the January 6 investigation, it was discovered that Shane Lamond, a Washington, D.C., police lieutenant who supervised its intelligence branch, had expressed his support for the Proud Boys in extensive communications with Enrique Tarrio over two years. Lamond allegedly leaked information to Tarrio regarding the police monitoring of Proud Boys social media, warning him to switch to encrypted apps. He also allegedly fed information to Tarrio regarding the D.C. police investigation into the burning of the Black Lives Matter banner during the December 2020 rally. Lamond was charged with obstruction of justice and lying to investigators about his communications with Tarrio.[83] Lamond pleaded not guilty, claiming through his attorney that maintaining contact with leaders of "extremist groups" was part of his official intelligence-gathering duties.[84]

Tarrio, whose warrant for the December Black Lives Matter banner burning was still outstanding, was arrested by D.C. police on January 4, 2021, when he came back into the city for the January 6 rally. When arrested, he was found willing and able to overthrow an election with force. After he was released on bond on January 5, Tarrio was ordered to stay out of D.C., but it was later determined he disregarded this order and met with the leader of the Oath Keepers in D.C. ahead of the January 6 attack.[85] At sentencing months later, the judge complained that the three months of incarceration that prosecutors requested was insufficient, sentencing Tarrio to five months instead.[86] Tarrio served his sentence and was released before being charged with seditious conspiracy in the January 6 attack. Tarrio had also previously served as an FBI informant.[87]

The failure by federal, state, and local police to manage the growing threat the Proud Boys posed, despite the public nature of their planning and illegal activities, highlights how poorly these agencies understand the methods that the violent white supremacist and far-right militant movement uses, and the threat they pose to law enforcement, much less to democracy. Law enforcement's willingness to ignore and even assist the Proud Boys' crime spree allowed the group to build influence within the broader white supremacist and far-right militant movement. It allowed the Proud Boys to develop a national and even international reputation for committing, and often leading, public violence at far-right demonstrations of all kinds, from pro-Trump and Blue Lives Matter rallies to anti-vaccine and anti-mask protests during the Covid shutdown. Law enforcement action, and inaction, allowed the Proud Boys to recruit, build networks, and establish the logistics necessary to mass thousands of like-minded militants at the U.S. Capitol on January 6, 2021, willing and able to overthrow an election with force.

Correcting the dangerously flawed approach to policing white supremacist groups is essential to the future security of our democracy. Since the January 6 arrests, the Proud Boys and other far-right militant groups have reconstituted their ranks and continue to menace elected officials and the general public, with little apparent law enforcement response. Though many Proud Boys leaders were convicted for leading the seditious conspiracy, the group is still active nationally and by some counts even larger, shifting its focus from instigating violence at public rallies to menacing people at school board meetings and drag shows. Compounding their threat, the Proud Boys and other far-right groups continue to recruit members from the ranks of law enforcement.

3

RACISM, WHITE SUPREMACY, AND FAR-RIGHT MILITANCY IN LAW ENFORCEMENT

Well-documented racial disparities pervade every step of the criminal justice process, from police stops, searches, arrests, shootings, and other uses of force to charging decisions and wrongful convictions.[1] As a result, many have concluded that a structural or institutional bias against people of color, shaped by long-standing racial, economic, and social inequities, infects the criminal justice system.[2] These systemic inequities can also instill implicit biases—unconscious prejudices that favor in-groups and stigmatize out-groups—among individual law enforcement officials, influencing their day-to-day actions while interacting with the public.

Police reforms, often imposed after incidents of racist misconduct or brutality, have focused on addressing these unconscious manifestations of bias. The U.S. Department of Justice, for example, has required implicit bias training as part of consent decrees it imposes to root out discriminatory practices in law enforcement agencies. Such training measures are designed to help law enforcement officers recognize these unconscious biases in order to reduce their influence on police behavior.[3]

These reforms, while well intentioned, leave unaddressed a more harmful form of bias that remains entrenched within law enforcement: explicit racism. Explicit racism in law enforcement takes many forms, from membership in or affiliation with violent white supremacist or far-right militant groups, to engaging in racially discriminatory behavior toward the public or law enforcement colleagues, to making racist remarks and sharing them in texts or on social media. While it is widely acknowledged that racist officers persist within police departments around the country, federal, state, and local governments are doing far too little proactively to identify them and take the necessary measures to protect the public from them. Addressing the danger these officers pose is essential to ensuring the integrity of the criminal justice system and providing equal protection of the law.

Efforts to address systemic and implicit biases in law enforcement are unlikely to be effective in reducing the racial disparities in the criminal justice system when explicit racism in law enforcement is allowed to endure. There is ample evidence to demonstrate that it does.

HISTORY REPEATING

In 1964, civil rights workers James Chaney, Andrew Goodman, and Michael Schwerner went missing in Mississippi during the Freedom Summer voter registration drive, shortly after being released from a Philadelphia, Mississippi, jail where they had been taken to pay a speeding fine.[4] President Lyndon Johnson ordered FBI director J. Edgar Hoover to send FBI agents to find them. Searchers found the bodies of eight Black men, including two college students who were working on the voter registration drive, before an informant's tip finally led the agents to an earthen dam where Chaney, Goodman, and Schwerner were buried. After local law enforcement refused to investigate the murders, the Justice Department charged nineteen Ku Klux Klansmen with conspiring to violate Chaney, Goodman, and Schwerner's civil rights. Two current and two former law enforcement officials were among those charged. An all-white jury convicted seven of the Klansmen but only one of the law enforcement officers.[5]

The Mississippi Burning case is one of the most notorious cases of racist violence involving law enforcement, and—perhaps because two of the victims were white—it brought national outrage and contributed to the passage of civil rights legislation in 1964 and 1965. But it wasn't the first or the last time law enforcement officers colluded with white supremacist groups. Far from being isolated incidents, these examples form part of an unbroken chain of law enforcement involvement in violent, organized racist activity right up to the present.

In the 1980s, the investigation of a KKK firebombing of a Black family's home in Kentucky exposed a Jefferson County police officer as a Klan leader. In a deposition, the officer admitted that he directed a forty-member Klan subgroup called the Confederate Officers Patriot Squad (COPS), half of whom were police officers. He added that his involvement in the KKK was known to his police department and tolerated so long as he didn't publicize it.[6]

In the 1990s, Lynwood, California, residents filed a class action civil rights lawsuit alleging that a gang of racist Los Angeles County sheriff's deputies known as the Lynwood Vikings perpetrated "systematic acts of shooting, killing, brutality, terrorism, house-trashing and other acts of lawlessness and wanton abuse of power."[7] A federal judge overseeing the case labeled the Vikings "a neo-Nazi, white supremacist gang" within the sheriff's department that engaged in racially motivated violence and intimidation against the Black and Latino communities. In 1996, the county paid $9 million in settlements.[8]

In 2001, two Texas sheriff's deputies were fired after they exposed their KKK affiliation in an attempt to recruit other officers.[9] In 2005, an internal investigation revealed that a Nebraska state trooper was participating in a members-only KKK chat room.[10] He was fired in 2006 but won his job back in an arbitration mandated by the state's collective bargaining agreement. On appeal, the Nebraska Supreme Court upheld his dismissal, determining that the arbitration decision violated "the explicit, well-defined, and dominant public policy that laws should be enforced without racial or religious discrimination, and the public should reasonably perceive this to be so."[11] Three police officers in

Fruitland Park, Florida, were fired or chose to resign over a five-year period from 2009 to 2014 after their Klan membership was discovered.[12] In 2015, a Louisiana police officer was fired after a photograph surfaced showing him giving a Nazi salute at a Klan rally.[13]

Only rarely do these cases lead to criminal charges. In 2017, Florida state prosecutors convicted three prison guards of plotting with their fellow KKK members to murder an inmate.[14] Federal prosecutions are even rarer. In 2019, the Justice Department charged a New Jersey police chief with a hate crime for assaulting a Black teenager during a trespassing arrest after several of his deputies recorded his numerous racist rants. "These [N-word] are like ISIS, they have no value," the chief said during the recorded conversation. "They should line them all up and mow 'em down. I'd like to be on the firing line."[15] This incident marked the first time in more than a decade that federal prosecutors charged a law enforcement official for an on-duty use of force as a hate crime.[16] A jury convicted the police chief of lying to FBI agents but was unable to reach a verdict on the hate crime charge, which prosecutors retried, resulting in another hung jury.[17] The police chief served thirteen months on the false statement charge and was released from prison in 2023.

The process required to address properly a police officer's involvement with groups like the Ku Klux Klan or neo-Nazi skinheads, which have decades-long histories of violence, might seem arduous, but these are actually the easy cases. Far more frequently, law enforcement officers express bias in ways that are more difficult for police administrators to navigate.

NEW GROUPS, OLD PATTERNS

New white supremacist and far-right militant groups can form spontaneously, then splinter, change names, and employ disinformation campaigns to mask their illicit activities. This subterfuge can sometimes make it difficult to determine whether an officer's affiliation with a particular group presents a conflict with law enforcement obligations. For example, a Virginia school resource officer, who as a teen had reportedly posted on the neo-Nazi website Stormfront, was found to be a "pledge coordinator" for the white nationalist group Identity Evropa, assisting new recruits in joining the organization. The group, which helped organize the 2017 Unite the Right rally, formed in 2016 with inspiration from the youth-focused European identitarian movement.[18] After the violence in Charlottesville showed the group's true colors, it renamed itself the American Identity Movement. The officer was fired in 2019.[19]

Other relatively new groups such as the Oath Keepers (formed in 2009) and Proud Boys (2016) had leaders who formally disavowed racism and white supremacy even if their members didn't always stay on message. These groups presented a potentially stronger lure to law enforcement officers and a more difficult problem for police leaders to navigate. But law enforcement should have looked more negatively on affiliation with the Proud Boys from its origins. Even though its members were not yet associated with deadly violence typically identified as terrorism, they called themselves a "gang," clearly promoted violence in their rhetoric, and committed it in public. Typically, gang affiliation is something law enforcement punishes severely. The Proud Boys' open recruitment of people with serious and often violent criminal records should have provided the evidence necessary for police leaders to address officer affiliations with these groups more aggressively, as they would in cases where evidence revealed police affiliation with Mafia or other gang activity.

The Oath Keepers were far more effective than the Proud Boys at recruiting law enforcement officials, which they made an organizational priority. The group, led by military veteran and Yale Law School graduate Stewart Rhodes, targeted law enforcement and military officials directly, claiming that the organization's mission was to uphold the oaths they swore to defend the Constitution when they entered government service, with an emphasis on protecting an expanded view of the Second Amendment right to bear arms. Those who didn't dig too deeply into the Oath Keepers' rhetoric or activities, and perhaps weren't as familiar with constitutional interpretation as they should have been as law enforcement officers, could understandably have been unwittingly drawn in early in the organization's existence.

In 2014, however, Oath Keepers joined with other far-right militant groups in a well-publicized armed standoff against federal law enforcement officials to prevent the execution of a duly authorized warrant to seize a Nevada rancher's cattle. This widely broadcast event fully exposed the group's violent character, already discernible from previous incidents: numerous Oath Keepers had been arrested over the years on firearms and explosives violations, and armed members were a menacing presence at several Black Lives Matter protests.[20] Yet leaks in 2020 and 2021 revealed applications from hundreds of law enforcement officers who sought to join the group and who offered to provide training in weapons and police tactics.[21] In Oregon, where more than two dozen law enforcement officers submitted applications to join the group, Oath Keepers participated in another armed standoff against federal agents at the Malheur Wildlife Refuge in 2016.[22] And it wasn't just the rank and file who sought association with this violent far-right group: among the 373 law enforcement officials whose applications leaked, the Anti-Defamation League identified 10 police chiefs and 11 sheriffs.[23] There has been no public accounting regarding the disciplinary measures, if any, taken against these officers.

In the aftermath of the January 6 investigations and prosecutions, evidence continues to emerge about close relationships between federal law enforcement and far-right groups. The ethics watchdog organization Citizens for Responsibility and Ethics in Washington (CREW) obtained internal emails between Secret Service agents and analysts describing their attempts to establish a working relationship with the Oath Keepers. The emails show the Secret Service agents disregarding the Oath Keepers' well-established criminal history and treating the group as a kind of adjunct security force. One agent, who self-identified as "the unofficial liaison to the Oath Keepers (inching toward official)," wrote in an email that the Oath Keepers are "very pro-LEO [law enforcement officer] and Pro Trump." The agent sought to assist with an Oath Keepers' request to deploy "security details" for a 2020 Trump speech in North Carolina, explaining that the Oath Keepers he spoke with were intending "to provide protection and medical attention to Trump supporters if they come under attack by leftist groups." Another Secret Service analyst who had been asked to provide intelligence about the Oath Keepers identified interviews in which Rhodes "denounced White Nationalist ideals while sharing his dislike of ANTIFA," but failed to report the Oath Keepers' highly publicized involvement in armed standoffs against federal agents.[24]

PROTEST POLICING EXPOSES FAR-RIGHT AFFINITIES

During the protests that followed the murder of George Floyd in May 2020, a number of officers across the country could be seen flaunting their affiliation or sympathies with far-right militant groups. Evidence of these affinities, most often recorded by journalists and civil rights groups, also brought attention to tepid responses by superiors.

A veteran sheriff's deputy monitoring a Black Lives Matter protest in Orange County, California, was photographed with patches affixed to his bulletproof vest featuring logos of the Oath Keepers and Three Percenters, the latter a violent far-right militant group that takes its name from the false idea that only 3 percent of American colonists took up arms against the British. It was only after a civil rights group publicized the photograph that the sheriff said it was "unacceptable" for the deputy to wear the patches and placed him on administrative leave pending an investigation.[25]

Similarly, in Chicago, a thirteen-year veteran of the Chicago Police Department was photographed, alongside a supervisor who apparently did not complain, wearing a face covering with a Three Percenters logo while on duty at a protest. After the photographs surfaced, causing a public scandal, the officer was placed under investigation.[26] The officer had reportedly been the subject of twenty-three complaints and several previous misconduct lawsuits, including an excessive-use-of-force suit following a nonfatal shooting. The city of Chicago paid $630,000 to settle those suits.[27] Twice, the police department closed investigations of the officer without taking disciplinary action, but after inquiries from the City Council and a request from the inspector general, the department opened a third investigation of the officer in March 2023.[28] The results of this investigation were not publicized, but Cook County State's Attorney Kim Foxx placed the police officer on a "Do Not Call" list, along with the officer found to have associated with Proud Boys and eight other officers whose names appeared on membership lists of the Oath Keepers.[29] Placement on this list prevents prosecutors from relying on these officers' testimony in court cases.

In Salem, Oregon, a police officer was recorded on video asking heavily armed white men dressed like militia to step inside a building or sit in their cars while the police arrested anti-racism protesters for failing to comply with curfew orders, "so we don't look like we're playing favorites." After a public outcry, the Salem police chief apologized for the appearance of favoritism, but determined the officer was only trying to gain the militants' compliance with the curfew.[30]

A police officer in Olympia, Washington, was placed under investigation for posing in a photograph with a heavily armed militia group called Three Percent of Washington. One of the militia members posted the photograph on social media, claiming that the officer and her partner had come over to thank them for guarding a local shopping center.[31]

The affinity some police officers have shown for armed far-right militia groups at protests is confounding given that many states, including California, Illinois, Oregon, and Washington, have laws barring unregulated paramilitary activities.[32] And it is most troubling because far-right militants have regularly attacked and killed police officers. No government agency officially documents these crimes, but the Anti-Defamation League identified fifty-one law enforcement officers killed by white supremacists and far-right militants from 1990 through 2017.[33] And the threat remains despite the far-right militants' feigned support for the Blue Lives Matter movement. In 2020, a series of shooting and bombing attacks against Federal Protective Service officers and sheriff's deputies in California by far-right militants intent on starting the "Boogaloo"—a euphemism for a new civil war—killed two and injured several others.[34] Another far-right militant associated with the Boogaloo movement was convicted of having fired an assault-style rifle into a Minneapolis police station during the protests following the murder of George Floyd.[35] Three others were arrested for manufacturing Molotov cocktails in preparation for an attack on law enforcement at a Black Lives Matter protest in Nevada, which was ultimately thwarted by the FBI.[36]

NONAFFILIATED RACISTS

Most people with white supremacist beliefs avoid joining identifiable organizations, even as they might socialize with them online or in person, support them, and even conspire with them to achieve their shared goals. Some simply don't have access to or interest in joining formal groups. Others seek to keep an arm's-length relationship in recognition of the social stigma and potential criminal liability that having one's name on the membership list of a violent group might create. Police officers would naturally be even more acutely aware of such risk.

In addition to those law enforcement officials with explicit white supremacist affiliations, many do not formally associate with white supremacist or militant groups at all, but do engage in overtly racist behavior toward the public, on social media, or over law-enforcement-only communication channels. In a 2019 report, the Plain View Project documented 5,000 patently bigoted social media posts by 3,500 accounts identified as belonging to current and former law enforcement officials. The report sparked dozens of investigations across the country.[37] The Philadelphia Police Department, for example, placed seventy-two officers on administrative duties pending an investigation into their racist social media activity, ultimately suspending fifteen with intent to dismiss. Other officers faced disciplinary action, including suspensions, but remained on the force.[38] Thirteen of twenty-five Dallas police officers investigated for objectionable social media postings received disciplinary actions ranging from counseling to suspensions without pay.[39] Only two of the twenty-two current St. Louis police officers identified in the report were terminated.[40]

The San Francisco Police Department attempted to fire nine officers whose overtly racist, homophobic, and misogynistic text messages were uncovered in a 2015 FBI police corruption investigation. After years of litigation, the California Supreme Court finally rejected the officers' appeal in 2018, which paved the way for disciplinary action to proceed.[41] As the case was pending, five other San Francisco police officers were found to have engaged in racist and homophobic texting, at times mocking the investigation of the earlier texts.[42] It is perhaps unsurprising, then, that in 2016 the Justice Department determined that San Francisco police officers stopped, searched, and arrested Black and Hispanic people at greater rates than white people even though they were less likely to be found carrying contraband.[43] In a positive development, when the texting scandal broke in 2015, the San Francisco district attorney established a task force to review three thousand criminal prosecutions that used testimony by the offending officers, dismissing some cases and alerting defense attorneys to potential problems in others.[44]

In June 2020, three Wilmington, North Carolina, police officers were fired when a routine audit of car camera recordings uncovered conversations in which the officers used racial epithets, criticized a magistrate and the police chief in frankly racist terms, and talked about shooting Black people, including a Black police officer. One officer said that he could not wait for a declaration of martial law so they could go out and "slaughter" Black people. He also announced his intent to buy an assault rifle in preparation for a civil war that would "wipe 'em off the [expletive] map." The officers confirmed making the statements on the recording, but claimed that they were not racist and were simply reacting to the stress of policing the protests following the killing of George Floyd. In addition to the officers' dismissal, the police chief ordered his department to confer with the district attorney to review cases in which the officers appeared as witnesses for evidence of bias against offenders.[45]

In July 2020, four police officers in San Jose, California, were suspended pending investigation into their participation in a Facebook group that regularly posted racist and anti-Muslim content. In a post about the Black Lives Matter protests, one officer reportedly responded, "Black lives really don't matter." In response, the San Jose Police Officers' Association president vowed to withhold the union's legal and financial support from any officer charged with wrongdoing in the matter, stating that "there is zero room in our department or our profession for racists, bigots or those that enable them."[46]

STATE INVESTIGATIONS REVEAL SYSTEMIC PROBLEMS

State government agencies that examined racism in local police departments also uncovered substantial evidence of racist misconduct. An audit of internal investigations at five California law enforcement agencies by the state auditor in 2022 discovered biased conduct targeting "communities of color, immigrants, women and LGBTQ people."[47] Though the audit did not uncover evidence indicating police officers were members of hate groups, it did identify six officers who had expressed support for violent far-right militant groups in public social media posts, including the Proud Boys and the Three Percenters militia.[48] The audit determined these police departments did not conduct proper investigations into allegations of biased conduct and did not have adequate policies to guard against bias within the forces.

The Minnesota Human Rights Commission investigated the Minneapolis Police Department and found that the department engaged in a pattern and practice of race discrimination in violation of the Minnesota Human Rights Act. The investigation found significant racial disparities particularly targeting Black people in uses of force, traffic stops, searches, citations, and arrests, and a culture in which police officers and supervisors used racist and sexist epithets with impunity. It also discovered police officers were using covert social media accounts to monitor and troll Black individuals, leaders, and organizations without any law enforcement or public safety purpose. Police officers did not use covert accounts to track white supremacist groups.[49]

FEDERAL LAW ENFORCEMENT NOT IMMUNE

Federal law enforcement is also infected with such misbehavior. In 2019, an internal U.S. Customs and Border Protection investigation revealed that sixty-two Border Patrol agents, including the agency's chief, participated in a secret Facebook group that included racist, nativist, and misogynistic commentary, including threats to members of Congress.[50] It is unclear whether disciplinary measures were taken against these agents. A 2019 report by *The Intercept* documented Border Patrol agents' tacit support of vigilante activities by border militia groups on the southwest border, groups that have demonstrated a propensity for illegal violence over many years.[51]

In 2022, a Defense Department contract administrator working on Intelink, a classified information sharing and communications platform used by federal intelligence and law enforcement agencies including the FBI, went public with allegations that the system was a "dumpster fire" of racist, Islamophobic, misogynistic, and anti-trans vitriol.[52] He was particularly alarmed by expressions of support for the January 6 insurrection by some intelligence agency employees. The contract administrator's attempts to document these violations of the system's terms of use policies and report them to the proper authorities for investigation resulted in his termination. A 2021 investigation by the inspector general of the intelligence community confirmed the "systemic" use of "derogatory and offensive language" and "inappropriate political and social commentary" on Intelink, but recommended that the FBI revoke the whistleblower's security clearance.[53] By contrast, according to the report, the inspector general did not investigate the intelligence community employees who had posted the racist and inappropriate content, claiming that it was "outside the scope" of its investigation.[54]

A 2023 examination by the Project on Government Oversight of leaked membership applications submitted to the Oath Keepers identified more than three hundred individuals claiming to be current or former employees of DHS agencies including "the Border Patrol, Coast Guard, Immigration and Customs Enforcement, and the Secret Service."[55] It is unclear whether the department took any disciplinary actions against these officers. A DHS working group organized by Homeland Security Secretary Alejandro Mayorkas in 2021 was tasked with conducting an evaluation to determine how to detect and respond to potential extremist threats within the department. The group issued a report in 2022 that said they found "very few instances of the DHS workforce having been engaged in domestic violent extremism," but indicated their review was impeded by the department's lack of an official definition of "domestic violent extremists," or guidance on how to detect domestic violent extremist activity within the department.[56] In July 2023, sixty-five congressional Democrats wrote to Secretary Mayorkas requesting more detailed information about what the department is doing to identify extremists within its ranks.[57] *USA Today* reported on September 18, 2023, that the members of Congress received no response, and Secretary Mayorkas has not provided a public statement on the matter.[58]

INSUFFICIENT LAW ENFORCEMENT RESPONSE TO RACISM IN THE RANKS

Law enforcement officers who associate with white supremacist and far-right militant groups or engage in racist behavior pose a threat to the communities they are sworn to serve. But few are fired. Internal investigations of citizen complaints against law enforcement officers often fail to sustain the accusations, and in many cases where misconduct is found, dismissals have been overturned by courts or in arbitration. Effective due process protections that ensure integrity and equity in the disciplinary process are necessary to protect falsely accused police officers from unjust punishments, but these procedures can easily be abused to protect racist officers.

In some cases, law enforcement officials who detect white supremacist activity in their ranks take no action unless the matter becomes a public scandal. For example, in Anniston, Alabama, city officials learned in 2009 of a police officer's membership in the League of the South, a white supremacist secessionist group that later helped organize the 2017 Unite the Right rally. The police chief, however, determined that the officer's membership in the group did not affect his performance and allowed him to remain on the job. In the following years the officer was promoted to sergeant and eventually lieutenant.[59]

The police department finally fired him in 2015, but only after the Southern Poverty Law Center published an article about a speech he gave at a League of the South conference in which he discussed his recruiting efforts among other law enforcement officers.[60] A second Anniston police lieutenant who attended the same League of the South rally was permitted to retire. The fired officer appealed, but after a three-day hearing a local civil service board upheld his dismissal. The officer then filed a lawsuit alleging that his firing violated his First Amendment free speech and association rights. A federal court affirmed the termination.

The Anniston example demonstrates the need for transparency, public accountability, and compliance with due process to resolve investigations of white supremacy in police departments. The Anniston Police Department and city officials knew about these officers' problematic involvement in a racist organization for years, but it took public pressure finally to compel action. The department responded more appropriately afterward, by dismissing the officer in a manner that provided the due process necessary to withstand judicial review. They also followed through with other positive steps to begin rebuilding public trust. The department implemented a policy requiring police officers to sign a statement affirming that they are not members of "a group that will cause embarrassment to the City of Anniston or the Anniston police department."[61] It requested conflict resolution training from the DOJ Community Relations Service.

But, as in many of these cases, the city's response failed to include a comprehensive evaluation or public accounting of the harms these avowed white supremacist police officers may have committed during the nine years they served in the Anniston Police Department, including in leadership positions. The Alabama NAACP requested that the DOJ and U.S. attorney examine the officers' previous cases for potential civil rights violations, but there is no evidence that either initiated such an investigation.[62] This decision forfeited yet another opportunity to restore public confidence in law enforcement and bring some measure of justice to those who may have been wrongly targeted by racist officers.

Failures to identify overtly racist police compounds their threat to the communities they serve. An Anti-Defamation League study identified seventy-three law enforcement officers whose affiliations with overtly racist groups—including the Ku Klux Klan, League of the South, Oath Keepers, Proud Boys, and Three Percenters militias—were publicly exposed from 2010 to 2021.[63] Forty-two percent of these individuals were fired or allowed to resign or retire. Forty percent were allowed to remain on duty. Several of those who were fired or resigned were able to find work at other law enforcement agencies.

Unfortunately, no central database lists all law enforcement officers fired for misconduct. As a result, some police officers dismissed for involvement in racist activity are able to secure other law enforcement jobs.[64] In 2017, the police chief in Colbert, Oklahoma, resigned after local media reported his decades-long involvement with neo-Nazi skinhead groups and his ownership of neo-Nazi websites.[65] A neighboring Oklahoma police department hired him the following year, claiming he had renounced his previous racist activities and held a clean record as a police officer.[66]

In 2018, the Greensboro, Maryland, police chief was charged with falsifying records so that he could hire a police officer who had previously been forced to resign from the Dover, Delaware, police department after kicking a Black man in the face and breaking his jaw.[67] After being hired in Greensboro, the officer was involved in the death of an unarmed Black teenager, which sparked an investigation that revealed twenty-nine use-of-force reports at his previous job, including some that found he used unnecessary force. The previous incidents had not been reported to the Maryland police certification board.[68]

Evidence also suggests that disciplinary investigations and adjudication of community complaints are themselves vulnerable to racial bias. A 2015 review of use-of-force and discourtesy complaints in eight medium-to-large U.S. cities found Black complainants were 29 percent less likely to have their allegations sustained than white complainants.[69] And Black police officers were 75 percent more likely to have complaints against them sustained than white officers.[70]

California recently took a positive step toward greater transparency, passing a state law requiring the publication of police disciplinary records. These records reveal that out of 3,500 citizen complaints of racial profiling from 2016 to 2019, only 2 percent were sustained.[71] Records analyzing police stops in California find Black drivers are stopped 2.5 percent more than white drivers, yet 250 police agencies that received racial profile complaints sustained none of them.[72] These included large agencies including the California Highway Patrol, Oakland Police Department, San Jose Police Department, and San Bernardino County Sheriff's Department. The Los Angeles Police Department sustained only 0.2 percent of racial profiling complaints.

Existing disciplinary systems have often proven insufficient in ridding law enforcement of racism, white supremacy, and far-right militancy and must be strengthened. It is also important to recognize that there will always be cases where an officer's misbehavior will not rise to a level justifying dismissal, or termination decisions will not be sustained on appeal. For these cases, law enforcement leaders must design other remedial policies to protect the public. Too often, if a police department's attempt to remove an officer for racist misconduct fails, it makes no further efforts to address the threat posed by that officer's continued employment. Police possess immense discretion to take a person's life and liberty. Leaving officers tainted by racist misbehavior in their jobs requires a detailed supervision plan to mitigate the potential threats they pose to the communities they police and to their fellow officers. And these plans must be implemented with sufficient transparency to restore public trust.

Multiple studies have shown that a relatively small number of officers generate a significant percentage of citizen complaints, but that repeat offenders with multiple, even dozens of complaints often remain on the job.[73] As a result, a manageable problem regarding a relatively small number of offenders is allowed to fester into a larger and more difficult one. Failing to address police misconduct can accelerate its spread within law enforcement peer groups.[74] A study of the Chicago Police Department found that 160 suspected police "crews"—networked groups of officers who coordinated their abusive or illegal activities— were responsible for almost 24 percent of all use-of-force complaints and for 20 percent of police shootings, despite making up just 4 percent of the force. This misconduct mostly targeted people of color: just 4 percent of officers received over 17 percent of all complaints by Black residents and 16 percent of complaints by Hispanic residents.[75]

More can and must be done on what is both a civil rights and national security issue. The federal government must take the lead. The FBI has primary jurisdiction for investigating domestic terrorism, including white supremacist and far-right militant violence. It also has primary jurisdiction in cases of civil rights violations, including by law enforcement officials. Unfortunately, the federal response to known connections of law enforcement officers to white supremacist and far-right militant groups has been strikingly insufficient.

4

HIDDEN IN PLAIN SIGHT

In 2015, the FBI's *Counterterrorism Policy Directive and Policy Guide* warned agents that "domestic terrorism investigations focused on militia extremists, white supremacist extremists, and sovereign citizen extremists often have identified active links to law enforcement officers."[1] This alarming declaration followed a 2006 intelligence assessment titled *White Supremacist Infiltration of Law Enforcement*, which identified several white supremacist groups that had encouraged members to infiltrate law enforcement. It noted that "active and retired law enforcement personnel are known to have joined the [neo-Nazi group National Alliance] and in some cases have held regional leadership roles in the organization."[2]

The 2006 assessment referenced two examples of law enforcement officers affiliated with white supremacist groups engaging in criminal activity. The first was a case in which the federal government leveled civil rights charges against a Boonsboro, Maryland, police officer allegedly affiliated with the Ku Klux Klan for making racist phone calls threatening to shoot Black schoolchildren and a Black city council member. The second highlighted the racketeering conviction of a California corrections officer for assisting the Nazi Low Riders in distributing drugs and committing assaults.[3] The 2006 assessment said the lack of consistent reporting on law enforcement officers engaged in white supremacist activity may be "an indication of successful infiltration that has gone undetected," a possibility that it considered a matter of "great concern."[4]

The FBI and the Department of Homeland Security have only belatedly recognized white supremacists as the most lethal domestic terrorist threat to the United States.[5] Just over the last decade, white supremacists have executed deadly shooting rampages in Overland Park, Kansas; Charleston, South Carolina; Roseberg, Oregon; Aztec, New Mexico; Parkland, Florida; Jeffersontown, Kentucky; Pittsburgh, Pennsylvania; Tallahassee, Florida; Poway, California; El Paso, Texas; Gilroy, California; Allen, Texas; Winthrop, Massachusetts; and Buffalo, New York.[6]

Any law enforcement officers associating with white supremacist and far-right militant groups should be treated as a matter of utmost concern. Operating under color of law, such officers put the lives and liberty of people of color, religious minorities, LGBTQ+ people, anti-racist activists, and their own colleagues at extreme risk, both through the violence they can mete out directly and by their failure to respond properly when these communities are victimized by other racist violent crime. Biased policing tears at the fabric of American society by undermining public trust in equal justice and the rule of law.

The FBI's 2006 assessment, however, took a narrower view. It identified the main problem as a risk to the integrity of FBI investigations and the security of its agents and informants. It claimed that "the primary threat" posed by the infiltration or recruitment of police officers into white supremacist or other far-right militant groups "arises from the areas of intelligence collection and exploitation, which can lead to investigative breaches and can jeopardize the safety of law enforcement sources or personnel."[7] The document does not address any of the potential harms these bigoted officers pose to communities of color they police or to society at large.

In a June 2019 hearing before the House Committee on Oversight and Reform, Rep. William Lacy Clay (D-MO) asked Michael McGarrity, the FBI's assistant director for counterterrorism, whether the bureau remained concerned about white supremacist infiltration of law enforcement since the publication of the 2006 assessment. McGarrity indicated he had not read the 2006 assessment.[8] When asked more generally about the issue, McGarrity said he would be "suspect" of white supremacist police officers, but that their ideology was a First Amendment–protected right. If he had read the 2006 assessment, however, he would have realized it addressed this concern. It correctly summarized Supreme Court precedent on the issue: "Although the First Amendment's freedom of association provision protects an individual's right to join white supremacist groups for the purposes of lawful activity, the government can limit the employment opportunities of group members who hold sensitive public sector jobs, including jobs within law enforcement, when their memberships would interfere with their duties."[9]

More importantly, the FBI's 2015 counterterrorism policy, which McGarrity was responsible for implementing, indicates not just that members of law enforcement might hold white supremacist views but also that FBI domestic terrorism investigations have often identified "active links" between the subjects of these investigations and law enforcement officials. Its proposed remedy was stunningly inadequate, however. The guide simply instructs agents to use the "silent hit" feature of the Terrorist Screening Center watch list so that police officers searching for themselves or their white supremacist associates could not ascertain whether they were under FBI scrutiny.

While it is important to protect the integrity of FBI terrorism investigations and the safety of law enforcement personnel, Congress has also tasked the FBI with protecting the civil rights of American communities often targeted with discriminatory stops, searches, arrests, and brutality at the hands of police officers. The issue in these cases isn't ideology but law enforcement connections to subjects of active terrorism investigations. The FBI's internal warning to its agents should have set off alarms within the broader law enforcement and intelligence communities. If the FBI had received information that U.S. law enforcement officials were actively linked to terrorist groups like al Qaeda or ISIS, or to criminal organizations like street gangs or the Mafia, it is unlikely it would have been similarly hesitant to act. Yet many of the white supremacist groups investigated by the FBI have longer and more violent histories than these other organizations.

To be clear, the FBI has at times aggressively investigated and successfully prosecuted law enforcement officers whose affiliations with white supremacist and far-right militant groups led to criminal activities. Many examples of these associations documented in this chapter came to light through FBI investigations. But these cases prove only that the FBI has the means and authorities it needs to tackle these crimes when FBI managers allow conscientious agents and analysts across the country to investigate them. FBI management has shown an appalling lack of interest in prioritizing these investigations, however, or even evaluating the scope of the problem.

In October 2020, Rep. Jamie Raskin chaired a congressional hearing investigating white supremacy in law enforcement. He asked the FBI to update its 2006 intelligence report regarding white supremacist infiltration of law enforcement and testify at the hearing.[10] An FBI representative instead disavowed the earlier intelligence report and declined the invitation to testify, stating that the bureau did not consider white supremacy in law enforcement a current problem.[11]

Just a few months later, thirty-nine sworn police officers from seventeen states were revealed to be among those who assaulted the Capitol on January 6, 2021, and at least six of them were charged with crimes, including an agent of the Drug Enforcement Agency.[12] He was not the only federal law enforcement official to be implicated in wrongdoing that day. Most of the U.S. Capitol Police and Washington, D.C., Metropolitan Police officers who were at the Capitol on January 6 fought valiantly to protect the Capitol and the members of Congress, staff, and journalists who were inside. More than 140 officers suffered injuries, one collapsed and died hours after the attack, and two others took their own lives in the following days.[13]

But, as Steve Schmidt suggested in a tweet during the attack, not all acted honorably. The Capitol Police suspended with pay six officers and placed another twenty-nine under investigation for their actions or in-actions during the January 6 attack.[14] Six were recommended for disci-pline.[15] One U.S. Capitol Police officer was charged with obstruction of justice for warning a riot participant to delete his photos from social media.[16] Two former FBI supervisors were also charged with crimes committed on January 6.[17] In 2023, the *Washington Post* reported that an active FBI agent had had his security clearance revoked for allegedly entering a restricted area outside the Capitol during the riot, but he has not been charged with a crime.[18] He has reportedly denied the allega-tion.

After the attack on the Capitol, ABC News reported on a leaked February 2021 memo from the FBI's San Antonio office warning that white supremacists inspired by a popular neo-Nazi newsletter were "very likely" seeking law enforcement affiliation and would "almost certainly" use these careers to gain access to law enforcement informa-tion.[19] The memo said it was based on information gathered from FBI investigations conducted from 2016 to 2020 and from informants who had "excellent access." It was the update of the 2006 intelligence note that Rep. Raskin had asked for months earlier. Raskin requested a meeting with the FBI to discuss this conflicted intelligence reporting, but no public response was received.[20]

This episode is a microcosm of the larger problem of bias in the FBI that contributed to its failure to prepare for the January 6 attack. When agents and analysts produce accurate intelligence that does not fit the policy preferences of FBI leaders, the leaders simply ignore or disavow it. Bias within the FBI, including at the top leadership levels, seems to have blinded the organization to the nature and scope of the threat. After the January 6 attack, a whistleblower warned the FBI associate deputy director that "there is . . . a sizeable percentage of the [FBI's] employee population that felt sympathetic to the group that stormed the Capitol."[21] It is unclear whether FBI management took any action to address this accusation.

The concern that high-level federal law enforcement officials may have supported the insurrection is not hypothetical. In September 2023, a Fulton County, Georgia, grand jury issued a racketeering indictment against former president Trump and eighteen others for attempting to overturn the Georgia election results. Among them was Jeffrey Clark, who, while serving as assistant attorney general in the Justice Department's Civil Division, conspired to open sham election fraud investigations to cast doubt on the results.[22]

Despite this clear evidence of at least some support within federal law enforcement for the militant groups that led the insurrection, there has not been a full public accounting of these agencies' failure to prepare adequately for the January 6 attack. The Justice Department plays a crucial role in protecting the rule of law and defending our democracy from criminal and national security threats. Its response to the attempted insurrection has been slow but workmanlike, producing thousands of charges against those who attacked police and ransacked the Capitol in an attempt to obstruct the electoral vote count. A special counsel has indicted former president Trump for conspiracy and obstruction for his attempts to overthrow the election. But there has not been a restructuring of priorities to focus on racism, white supremacy, and far-right militancy in law enforcement agencies: federal, state, and local. All evidence indicates this remains a persistent problem.

FEDERAL ATTENTION IS NEEDED TO LAW ENFORCEMENT MISCONDUCT

In August 2023, six white Rankin County, Mississippi, sheriff's deputies pled guilty to federal civil rights violations and obstruction of justice for breaking into a home and torturing two Black men, shooting one of them, because they were staying in a house with a white woman.[23] Some of the officers, who called themselves the "Goon Squad," were implicated in previous questionable assaults on Black men, two of whom were killed during the encounters.[24]

Four days later, the FBI arrested ten officers from the Antioch and Pittsburg, California, police departments for a variety of misconduct, including several civil rights violations.[25] The investigation initially targeted a fraud scheme in which officers falsified educational accomplishments to get unearned pay increases. But it uncovered local police officers and supervisors engaging in widespread use of racist, misogynistic, and anti-trans language over law enforcement text messaging services. Almost half of the ninety-nine officers in the Antioch police department were implicated in the racist text messaging scandal.[26] Antioch police officers used epithets to describe Black people and deliberately targeted them with excessive force, including allowing K-9s to bite them and shooting them with less-lethal baton rounds.[27]

These cases again show that federal law enforcement has the tools it needs to bring effective prosecutions but that they are too rarely used. The Justice Department fails to prioritize these police misconduct investigations or utilize all the necessary resources to address police violence and racism as a systemic national problem.[28] Federal prosecutors declined to prosecute 96 percent of FBI civil rights investigations involving police misconduct from 1995 to 2015, turning down more than 12,700 complaints, according to a Reuters analysis of DOJ records.[29]

Federal prosecutors do face a high evidentiary bar when bringing criminal cases against law enforcement officials, which require proof that the officers willfully intended to violate the victim's civil rights in their use of force.[30] It is not enough to prove that an officer's intentional use of excessive force resulted in a denial of a victim's constitutional rights. The federal civil rights statute that covers police brutality, called Deprivation of Rights Under Color of Law, requires prosecutors to prove that police officers intended to use excessive force *and* that they did so "willfully," that is, with the specific intent to violate the victim's constitutional rights.[31]

This "willfully" standard is higher than that required in other criminal prosecutions and tends to dissuade federal prosecutors from bringing these cases to court, out of concern that a conviction isn't certain. The George Floyd Justice in Policing Act, which was introduced in Congress in 2020, would have changed this standard to "knowingly or recklessly."[32] It passed in the House of Representatives in 2020, and again in 2021, but failed both times after it was not advanced in the Republican-controlled Senate.

The "willfully" standard is not a complete bar to successful prosecutions of racist police misconduct, however, as the 1992 convictions of the LAPD officers who beat Rodney King and the 2023 guilty pleas entered by the Mississippi sheriff's deputies demonstrate. A successful prosecution just requires a deeper and more exacting search for evidence of racist intent. Unfortunately, civil rights investigations against law enforcement officials are not a top priority in the FBI, whose agents often rely on state and local police for support in more highly ranked programs, like terrorism, drugs, and organized crime.

Part of the reason federal prosecutors decline to file charges in such cases has to do with the routine way the FBI investigates civil rights complaints against officers. Typically, the receiving agent takes a complaint from a victim, obtains the police report, checks the officer's name against previous FBI investigations, interviews witnesses if there are any, asks the accused officer to submit to interviews (which inevitably is declined when the officer chooses to stand on the police reports), puts it together in a memo, and sends the package up to the U.S. attorney's office for a prosecutive opinion. In most of these cases, it is the victim's word against the officer's. So it isn't surprising the declination rate is so high. Evidence of racism and bias is often available in previous complaints, misconduct investigations, civil rights lawsuits, and other police department data, but this evidence is not systematically collected in a manner that agents investigating civil rights violations could easily access and use.

The Justice Department has so far failed to develop a federal database that tracks racist law enforcement misconduct and affiliation with white supremacist or far-right militant groups, which makes discovering evidence of racist intent in individual cases more difficult. The FBI only began collecting data on law enforcement uses of force in 2018, after Black Lives Matter and other police accountability groups pushed for more federal oversight of police violence against people of color.[33] This is a positive step, but the data rely on voluntary reporting by law enforcement agencies, a methodology that has led to serious deficiencies in other areas, particularly hate crime reporting. The FBI also fails to document forms of police racial misconduct that do not involve use of force.

The FBI and Justice Department should actively collect data about police misconduct as they would for any other potentially criminal activity, rather than wait passively for police to self-report inappropriate uses of force. Civil rights complaints filed by community members and racial discrimination claims by law enforcement employees could provide the predicate for misconduct investigations, which could in turn inform a national strategic plan to protect communities from racist police violence more effectively. In the Antioch and Pittsburg cases, it took an investigation into government fraud to discover inadvertently that a dozen members of two police departments had been racially terrorizing their communities for years. The community members they abused certainly knew.

In addition to criminal penalties, the Justice Department has the authority to bring civil suits against law enforcement agencies if it can demonstrate a "pattern or practice" of civil rights violations.[34] Civil suits have a lower evidentiary bar, and they target department-wide problems rather than individual officers' misconduct. These cases often reach settlement agreements or "consent decrees," which provide for a period of DOJ oversight of agreed-upon reform efforts. The Obama administration opened twenty pattern-and-practice investigations of police departments, doubling the number initiated by the Bush administration, and entered into at least fourteen consent decrees with police agencies.[35] However, the Justice Department has not developed metrics to evaluate the effectiveness of these efforts in curbing police violence or civil rights abuses.[36] Some evidence indicates that consent decrees may have a positive effect in reducing misconduct and civil rights lawsuits.[37] Even where they fail to reduce civil rights violations, they can compel transparency and provide a means of accountability.

For example, in 2014, the Justice Department entered a settlement agreement with the Portland Police Bureau after a civil rights investigation found it engaged in a pattern and practice of using excessive force against people suffering from mental illness. The Portland police agreed to enact a series of reforms, including tightening its use of force policies and improving oversight, documentation, and training. During the 2020 protests following the police killing of George Floyd, however, the Justice Department found that Portland officers had used force six thousand times, often indiscriminately and in violation of policy, and was therefore out of compliance with the settlement agreement.[38] The Justice Department is now seeking a new set of reforms, including body cameras, civilian oversight of police training, and a community oversight board.[39]

The Trump administration abandoned police reform efforts championed by Obama's Justice Department. Attorney General Jeff Sessions ordered a review of civil rights pattern-and-practice cases and, on his last day in office, signed a memo establishing more stringent requirements for Justice Department attorneys seeking to open them, which limited the utility of this tool in curbing systemic police misconduct.[40] Sessions also killed a program operated by the DOJ Office of Community Oriented Policing Services that evaluated police department practices and offered corrective recommendations in a more collaborative way that avoided litigation. Attorney General William Barr indicated similar disdain for law enforcement oversight, once threatening that communities that do not give support and respect to law enforcement "might find themselves without the police protection they need."[41]

The Biden administration has taken steps to improve the Justice Department's performance on these matters, issuing an executive order to advance accountable policing in 2022.[42] The executive order instructs the Justice Department to establish a National Law Enforcement Accountability database, which will collect records of law enforcement misconduct, including sustained complaints, disciplinary actions, and civil judgments. In December 2023, the Justice Department announced its establishment of this database, but it will include misconduct records only for federal law enforcement officers, and it can be used by federal law enforcement agencies only to determine suitability for hiring in law enforcement positions.[43]

The Biden executive order also establishes a working group to develop law enforcement applicant screening procedures, consistent with the First Amendment, "to help avoid the hiring and retention of law enforcement officers who promote unlawful violence, white supremacy, or other bias against persons based on race, ethnicity, national origin, religion, sex (including sexual orientation and gender identity), or disability."[44] Specifically identifying white supremacy and law enforcement bias as the issues to be addressed is essential to developing a sound and effective policy.

The cases in Mississippi and California may be evidence that these policies are giving the Justice Department new energy to tackle racist violence by law enforcement. But it will take pressure from Congress and the public to ensure that the working group develops sound recommendations, and that the administration implements them effectively. It is important to get these policies in place quickly so that a change in administrations does not take another direction and impede progress.

IMPLICIT BIAS TRAINING IS INSUFFICIENT

The Justice Department offers civil rights and implicit bias training to law enforcement and often mandates it in consent decrees following pattern and practice lawsuits. While this training may be important to help sensitize law enforcement to unconscious bias, its effectiveness in curbing police bias remains unproven.[45] An obvious deficiency in implicit training sessions is the failure to address *overt* racism and white supremacy within law enforcement. A police trainer quoted in *The Atlantic* said overt racism is "just something that you don't admit . . . If we admit that, then what does it mean about how we serve the public?"[46] Another told *The Forward*, "If [anti-bias training] is not presented in a very nimble way, officers will assume that what you're saying is that officers are racist. . . . In my experience, that has tended to close officers up to whatever content you provide."[47] A third trainer told *Popular Science*, "When they walk into the classroom, the officers are somewhere between defensive and downright hostile. They think we're gonna shake our fingers at them and call them racist."[48] Some studies suggest that implicit bias training can even be counterproductive by reinforcing racial stereotypes.[49]

During the June 2019 House oversight committee hearing, Rep. Clay asked Deputy Assistant Director Calvin Shivers, who manages the FBI's civil rights section, whether the bureau provided any resources or training to state and local police departments to help them identify white supremacists attempting to infiltrate their agencies.[50] Shivers said the training that the FBI's civil rights section provides to law enforcement is focused on helping them identify hate crimes that may occur within their jurisdictions. He did not identify any training focused on identifying and weeding out officers who actively participate in white supremacist and far-right militant groups.

The continued presence of even a small number of far-right militants, white supremacists, and other overt racists in law enforcement has an outsized impact on public safety and on public trust in the criminal justice system and cannot be ignored. Leaving individual agencies to police themselves in a piecemeal fashion has not proven effective at restoring public confidence in law enforcement. Instead, the country needs a comprehensive plan—one that involves federal, state, and local governments—to ensure that law enforcement agencies do not tolerate overtly racist conduct.

THE PROSECUTOR'S ROLE

Prosecutors have an important role in protecting the integrity of the criminal justice system from the potential misconduct of explicitly racist officers. The landmark 1963 Supreme Court ruling in *Brady v. Maryland* requires prosecutors and the police to provide criminal defendants with all exculpatory evidence in their possession.[51] A later decision in *Giglio v. United States* expanded this requirement to include the disclosure of evidence that may impeach a government witness.[52] Prosecutors keep a register of law enforcement officers whose previous misconduct could reasonably undermine the reliability of their testimony and therefore would need to be disclosed to defense attorneys. This register is often referred to as a "Brady list" or "no-call list."

As Georgetown law professor Vida B. Johnson has argued, evidence of a law enforcement officer's explicitly racist behavior could reasonably be expected to impeach his or her testimony.[53] Prosecutors should be required to include these officers on Brady lists to ensure that defendants against whom they testify have access to the potentially exculpating evidence of the officers' explicitly racist behavior. This reform would be an important measure in blunting the impact of racist police officers on the criminal justice system. In 2019, progressive St. Louis prosecutor Kimberly Gardner placed all twenty-two of the St. Louis police officers that the Plain View Project identified as posting racist content on Facebook on her office's no-call list.[54] As previously mentioned, Kim Foxx, the Cook County, Illinois, state's attorney, placed ten Chicago police officers who had affiliations with far-right militant groups on her office's no-call list in 2023.[55]

Of course, prosecutors are not above reproach and must also be held to account. In May 2023, a county judge held that the Contra County, California, district attorney's charging decisions were influenced by racial bias. The judge found the district attorney's office charged Black defendants with special enhancements, which can "impose a mandatory life sentence without the possibility of parole," forty-four times more often than for other defendants. The lawsuit was the result of a 2020 California police reform law that allows criminal defendants to allege that bias influenced charging, conviction, and sentencing decisions. The city of Antioch, California, where dozens of police officers were found to have engaged in racist misconduct, is in Contra County.[56]

In Florida, an assistant state attorney in rural Jefferson County issued a written policy directing the all-white staff of approximately fifty prosecutors to seek more severe punishments for Hispanic defendants. The policy, in place in 2022 and 2023, instructed prosecutors to seek guilty verdicts and court costs for Hispanic people caught driving without a license, but deferred prosecution for others. The assistant prosecutor who reported the memo said it was part of a broader racist and anti-immigrant attitude within the office, but the state attorney claimed it was just a poor choice of words. The policy, he said, was intended to cover undocumented migrant workers, rather than a racial group. He reprimanded but did not fire the junior-level prosecutor who wrote it.[57]

HITTING SNOOZE ON THE JANUARY 6 WAKE-UP CALL

After a white Minneapolis police officer was filmed kneeling on an unarmed Black man's neck for the nine minutes and twenty-nine seconds it took to kill him, Americans across the country poured into the streets to demand an end to racist police violence. The following year, when dozens of current and former police officers, members of the military, and elected representatives were among the mob that attacked the Capitol, assaulted police officers, and attempted to overthrow a democratic election, the presence of white supremacist and far-right militancy in our security agencies was widely recognized as a serious threat that demanded a solution.

Progress has been made. In the largest criminal investigation in history, the FBI and Justice Department have charged over 1,200 people, including six Oath Keepers and four Proud Boys who were convicted of seditious conspiracy, the most serious charges to date. At least twenty of those charged were current or former law enforcement officers. In 2023, the FBI charged police officers in Mississippi and California with civil rights violations for racist police violence. The Justice Department has resumed its use of civil rights pattern-and-practice lawsuits to hold police departments more accountable. These cases prove that federal law enforcement has the tools it needs to address this problem if it is given the appropriate resources and prioritizes their use.

Likewise, in 2021, the secretary of defense ordered a department-wide stand-down to reiterate the need to address extremism in the ranks and to receive training on how to report it.[58] That year, the department issued new policies to clarify what conduct is prohibited and new screening measures for recruits.[59] The Secretary of Homeland Security also established a working group to address extremism within his department. Over the last several years, some police leaders who have discovered officers affiliating with white supremacist or far-right militant groups have taken swift action, conducting investigations, and, where warranted, dismissing those officers from the force.[60]

Public pressure demanding reforms from elected representatives has also produced results. State legislatures have passed hundreds of police reform bills in all but a handful of states. President Biden issued an executive order establishing reforms for federal law enforcement and creating a database to collect national data about police misconduct.

But, as in the past, successful efforts to challenge white supremacy have been met with resistance and retrenchment. A sharply divided U.S. Congress failed to pass a federal police reform bill.[61] Many of the successful efforts at the state level have been rolled back or lost funding.[62] The Defense Department efforts to reduce extremism met resistance internally and from Republicans in Congress. The ordered reforms were not fully imposed, and enhanced screening efforts were quietly abandoned.[63] Similar efforts to stem extremism within DHS likewise appear to have faltered. No similar effort at the FBI or Justice Department was ever announced.

Despite the January 6 prosecutions, militant groups such as the Proud Boys have reorganized and continue to menace local communities across the United States with little intervention from law enforcement.[64] In 2021, a Fresno, California, police officer was photographed marching with Proud Boys at local protests. He admitted to having been a member of the Proud Boys in the past, but claimed he had left them to form his own group of "gentleman combatants."[65] And law enforcement officials continue to engage in racist misconduct with little apparent concern that their colleagues will report them. Also in 2021, Torrance, California, police officers were suspended after the *Los Angeles Times* reported they shared racist, anti-Black, anti-Semitic, and sexist text messages, and engaged in excessive force and other misconduct.[66] Prosecutors were forced to dismiss criminal charges in ninety cases in which these officers provided evidence.

The successes show what can be done, but a sustained and unified effort involving law enforcement, prosecutors, judges, and elected officials will be required to address the problem effectively. The piecemeal approach taken thus far shows that the tools all work when they are used. But a comprehensive effort to document racist misconduct by law enforcement officials is necessary to demonstrate the full scope of the problem so that more fulsome reforms can be enacted and, more importantly, sustained.

Part Two

A STRATEGY FOR CHANGE

5

RESETTING FEDERAL LAW ENFORCEMENT PRIORITIES

Violence by white supremacists is a manageable problem when law enforcement and government leaders focus on reducing it. Despite their outsized impact, these types of attacks constitute only a tiny fraction of violence in American society. The FBI and other federal agencies have all the tools necessary to investigate cases, prosecute the perpetrators, and dismantle the networks that support them. But the Justice Department has chosen as a matter of policy not to prioritize this threat.

In June 2021, the Biden administration issued the U.S. government's first National Strategy for Countering Domestic Terrorism. While a positive step, the strategy has flaws, its implementation has been sluggish, and its ultimate effects to date are unmeasured.[1] What the Justice Department needs—and what it has so far refused to produce—is a strategy that explicitly targets white supremacist violence and prioritizes addressing this threat as a matter of national security.

Federal law enforcement's mandate to address white supremacist violence dates back to the 1870s, when Congress passed the Act to Establish the Department of Justice. The first task of this new federal body was to address violence by groups who opposed the Thirteenth, Fourteenth, and Fifteenth Amendments, which granted citizenship and civil rights protections to formerly enslaved African Americans.[2] The most serious threat, according to the history published on the Justice Department's website, came from the Ku Klux Klan, which "often carried out lawless acts of violence and aggression, terrorizing African Americans for exercising their right to vote, running for public office, and serving on juries."[3]

In 1871, Congress passed what was arguably the first domestic terrorism law, the Ku Klux Klan Act.[4] The law, one of four new civil rights statutes known as the Enforcement Acts, granted the federal government expanded powers, including using the military to enforce constitutional rights, as there was no federal law enforcement agency capable of performing this function at the time.[5] The Justice Department website proudly enumerates the successful prosecutions in the early 1870s under President Ulysses S. Grant and the first attorney general, former Confederate officer Amos T. Akerman:

> In the first years of Grant's first term in office as President, there were over 1,000 indictments against Klan members with over 550 convictions won by new Department of Justice lawyers. By late 1871, there were more than 3,000 indictments and 600 more convictions. Due to the initial and highly successful efforts of the new Department of Justice and Attorney General Akerman, there was a dramatic decrease in violence in the South by the time he left office in 1872. This would prove to be just the beginning to a celebrated 150 years of federal law enforcement by the officials and employees of our Department of Justice. [6]

The federal government's Reconstruction-era focus on fighting white terror was short-lived. Despite the success of these federal prosecutions in crippling the original Klan—or perhaps because of it—the Supreme Court issued a series of opinions from 1873 through 1876 that limited the application of the Fourteenth Amendment, and therefore weakened the utility of the Ku Klux Klan Act in protecting civil rights. The end of Reconstruction and the removal of federal forces as a bulwark against white terrorism enabled the return of white supremacy in law and practice.[7] The Equal Justice Initiative has documented over 4,400 "racial terror lynchings" from the end of the Civil War through World War II, a form of vigilante violence designed to maintain existing white power structures that was "largely tolerated by state and federal officials."[8] The Ku Klux Klan was revived in 1915 and has persisted ever since. But the Klan is only one of scores of white supremacist and far-right militant organizations whose violent attacks still threaten communities of color, immigrants, LGBTQ+ people, women, and religious minorities.

The Justice Department and its primary investigative arm, the FBI, have a constitutional mandate to ensure that these communities receive equal protection under the law. But throughout its history, the Justice Department has not prioritized the threat in a manner that the level of violence demanded. While the FBI and DOJ could point to hundreds of cases prosecuted over the decades, these represent just a tiny fraction of the racist, homophobic, anti-Semitic, and anti-immigrant violence that has gone unreported, unprosecuted, and uncounted.

Current U.S. Department of Justice policies reflect priorities established after the al Qaeda attacks of September 11, 2001, when Attorney General John Ashcroft named terrorism prevention—international and domestic—as its number one mission.[9] In a 2001 Senate hearing, Ashcroft vowed to protect Americans from "international terrorists" who target American citizens "both at home and abroad," adding that "the risk of terrorism within our borders does not result solely from persons of foreign origin." As an example of "acts of terrorism perpetrated by disaffected citizens," he cited the 1995 bombing of the Alfred P. Murrah Federal Building in Oklahoma City by far-right extremist Timothy McVeigh, which killed 168 people.[10]

In practice, however, the post-9/11 counterterrorism infrastructure overwhelmingly prioritized what it calls "international terrorism" investigations, which primarily targeted Muslims, over "domestic terrorism," which did not.[11] By 2004, more than six thousand FBI field agents worked counterterrorism, as reported by an inspector general's audit on the effects of reprioritization.[12] According to an audit from 2010, the last year these figures were published, from 2005 through 2009 the FBI assigned fewer than 330 of these thousands of field agents to domestic terrorism.[13] In 2019, FBI assistant director for counterterrorism Michael McGarrity testified that 80 percent of counterterrorism resources are devoted to international terrorism, and 20 percent to domestic terrorism.[14] In December 2023, FBI director Christopher Wray indicated that though the FBI had doubled the number of its domestic terrorism investigations since 2020, it still considered international terrorism the primary threat. Wray indicated that as of November 2023, the FBI had 2,700 open domestic terrorism investigations as compared to 4,000 international terrorism investigations.[15]

This skewed distribution of resources does not reflect an objective evaluation of threats from different groups. Instead, federal law enforcement priorities are driven by exaggerated perceptions of threats from groups like al Qaeda, along with Islamophobic perceptions of American Muslims as threatening "persons of foreign origin," to borrow Ashcroft's language. Some FBI agents risk their lives pursuing real threats from international organizations with a track record of deadly violence. But many other so-called international terrorism investigations needlessly devote resources to aggressive monitoring and infiltration of Muslim, Arab, Middle Eastern, South Asian, and African American communities throughout the United States. The rationale is to identify preemptively and prosecute selectively "radicalized" individuals who have not committed terrorist acts but whom the government believes, based on a flawed theory of terrorist radicalization, may do so sometime in the future.[16]

Further, for the several hundred agents assigned to domestic terrorism, the FBI prioritized investigations of environmental activists and racial justice protesters, who rarely, if ever, engaged in deadly violence—a key element of the federal definition of terrorism. In 2005, for example, the FBI declared ecoterrorists the number one domestic threat, despite not a single fatal attack in the United States[17] In 2016, the Justice Department went all out in its ultimately failed attempt to prosecute more than two hundred activists protesting Trump's inauguration, in stark contrast to the handful of federal charges that came out of violent far-right riots taking place all across the country in which white supremacists and far-right militants stabbed, shot, and beat anti-racism protesters.[18]

Overall, the federal government's domestic terrorism efforts have investigated and prosecuted only a tiny percentage of the violent acts committed by far-right militants. Exactly how many is impossible to say, because the Justice Department does not collect or publish data that would measure the true nature or scope of this problem. A May 2021 report required by the National Defense Authorization Act of 2020 confirmed that the FBI does not track the annual incidents of lethal and nonlethal violence committed by groups it categorizes as "domestic violent extremists."[19]

To fill this gap, academic institutions, advocacy organizations, and think tanks have developed their own analyses of terrorism incidents. Arie Perliger at West Point's Combating Terrorism Center, for example, documented 607 fatalities from 1990 through 2011 arising from violent attacks "intended to promote ideas compatible with far-right ideology," including hate crimes.[20] Other studies use different criteria to define domestic and international terrorist threats, cover different time frames, or focus on specific victim sets, which means the data vary significantly, making it difficult to gain a comprehensive understanding of the impact of far-right violence. Professors Joshua D. Freilich and Steven M. Chermak, who founded the Extremist Crime Database, for example, identified 448 *law enforcement officers* who were killed in thirty-seven incidents from 1990 through 2008 "in which at least one of the suspects was a far-rightist."[21]

Despite these obstacles, two facts become clear from comparing the most comprehensive studies. First, when measured according to the number of resulting fatalities, far-right violence poses a threat as great as, or greater than, any other threat categorized as terrorism, domestic or international. Second, hate crimes—in the form of racist, Islamophobic, anti-Semitic, homophobic, and anti-immigrant violence—are severely underaddressed by federal law enforcement.

"NOT A POLITICAL ACT"

For many Americans, the Justice Department's failure to prioritize violence by white supremacists became evident when Dylann Roof assassinated Reverend Clementa Pinckney, a sitting state legislator, and eight members of Pinckney's Mother Emanuel African Methodist Episcopal Church in Charleston, South Carolina, in June 2015. Early evidence showed Roof was motivated by timeworn white supremacist tropes: friends reported his saying before the attack that he wanted to start a "race war," and according to accounts by survivors, during the shooting he said, "I have to do it. You rape our women and you're taking over our country."[22] But in interviews, FBI director James Comey refused to call the attack an act of terrorism.[23] Comey said, "Based on what I know so far, I don't see it as a political act."[24]

In the aftermath of the attack, journalists and public figures observed that federal officials readily use the terrorism label to describe criminal activity by Muslims, even in the absence of clear evidence of political motive. Many commentators also asked why terror directed at Black communities is so rarely called terrorism. Jelani Cobb noted that the FBI's description of Timothy McVeigh's Oklahoma City bombing as "the worst act of homegrown terrorism in the nation's history" overlooks the 1921 Tulsa Race Massacre, in which a white mob murdered as many as three hundred Black residents of the Greenwood neighborhood. "From one perspective, the Murrah bombing was the worst act of domestic terrorism in our history," Cobb writes in the *New Yorker,* "but, as the descendants of the Greenwood survivors know, it was likely not even the worst incident in *Oklahoma's* history."[25] The Tulsa massacre was only one of many massacres of Black communities in the "Red Summer" of 1919 and continuing through 1920 and 1921—a surge of white racist terror that J. Edgar Hoover's Bureau of Investigation all but ignored, choosing instead to investigate whether the Black resistance to these attacks was influenced by Bolshevik propaganda.[26]

Words matter when a federal official describes an act of violence. Failing to regard deadly racist violence perpetrated by white supremacists as "terrorism," when both violent and nonviolent crimes perpetrated by Muslims are routinely treated as such, sends a public message that the security of minority communities is not a top priority. It undermines trust in law enforcement, particularly among Black and Muslim Americans, who are overpoliced as terrorism suspects and underserved as terrorism victims.

Failure to employ the "terrorism" label also reduces the relative import of far-right violence in the Justice Department bureaucracy. As part of post-9/11 reprioritization, the FBI established a ranked list of eight priorities. Terrorism is first on this list, and these investigations are well resourced and prioritized. Investigators tend to look broadly to determine if an ongoing criminal organization may have supported the attack or is planning new ones. In contrast, civil rights violations, including hate crimes, rank fifth out of eight priorities. Investigations tend to focus narrowly on a particular attack or attacker, seeking to identify evidence to prove the biased motive for the attack.

What's more, federal hate crime investigations are very rare. Crime victim surveys conducted from 2004 to 2015 estimated that approximately 230,000 violent hate crimes occur annually but, despite five federal hate crime statutes, the Justice Department prosecuted only about twenty-five defendants each year.[27] In 2017 and 2018, during the Trump administration, only six prosecutions were reported each year.[28] Hate crime prosecutions rose again during the Biden administration, with ninety defendants charged from January 2021 through August 2023, but this is still a tiny fraction of the hate crimes that occur in the United States.[29]

The relatively small number of Justice Department prosecutions is a result of its long-standing policy of deferring investigations of hate crimes to state and local law enforcement. This route is often a dead end for victims seeking justice: despite the vast number of reported hate crimes, only a small percentage of police agencies (14 percent in 2019) acknowledge in federal crime reports that hate crimes occur in their jurisdiction.[30] And while state prosecutions may be appropriate in some cases, many states rarely use their hate crime laws, and some, including South Carolina, don't have them at all.[31]

Roof was charged with nine counts of murder in South Carolina state court and thirty-three acts of hate crimes and firearms offenses in federal court.[32] In 2017, he became the first person sentenced to death for a federal hate crime.[33] But labeling a crime by a white supremacist "terrorism" has import beyond the severity of the punishment. White supremacist attacks often fit the federal definitions of both domestic terrorism and hate crimes, as well as state violations such as murder. Labeling a far-right crime "terrorism" signals it is top priority within the post-9/11 bureaucracy and recognizes the organized nature of white supremacist violence, even in a case where an attacker acted alone, as Roof did. Roof's attack later served as an inspiration to white supremacist mass shooters across the United States and abroad, as well as others charged in terrorism-related crimes.[34]

It is also important to clarify that a crime may be labeled terrorism and still also be charged as a hate crime. This fact became obscured and confused in the debate that followed the attack on Mother Emanuel Church. In the July 2015 press conference announcing the federal grand jury indictment on hate crimes charges, Attorney General Loretta Lynch was asked whether "domestic terrorism charges had been considered."

Attorney General Lynch responded, "As you know, there is no specific domestic terrorism statute." She then explained, "However, hate crimes . . . are the original domestic terrorism. And we feel that the behavior that is alleged to have occurred here is archetypal behavior that fits the hate crimes statutes and vindicates their purpose."[35]

As Lynch's comments expressed, terror by white supremacists is the violence that has threatened America since its origins. The murder of nine Black churchgoers should have shifted Justice Department priorities to address the unbroken chain of attacks that have long been neglected by federal authorities. But instead, federal officials seized on the fact that, as Attorney General Lynch pointed out, there is no specific federal charge called "domestic terrorism." The reason they couldn't appropriately address white supremacist violence, some argued, is that their hands were tied by insufficient powers to prosecute white supremacists as domestic terrorists.

These calls for greater powers echoed federal law enforcement's stance after 9/11, when FBI leaders blamed their intelligence failures on legal restraints designed to protect Americans' constitutional rights, and used these false pretenses to wring broad new domestic spying authorities from Congress. But federal law enforcement needs a new approach to fighting far-right violence and hate crimes, not a deeper investment in failed methods. Efforts to expand legal powers to prosecute domestic terrorism represent the wrong approach to policing white supremacy effectively. The FBI and Justice Department prosecutors, along with their state and local law enforcement partners, already have all the legal tools they need to investigate and prosecute violence by white supremacist militants. They just need to prioritize these cases.

MISGUIDED CALLS FOR A NEW DOMESTIC TERRORISM STATUTE

After the attack on Mother Emanuel Church, Justice Department officials in the Obama administration forwarded a legislative proposal that would create a domestic terrorism offense, perhaps modeled on the laws governing international terrorism. Mary McCord, the former head of the Justice Department's National Security Division, stated that passing enactment of a new federal crime of domestic terrorism was necessary to make it the "moral equivalent" of international terrorism.[36] Thomas Brzozowski, the Justice Department's Counsel for Domestic Terrorism, claimed that the lack of a federal statute "that is entitled 'domestic terrorism' " sows confusion, and that creating one would help establish a "common vocabulary."[37]

In fact, the opposite is true. While there isn't a specific federal crime called "domestic terrorism," the same is true for "international terrorism."[38] Instead, an entire chapter of the U.S. Criminal Code is titled "Terrorism." This chapter defines both international and domestic terrorism and then lists fifty-seven "federal crimes of terrorism." Fifty-one of these laws apply to acts of domestic terrorism. The code also contains two separate "material support for terrorism" provisions. It can be a bit confusing, but it simply isn't accurate to say there is no domestic terrorism law. There are lots of them.

Terrorism has always been a contentious and politically freighted term that has defied a precise definition.[39] It is a pejorative label, best used as a rhetorical device for describing violence a government or society particularly despises. Its use in legal proceedings is controversial because it is a political term—a government may consider an act committed by one person against a particular target terrorism, but not the same act committed by another against a different target. Rather than trying to craft a statute creating a new crime called "terrorism," every element of which would need to be proven beyond a reasonable doubt in a court of law, Congress identified the criminal offenses terrorists often committed, such as bombings, air piracy, kidnappings, assaults on government officials, and the possession or use of certain weapons, among others, and labeled them "federal crimes of terrorism."[40]

The legal framework for federal counterterrorism prosecutions is set forth in the "Terrorism" chapter of the U.S. Criminal Code.[41] The chapter begins with definitions of both international and domestic terrorism. Domestic terrorism is defined as activities that "involve acts dangerous to human life that are a violation of the criminal laws of the United States or of any State, appear to be intended to intimidate or coerce a civilian population; to influence the policy of a government by intimidation or coercion; or to affect the conduct of a government by mass destruction, assassination, or kidnapping, and occur primarily within the territorial jurisdiction of the United States."[42] Despite FBI director Comey's reticence to describe Roof's racist attack as an act of domestic terrorism, it clearly fits within this definition—a criminal act dangerous to human life intended to intimidate a civilian population.

The definition of international terrorism uses the same descriptive language, but states that acts must occur outside the territorial jurisdiction of the United States or "transcend national boundaries in terms of the means by which they are accomplished, the persons they appear intended to intimidate or coerce, or the locale in which their perpetrators operate or seek asylum."[43] So, according to the statute, the difference between international and domestic terrorism is purely geographical.

Neither definition assigns criminal penalties, as that is not the role of the definition sections of statutes.[44] Charges that may be used to prosecute terrorist acts are instead found in the chapter's fifty-seven statutes, listed under the heading of "federal crimes of terrorism." Fifty-one of these charges apply to acts committed inside the United States, thereby meeting the definition of domestic terrorism.

One of the federal crimes listed in the terrorism chapter establishes criminal penalties for "acts of terrorism transcending national boundaries."[45] Some believe that this crime can be applied only to international terrorism cases, but that is not accurate; the statute prohibits violent acts in the United States that create a substantial risk of serious bodily injury in circumstances that may obstruct interstate or foreign commerce and are calculated to affect the U.S. government.[46] Though it is used primarily to target "international" terrorism, this crime is also applicable to what the Justice Department regards as "domestic" terrorism, so long as some part of the crime occurs outside the United States or has an effect on foreign commerce.[47]

OVERBROAD MATERIAL SUPPORT STATUTES

The primary distinction between international and domestic terrorism in the U.S. Code can be found in the law that criminalizes material support for a foreign terrorist organization.[48] This law imposes severe penalties on anyone, regardless of their nationality, who knowingly provides funding or other forms of aid to a group, organization, or individual that the U.S. government has identified as a "specially designated global terrorist" or "foreign terrorist organization." Federal law gives the government nearly unfettered authority to apply these designations, requiring only a "reasonable suspicion" that the entity is involved in terrorism. This is a very low legal standard that can be based on secret evidence the designated group or individual is unable to see or rebut.[49]

The law provides the government with its justification for categorizing American Muslims as "international" terrorists and subjecting them to broader, more secretive, and less accountable investigations than those available in domestic terrorism cases.[50] Linking a person to an international group, even if only through an alleged "inspiration," grants access to an array of national security tactics, including electronic surveillance tools designed to capture foreign spies. These include the Foreign Intelligence Surveillance Act wiretaps and physical searches, and National Security Letters, which may be used to obtain subscriber information from telecommunications companies, credit reporting agencies, and financial institutions. Using these powers requires less independent scrutiny than traditional criminal warrants and grand jury subpoenas, which are approved by judges or authorized by grand juries and often made part of the public record.[51]

When they were first introduced in the 1980s and early 1990s, material support bills faced significant bipartisan resistance, based on their potential to infringe on Americans' First Amendment rights.[52] Democratic senator Howard Metzenbaum called the bills "a throwback to the McCarthy era."[53] Republican senator Jeremiah Denton concluded that the initial proposal was "too loosely written" and "seemed to include even speech."[54] Given such criticisms, early bills failed.[55] But in 1994, the first material support for terrorism prohibition became law. This statute, called Providing Material Support to Terrorists, prohibits providing funding or other assistance toward the commission of any one of the fifty-seven terrorism-related criminal offenses.[56] It can be applied to acts of both domestic and international terrorism.

In 1996, Congress passed the Antiterrorism and Effective Death Penalty Act, which established a second, more controversial material support prohibition.[57] Where the original statute criminalized material support for terrorism crimes, the 1996 statute criminalized "providing material support to designated foreign terrorist organizations." The criminal intent, or mens rea, requirements also differ. The first material support statute criminalized only support that the defendant knows will be used to further a terrorism-related criminal offense. By contrast, the second statute was much broader, prohibiting the provision of any support, expert advice, or resources to a group the defendant knows has been designated a foreign terrorist organization, even if such support did not assist the group's criminal or terrorist activities and was not intended to. Simply joining an organization, advocating on its behalf, or providing

humanitarian assistance to needy people in an area controlled by a foreign terrorist organization can be considered material support under this
second provision.

As lawmakers recognized in their initial hesitancy about material
support laws, the First Amendment's free speech and association rights
prevent Congress from prohibiting Americans from joining or advocating on behalf of domestic groups. For this reason, the material support statute that prohibits resources for organizations—not just acts of
terrorism—applies only to those groups designated as foreign terrorist
organizations and not to domestic organizations.

Within the ill-defined "international terrorism" sphere, the statute
prohibiting material support for foreign terrorist organizations has led
to the kinds of abuses that First Amendment advocates feared, with
Muslim Americans as a frequent target. In a 2004 case widely criticized
by human rights groups, the Justice Department used the material support for foreign terrorist organizations statute to charge and convict five
leaders of the Holy Land Foundation, formerly the largest Muslim char-
ity in the United States. The Holy Land Foundation was founded as a
U.S. not-for-profit in 1989 to fund charitable efforts throughout the
world, and particularly to bring humanitarian relief to Palestinians living under Israeli occupation in the West Bank and Gaza. At issue in the
trial was $12 million in donations to six West Bank "zakat committees,"
organizations set up to distribute charitable aid in the Muslim tradition.
The U.S. government had not designated these entities as terrorist; indeed, the zakat committees had also received funding from the U.S.
Agency for International Development.[58] But federal prosecutors claimed
at trial that the zakat committees were controlled by Hamas, a designated foreign terrorist organization, and that the Holy Land Foundation
should have known.

In the trial, prosecutors did not allege that Holy Land financed
Hamas directly, that its charitable donations were diverted to Hamas,
or that it otherwise supported acts of violence in the Palestinian

territories. The government acknowledged the Holy Land funds went to their intended charitable recipients. Instead, the government argued that Holy Land's humanitarian assistance to the zakat committees benefited Hamas by helping it win the "hearts and minds" of the Palestinian people. Prosecutors also made the case that Holy Land's donations to the zakat committees freed Hamas, which as the governing authority in Gaza also provided some social services to Gaza residents, to use a greater portion of its funds for militant activities.[59] The five defendants were convicted and sentenced to a total of 180 years in prison, sending a deep chill throughout the charitable sector.[60]

The material support for foreign terrorist organizations statute has also been used in FBI sting operations that manufacture terrorism threats to produce statistical accomplishments. This unfortunate practice is due in part to the overresourcing of international terrorism investigations: agents assigned to disrupt international terrorist plots are pressured to demonstrate their success, even if no genuine plots exist.

For instance, the FBI conducted a five-year sting operation targeting Nicholas Young, a Muslim American police officer in Washington, D.C., using multiple informants to entice him into committing a crime. After cementing a relationship with Young over a two-year period, one informant pretended to join ISIS in Syria and reached out to Young pleading for money. In July 2016, Young sent the informant a $245 Google Play gift card. Despite the tiny amount of money involved and the fact that it went to an FBI informant who wasn't really a member of a foreign terrorist organization, Young was charged with attempting to provide material support to ISIS and sentenced to fifteen years in prison.[61]

An analysis of ISIS-related international terrorism cases from 2014 to 2017 revealed that the majority involved material support charges, and 61 percent relied on undercover agents or informants. This includes every case in which the FBI claimed to have interdicted alleged terrorist plots.[62] Clearly, not all of these cases involve punishing charitable donations in conflict zones, as in the Holy Land Foundation prosecution, or manufacturing crimes, as in the Young case. But given such problematic examples, use of the material support for foreign terrorist organizations statute deserves heightened scrutiny.[63]

Troublingly, the overly broad authority that the FBI has abused in the international terrorism context appears to be what the Justice Department has aimed to mirror in a new domestic terrorism statute, a proposal that continued through the Trump administration. In April 2018, Thomas O'Connor, the head of the FBI Agents Association, urged Congress to "fix the problem by amending the U.S. Code to make domestic terrorism a crime."[64] FBI director Christopher Wray concurred that the FBI "can always use more tools in the toolbox" in the "domestic terrorism space."[65]

In light of abuses of the law prohibiting material support for foreign terrorist organizations, there is reason to fear that expanding the Justice Department's counterterrorism powers—by extending the power to designate groups of U.S. citizens as "domestic terrorist organizations" and criminalize providing material support to them—would have serious implications for Americans' rights to free speech, association, and equal protection. While Justice Department officials have used notorious incidents of white supremacist violence, including the attack on Mother Emanuel Church, to push for a new domestic terrorism statute, the Department itself continues to deprioritize far-right violence and focus its most aggressive tactics instead against environmentalists, political protesters, and communities of color. It isn't hard to guess who would likely be targeted with new domestic terrorism laws.

The calls for new powers also ignore the fact that existing statutes have long provided substantial authority for the federal government to investigate and prosecute acts of domestic terrorism. This authority has been obscured by the arbitrary distinctions between international and domestic terrorism that guide Justice Department policy and practice.

STATUTORY TERRORISM DEFINITIONS IGNORED

According to the terrorism definitions in the U.S. Criminal Code, terrorist acts should be considered "international" when they occur outside the territorial jurisdiction of the United States or "transcend national boundaries." In practice, however, the Justice Department ignores statutory definitions and distinguishes cases as domestic or international primarily based on the perpetrators' race, ethnicity, and perceived ideologies, without regard to the nationality of the attacker or the location of the attack.

In the informal definitions that appear on its website and in reports, the FBI has characterized domestic terrorism as violent acts perpetrated "by individuals and/or groups inspired by or associated with primarily U.S.-based movements that espouse extremist ideologies of a political, religious, social, racial, or environmental nature."[66] More simply, it has suggested domestic terrorism is "Americans attacking Americans based on U.S.-based extremist ideologies."[67] In contrast, it defines international terrorism as acts perpetrated by those affiliated "with designated foreign terrorist organizations or nations (state-sponsored)."[68]

These informal definitions are misleading, however, as ideologies and ideological movements are not cabined by national borders.[69] American white supremacists, for example, are influenced by British Israelism (a racist interpretation of Christianity justifying British colonization of nonwhite nations), National Socialism (a German political philosophy), and Odinism (an ancient Norse religion). These ideologies clearly did not originate in and are not exclusive to the United States.

The white supremacist conspiracy theory known as "white genocide," or the "great replacement," also crosses national boundaries. This racist and anti-Semitic conspiracy theory, promoted in Pat Buchanan's *Death of the West*, has animated the global white supremacist movement for decades. "The Great Replacement" frames white people as victims in need of protection and urges preventive action—conveniently characterized as defensive rather than offensive—to protect white social, political, and economic dominance. Its current incarnation claims that there is a leftist (or sometimes Jewish) plot to displace white Americans in the United States through nonwhite immigration, race mixing, and increased birth rates in communities of color. David Lane, convicted member of the 1980s terrorist group The Order, summarized the white supremacist mission statement in fourteen words: "We must secure the existence of white people and a future for white children." [70]

This "mission" resonates with white supremacists around the world. An Australian white supremacist who in 2018 attacked a mosque in Christchurch, New Zealand, killing fifty people, titled his manifesto "The Great Replacement," and referenced both the 2015 Charleston attack and a 2011 white supremacist mass killing in Norway as inspiration. The mass shooters who killed twenty-three people in El Paso, Texas, and ten people at Tops Market in Buffalo, New York, modeled their attacks on the Christchurch shooting and wrote their own manifestos, cribbing heavily from the Christchurch attacker's.

Collaborations extend internationally. U.S.-based white supremacist, anti-Semitic, fascist, and ethno-nationalist groups regularly associate with like-minded groups in Canada, Europe, Russia, and elsewhere. The FBI busted an AWOL Canadian soldier along with several Americans who had conspired to commit terrorist acts as members of a neo-Nazi accelerationist group called The Base, whose leader is alleged to be living in Russia. [71] The British white nationalist who murdered Jo Cox, a member of the U.K. Parliament, was reportedly a supporter of an American neo-Nazi group. [72] Some violent white supremacist groups such as Volksfront, Blood and Honor, and Hammerskins maintained international chapters or factions. British, American, European, and Australian nationalists have joined Nazi-affiliated fighting groups in Ukraine, such as Right Sector and Azov Battalion. [73] The far-right Proud Boys have international chapters.

Though many of these foreign white supremacist and far-right militant groups are violent and treated as terrorists in their own countries, the United States designates few of them as foreign terrorist organizations, so American support for or association with these groups is not treated as "international terrorism." Interestingly, the Trump administration's National Strategy for Counterterrorism, unveiled on October 4, 2018, acknowledged for the first time that some of these nationalist and neo-Nazi organizations threaten American lives, naming the Nordic Resistance Movement and Britain's banned National Action Group as two examples.[74] Neither appears on the U.S. State Department's list of foreign terrorist organizations, however.[75] Instead, the Trump administration in 2020 formally listed the Russian Imperial Movement as a Specially Designated Global Terrorist organization. This group, which has allegedly provided paramilitary-style training to white supremacists and neo-Nazis in Europe, became the first white supremacist group that the United States officially sanctioned as terrortists.[76] The State Department did not designate Russian Imperial Movement as a Foreign Terrorist Organization, however, which would have barred individuals from providing it material support.[77]

The Justice Department characterizes American Muslims plotting violence in the United States with no assistance from foreign groups as "international" terrorists by arguing that they are "inspired by" foreign terrorist ideologies. Often this is based on scant evidence, such as visiting a website or watching a video. For instance, former FBI director Comey did not hesitate to label a July 2015 mass shooting that killed three U.S. Marines and a Navy sailor in Chattanooga, Tennessee, a terrorist attack "motivated by foreign terrorist organization propaganda."[78] He acknowledged, however, that the FBI could not determine which terrorist group's messaging might have influenced the shooter, Muhammad Abdulazeez, who was killed at the scene and left behind no explanation for his actions.[79] Like Roof, Abdulazeez was an American citizen who acted alone, entirely inside the United States, with no support from any foreign terrorist groups. The crucial difference that led the FBI to label him an international terrorist rather than a domestic one was that Abdulazeez was Muslim and Roof was not.

American Muslims acting in the United States with no direct connection to foreign terrorist groups are categorized not as "domestic" terrorists but as "homegrown violent extremists" (HVEs). This nomenclature has no connection to any statutory definition. Instead, violence by Muslims is treated as a form of "international" terrorism due to purported "inspiration" from designated foreign terrorist groups. In written testimony provided for the Senate Homeland Security Committee on October 10, 2018, FBI director Christopher Wray reiterated the FBI's assessment that "HVEs are the greatest threat to the Homeland."[80]

The Justice Department demonstrated its politicized promotion of "international" terrorism prosecutions in a January 2018 report, which alleged that 73 percent of defendants convicted on terrorism-related charges were immigrants or visitors to the United States.[81] Only by excluding domestic terrorism cases involving U.S. citizens could this misleading figure be achieved. The Justice Department now acknowledges that the report, which was issued to justify the Trump administration's "Muslim ban" and other policies aimed at restricting immigration, was inaccurate and misleading.[82] It has refused to withdraw or correct the data, however.

Despite these claims, the Justice Department's own records suggest that domestic terrorist groups are more active than "international" terrorists. Prosecution statistics produced by the Executive Office for U.S. Attorneys indicate that between 2009 and 2018, federal prosecutors filed 892 "domestic" terrorism cases, more than double the 442 "international" terrorism prosecutions they filed over the same period.[83] This is a particularly striking number in light of 2017 testimony that the FBI devotes 80 percent of its counterterrorism resources to international investigations. With just one-fifth of the resources, domestic terrorism investigations produced more than twice the number of indictments.

The FBI investigations and Justice Department prosecutions related to the January 6, 2021, insurrection have been worked under the domestic terrorism program. Due to the high number of people involved, these cases create a statistical anomaly that is both enlightening and potentially misleading. More than 1,200 people have been charged with crimes related to the assault on the Capitol, making it by far the largest criminal incident ever investigated by the FBI, surpassing in two years the number of domestic terrorism cases prosecuted over the previous ten. But because the FBI and Justice Department initially prioritized charging people who trespassed into restricted areas in and around the Capitol, most of the charges were mere misdemeanors for conduct that would not normally be considered terrorism-related. Hundreds of people who engaged in violence at the Capitol on January 6 have yet to be charged, even though private internet sleuths who call themselves sedition hunters have identified many of them.[84]

Looking at the data standing alone, it would seem to suggest that the FBI and Justice Department priorities toward domestic terrorism changed significantly in 2021 and 2022. But the prosecutions arise from a single, albeit very large, criminal event. There is little evidence to indicate that the FBI or Justice Department is any more aggressive in investigating and prosecuting ongoing violence from white supremacists and far-right militants, who continue to engage in public violence around the country with little apparent law enforcement response.

The January 6 prosecutions have demonstrated the variety of laws available to prosecute white supremacist and far-right militant violence, however, including convictions obtained for the most serious charges: the seditious conspiracy counts against members of the Proud Boys and Oath Keepers. The confusion the Justice Department previously sowed by claiming the lack of a domestic terrorism law had to be corrected when federal prosecutors sought to keep these defendants in custody pending trial. In both cases, the prosecutors had to remind the judges overseeing the detention hearings that several of the defendants were charged with "crimes of terrorism," contradicting earlier claims that there was no domestic terrorism crime.[85]

TOOLS IN THE COUNTERTERRORISM TOOLBOX

Fortunately, Congress has already done the work necessary to provide federal law enforcement with all the tools it needs to address white supremacist and far-right militant violence effectively. I know, because I worked successful domestic terrorism investigations as an FBI undercover agent in the 1990s, using investigative tools that enabled my colleagues and me to seize illegal weapons, solve bombings and hate crimes, and prevent future acts of violence.

In their arguments, proponents of a new domestic terrorism law mischaracterized how FBI agents use these tools in the context of domestic terrorism investigations, suggesting they must rely only on charges with "terrorism" in their name. The undercover operation I was assigned to was categorized as a domestic terrorism investigation, worked by the Los Angeles Joint Terrorism Task Force. But that didn't mean we were limited to charging only the crimes listed in the terrorism chapter of the U.S. Criminal Code. The entire code book was available, as it is with any investigation: for instance, an investigation opened as a drug trafficking case might discover money laundering or tax violations instead. Agents might start an investigation with an allegation or indication that a particular violation occurred, but the evidence discovered during that investigation dictates what charges, if any, are applied at the end. It's also possible that the evidence gathered supports no federal charges but only state violations. The case can then be passed to state or local law enforcement.

The development of law enforcement task forces, such as the Los Angeles Joint Terrorist Task Force that conducted my undercover operation, was to ensure seamless cooperation between federal, state, and local law enforcement agencies. Our investigation discovered numerous federal violations involving the manufacture, sale, and transfer of illegal firearms, silencers, and explosives. We also solved a series of bombings, some of which were charged as hate crimes, including an attempted firebombing of a local synagogue. In addition, some of the defendants were charged with conspiracy for planning a bombing and mass shooting attack on a local African Methodist Episcopal church that had not yet taken place. Task force officers brought state firearms charges in a number of cases where federal charges were unavailable. No one suggested during that operation that there were not sufficient legal authorities to prosecute the crimes we uncovered.

The tools we used back in the 1990s remain effective today. Statutes used in successful domestic terrorism prosecutions in recent years include the fifty-one federal crimes of terrorism that apply to acts committed in the United States, along with the material support statute that prohibits support for terrorist acts. They also include dozens of other civil rights, organized crime, violent crime, and conspiracy statutes that prosecutors regularly use in domestic terrorism cases, including cases involving far-right violence. These laws are listed in Figures 1–5 on the following pages, and examples of their use are described below. All the necessary tools are available to prevent, prosecute, and punish far-right violence effectively; what's missing is the federal will to employ them in a consistent and strategic manner.

CHARGING FEDERAL CRIMES OF TERRORISM

Kevin Harpham, who in 2011 planted a bomb along the route of a Martin Luther King memorial march, pled guilty to attempting to use a weapon of mass destruction, one of the fifty-one federal crimes of terrorism that apply in domestic acts.[86] Likewise, Taylor Michael Wilson, a white supremacist who had attended the Unite the Right rally, later breached the secure area of an Amtrak train while armed with a gun and ammunition. He was charged via a statute called "Terrorist

Figure 1. Federal Crimes of Terrorism That Can Apply in Cases of Domestic Terrorism

No.	Predicate Offense Listed in 18 U.S.C. § 2332b(g)(5), incorporating § 2339A, as Codified in the U.S. Code	Summary of Offense
1	18 U.S.C. § 32	Destruction of aircraft or aircraft facilities
2	18 U.S.C. § 37	Violence at international airports
3	18 U.S.C. § 81	Arson within special maritime and territorial jurisdiction
4	18 U.S.C. § 175	Prohibitions with respect to biological weapons
5	18 U.S.C. § 175b	Possession of a biological agent or toxin by restricted persons, including those with criminal background or mental incompetency
6	18 U.S.C. § 175c	Knowing production or transfer of the variola virus
7	18 U.S.C. § 229	Prohibitions on the development, acquiring, or transfer of any chemical weapon
8	18 U.S.C. § 351	Congressional, cabinet, or Supreme Court assassination, kidnapping, or assault
9	18 U.S.C. § 831	Prohibited transactions involving nuclear materials
10	18 U.S.C. § 832	Participation in nuclear and weapons of mass destruction threats to the United States
11	18 U.S.C. § 842(m)	Import or export of any plastic explosive without a detection agent
12	18 U.S.C. § 842(n)	Ship, transport, receive, possess any plastic explosive without a detection agent
13	18 U.S.C. § 844(f)	Maliciously damage or destroy by means of fire or explosive any building or other real or personal property of the United States
14	18 U.S.C. § 844(i)	Maliciously damage or destroy by means of fire or explosive any building or other real or personal property used in interstate or foreign commerce
15	18 U.S.C. § 930(c)	Killing any person with a firearm or other dangerous weapon in federal facilities
16	18 U.S.C. § 1030(a)(1)	Knowingly access a computer and obtain restricted information with reason to believe that it could be used to injure the United States or advantage a foreign nation

No.	Predicate Offense Listed in 18 U.S.C. § 2332b(g)(5), incorporating § 2339A, as Codified in the U.S. Code	Summary of Offense
17	18 U.S.C. § 1030(a)(5)(A) with damage as listed in 1030(c)(4)(A)(i)(II)–(VI)	Knowingly transmit program or code that intentionally causes damage to a protected computer, where damage either causes physical injury, modification or impairment of medical treatment, threat to public health or safety or damage affects computer used in furtherance of justice, national defense, or national security
18	18 U.S.C. § 1091	Genocide, whether in time of peace or war, with specific intent to destroy, in whole or in substantial part, a national, ethnic, racial, or religious group
19	18 U.S.C. § 1114	Killing or attempting to kill any officer or employee of the United States
20	18 U.S.C. § 1116	Murder or manslaughter of foreign officials, official guests, or internationally protected persons
21	18 U.S.C. § 1203	Hostage taking
22	18 U.S.C. § 1361	Willful injury or depredation against any property of the United States
23	18 U.S.C. § 1362	Willful or malicious destruction of any of the works, property, or material of any communication line, station, or system
24	18 U.S.C. § 1363	Willful and malicious destruction or injury of property within special maritime or territorial jurisdiction of the United States
25	18 U.S.C. § 1366	Destruction of an energy facility
26	18 U.S.C. § 1751	Presidential and presidential staff assassination, kidnapping, or assault
27	18 U.S.C. § 1992	Terrorist attacks and other violence against railroad carriers and against mass transportation systems on land, on water, or through the air
28	18 U.S.C. § 2155	Destruction of national defense materials, premises, or utilities
29	18 U.S.C. § 2156	Production of defective national defense material, premises, or utilities
30	18 U.S.C. § 2280	Violence against maritime navigation

No.	Predicate Offense Listed in 18 U.S.C. § 2332b(g)(5), incorporating § 2339A, as Codified in the U.S. Code	Summary of Offense
31	18 U.S.C. § 2280a	Violence against maritime navigation and maritime transport involving weapons of mass destruction
32	18 U.S.C. § 2281	Violence against maritime fixed platforms
33	18 U.S.C. § 2281a	Use of explosive or radioactive material or noxious substance against or on fixed platform when purpose is to intimidate a population or compel government or organization to do or abstain from an act
34	18 U.S.C. § 2332a	Use of weapons of mass destruction within the United States
35	18 U.S.C. § 2332b	Acts of terrorism transcending national boundaries
36	18 U.S.C. § 2332f	Bombings of places of public use, government facilities, public transportation systems, or infrastructure facilities
37	18 U.S.C. § 2332g	Missile systems designed to destroy aircraft
38	18 U.S.C. § 2332h	Radiological dispersal devices
39	18 U.S.C. § 2332i	Acts of nuclear terrorism
40	18 U.S.C. § 2339	Harboring or concealing terrorists, with respect to certain statutes
41	18 U.S.C. § 2339C	Unlawfully or willingly provide or collect funds with intention that they be used to carry out an act intended to cause death or substantial bodily injury to a civilian, when purpose is to intimidate a population or compel a government or international organization to do or abstain from an act
42	42 U.S.C. § 2122	Prohibitions governing atomic weapons
43	42 U.S.C. § 2283	Protection of nuclear inspectors
44	42 U.S.C. § 2284	Sabotage of nuclear facilities or fuel
45	49 U.S.C. § 46502	Aircraft piracy
46	49 U.S.C. § 46504	Assault of a flight crew members or attendant with a dangerous weapon
47	49 U.S.C. § 46505(b)(3)	Placing or attempting to place an explosive or incendiary device on an aircraft

No.	Predicate Offense Listed in 18 U.S.C. § 2332b(g)(5), incorporating § 2339A, as Codified in the U.S. Code	Summary of Offense
48	49 U.S.C. § 46505(c)	Using dangerous weapon during flight, placing or attempting to place dangerous weapon, loaded firearm, or explosive or incendiary device during flight, with willful or reckless disregard for safety of human life
49	49 U.S.C. § 46506	Application of certain criminal laws to acts on aircraft if homicide or attempted homicide is involved
50	49 U.S.C. § 60123	Knowing and willful violation of (a) marking requirements of pipeline facilities in the vicinity of demolition, excavation, tunneling, or construction, (b) safety standards, inspection or maintenance requirements, allowing access to records, conduct risk analysis, and integrity management, or (c) unauthorized disposal within right-of-way of pipeline
51	49 U.S.C. § 60123(b)	Knowing and willful damaging or destroying of interstate gas pipeline facility

(Fig. 1 does not include six other statutes listed in 18 U.S.C. § 2339A that apply only to international terrorism.[87])

Figure 2. List of Statutes Used as Lead Charges in Four or More Domestic Terrorism Prosecutions from FY 2013 to FY 2017 That Are Not Listed as Predicate Offenses in 18 U.S.C. § 2339A

No.	U.S. Code	Summary of Statute	No. of Prosecutions Listing Statute as Lead Charge	Percentage of Total Prosecutions Listing Statute as Lead Charge
1	18 U.S.C. § 372	Conspiracy to impede or injure person holding public office	57	13.8%

No.	U.S. Code	Summary of Statute	No. of Prosecutions Listing Statute as Lead Charge	Percentage of Total Prosecutions Listing Statute as Lead Charge
2	18 U.S.C. § 875	Transmittance of interstate communication containing demand for ransom for kidnapped person, extortion, threat to kidnap, or threat to injure property or reputation	43	10.4%
3	26 U.S.C. § 5861	Manufacturing, importing, or dealing in firearms without paying tax	21	5.1%
4	18 U.S.C. § 922	Importing, manufacturing, or dealing in firearms or ammunition in interstate commerce without a license	18	4.4%
5	18 U.S.C. § 871	Threats against president and successors to the presidency	17	4.1%
6	18 U.S.C. § 115	Influencing, impeding, or retaliating against a federal official by threatening or injuring a family member	16	3.9%
7	18 U.S.C. § 371	Conspiracy to defraud the United States	13	3.2%
8	18 U.S.C. § 876	Mailing threatening communications	11	2.7%
9	18 U.S.C. § 1038	False information and hoaxes	10	2.4%
10	18 U.S.C. § 111	Assaulting, resisting, or impeding certain officers or employees	7	1.7%
11	18 U.S.C. § 1521	Retaliating against a federal judge or federal law enforcement officer by false claim or slander of title	7	1.7%

No.	U.S. Code	Summary of Statute	No. of Prosecutions Listing Statute as Lead Charge	Percentage of Total Prosecutions Listing Statute as Lead Charge
12	18 U.S.C. § 1001	Falsifying, concealing, or making material false statement within the jurisdiction of the executive, legislative, or judicial branch of government	4	1.0%
13	18 U.S.C. § 1343	Fraud by wire, radio, or television	4	1.0%
14	18 U.S.C. § 1951	Interference with commerce by threats or violence	4	1.0%
15	18 U.S.C. § 43	Force, violence, or threats involving animal enterprises	4	1.0%
16	18 U.S.C. § 514	False or fictitious instrument, document, or obligations	4	1.0%
17	21 U.S.C. § 841	Manufacturing, distributing, or dispensing a controlled substance	4	1.0%

Figure 3. Federal Hate Crimes Laws

No.	U.S. Code	Title of Statute	Summary of Statute	No. of Times Was Lead Charge in LIONS Hate Crimes Program Areas from FY 2013 to FY 2017
1	18 U.S.C. § 249	The Matthew Shepard and James Byrd Jr. Hate Crimes Prevention Act of 2009	Criminalizes willful case of bodily injury using a dangerous weapon because of the victim's actual or perceived race, color, religion, national origin, gender, sexual orientation, gender identity, or disability.	36
2	42 U.S.C. § 3631	Criminal Interference with Right to Fair Housing	Criminalizes the use or threat to use force to interfere with housing rights because of the victim's race, color, religion, sex, disability, familial status, or national origin.	0
3	18 U.S.C. § 247	Damage to Religious Property, Church Arson Prevention Act	Criminalizes the intentional defacement, damage, or destruction of religious real property because of the religion or because of the race, color, or ethnic characteristics of the people associated with the property. Also criminalizes obstruction of any person in their free exercise of religious beliefs.	3

No.	U.S. Code	Title of Statute	Summary of Statute	No. of Times Was Lead Charge in LIONS Hate Crimes Program Areas from FY 2013 to FY 2017
4	18 U.S.C. § 245	Violent Interference with Federally Protected Rights	Criminalizes the use of force or willful interference in a person's participation in a federally protected activity like public education, employment, and jury service, among others, because of their race, color, religion, or national origin.	5
5	18 U.S.C. § 241	Conspiracy Against Rights	Criminalizes conspiracy to injure, threaten, or intimidate a person in the free exercise or enjoyment of any right or privilege secured under the Constitution or laws of the United States.	12

Figure 4. Federal Statutes Not Included in the Five Federal Hate Crimes Laws Identified by DOJ That Were Used to Prosecute Hate Crime Incidents from FY 2013 to FY 2017

No.	U.S. Code	Summary of Statute	No. of Times Was Lead Charge in LIONS Hate Crimes Program Areas from FY 2013 to FY 2017
1	18 U.S.C. § 371	Conspiracy to defraud the United States	4

No.	U.S. Code	Summary of Statute	No. of Times Was Lead Charge in LIONS Hate Crimes Program Areas from FY 2013 to FY 2017
2	22 U.S.C. § 2778	Control of arms exports and imports	4
3	18 U.S.C. § 1951	Interference with commerce by threats or violence	3
4	18 U.S.C. § 875	Transmittance of interstate communication containing demand for ransom for kidnapped person, extortion, threat to kidnap, or threat to injure property or reputation	3
5	8 U.S.C. § 1325	Improper entry by alien	2
6	18 U.S.C. § 844	Importing, manufacturing, dealing, transporting, or distributing explosive materials or withholding information or making fictitious statements regarding explosive materials	2
7	18 U.S.C. § 922	Importing, manufacturing, or dealing in firearms or ammunition in interstate commerce without a license	2
8	18 U.S.C. § 2261A	Stalking	1
9	18 U.S.C. § 876	Mailing threatening communications	1

Figure 5. Conspiracy Statutes Listed as the Lead Charge in Domestic Terrorism and Hate Crimes Cases from FY 2013 to FY 2017

No.	U.S. Code	Summary of Statute	No. of Prosecutions Listing Statute as Lead Charge
1	18 U.S.C. § 241	Conspiracy to injure, threaten, or intimidate a person in free exercise or enjoyment of any right or privilege secured under the Constitution or U.S. laws	12
2	18 U.S.C. § 371	Conspiracy to defraud the United States	17
3	18 U.S.C. § 372	Conspiracy to impede or injure person holding public office	57

Attacks and Other Violence Against Railroad Carriers and Against Mass Transportation on Land, on Water, or Through the Air," which, unsurprisingly, is listed as one of the federal crimes of terrorism.[88] While not every act prosecuted under these statutes fits the definition of terrorism or rises to the level of seriousness that most people would consider terrorism, these examples certainly did. Justice Department officials did not hesitate to describe these crimes as acts of terrorism in public statements and in the courtroom.[89] The fifty-one federal crimes of terrorism that apply to domestic acts (outlined in Figure 1) provide substantial authority to prosecute and punish domestic terrorists.

Indeed, the Justice Department has used one of the predicating offenses—the prohibition against "transnational" terrorism—to prosecute a case against a U.S. citizen whose animus against the U.S. government was personal rather than political. Edward Nesgoda, a former New Jersey police officer, stockpiled firearms and explosives and threatened to blow up a county courthouse in a child support dispute. The federal indictment alleged this act "would have obstructed, delayed or affected interstate or foreign commerce had the offense been consummated." Nesgoda pled guilty to possession of an unregistered explosive device.[90] During Nesgoda's state prosecution for assaulting two police officers during the search of his residence, New Jersey State Police reportedly referred to him as a "domestic terrorist."[91]

It is worth noting that thirteen of the fifty-one offenses in Figure 1 involve chemical, biological, radiological, or nuclear weapons.[92] While offenses involving such weapons may seem more relevant to cases of "international" terrorism than "domestic" ones, the opposite is true. According to one study analyzing post-9/11 terrorism cases, not a single "homegrown jihadist extremist" is known to have acquired or used chemical, biological, radiological, or nuclear weapons in the United States. On the other hand, sixteen so-called domestic terrorists have "deployed, acquired, or tried to acquire" such weapons during this period, including thirteen labeled as "right-wing," one labeled "left-wing," and two labeled "idiosyncratic."[93]

Plots in which neo-Nazis obtained radiological materials to manu-facture "dirty" bombs were thwarted by pure chance. In 2009, a Maine neo-Nazi planning to detonate a dirty bomb at President Barack Obama's inauguration succeeded in having radioactive materials sent to his home by impersonating a doctor, but he was killed in a domestic dispute before the weapon was constructed.[94] In 2017, a Florida cell of the neo-Nazi group Atomwaffen obtained radiological materials and bomb-making equipment, but their plans were disrupted when one dissident member killed two of his colleagues.[95] A Texas militiaman's cyanide bomb, capable of killing thirty thousand people, likewise was discovered inadvertently in 2004, when police searched his storage locker after he sent a set of false identification documents to the wrong address.[96] These narrowly avoided disasters demonstrate the militant far right's intentions and capabilities in obtaining the materials to manufacture weapons of mass destruction.

PROVIDING MATERIAL SUPPORT TO DOMESTIC TERRORISM

One U.S. citizen who tried to create such a weapon was Glendon Scott Crawford, a mechanic at General Electric in Schenectady, New York, whose 2013 case became a rare example of Justice Department prose-cutors applying the material support statute in a domestic terrorism prosecution. According to reporting by Trevor Aaronson in *The Inter-cept*, Crawford "wanted to build a 'death ray,' a portable, remote-controlled, radiological weapon made from medical equipment and off-the-shelf electronics." He planned to use this device to attack Mus-lims at a local mosque, using a smartphone to detonate it.[97]

The government's charging documents indicate that Crawford, a self-described member of the United Northern and Southern Knights of the Ku Klux Klan, traveled to North Carolina in August 2012 seeking financial assistance from a local Klan leader to build the radiation emitting device.[98] The Klan leader, who Aaronson identified as Loyal White Knights Imperial Wizard Chris Barker, had previously been charged with an unrelated state firearms violation. Barker offered to cooperate with the FBI in exchange for leniency on the firearms case, and introduced Crawford to two FBI undercover agents.[99] The agents, one posing as a Klansman and the other as "a wealthy, like-minded businessperson," agreed to provide financial support and materials for Crawford to construct his "death ray" weapon.

In November 2012, the FBI agents met with Crawford and his "software guy," Eric J. Feight, an engineer who had agreed to build a remote control for the weapon. For this meeting, Aaronson writes, "Crawford came up with code names. He was 'Dmitri.' Feight was 'Yoda.' The undercover agents were 'Robin Hood' and 'Daddy Warbucks.' The 'death ray' was 'the Baby.' They even had a code phrase for killing Muslims: 'sterilizing medical waste.' "[100] The FBI wired the warehouse where Crawford and Feight began work on their device, and on June 18, 2013, an FBI SWAT team arrested Crawford there. Feight was arrested soon after.

Feight was charged with providing material support toward the commission of a terrorist act, pled guilty, and received about eight years in prison. Crawford was also charged with violating this same material support statute, but the charge was later changed to conspiracy to use a radiological dispersal device and a weapon of mass destruction, for which he was sentenced to thirty years in prison.[101]

This use of the material support statute in a domestic terrorism case was well within the Justice Department's power but was an anomaly. The exclusive use of the 1996 material support statute to bar support for foreign terrorist groups has apparently led to a misperception that the 1994 material support statute, which bans material support for terrorist acts, does not apply to domestic terrorism cases.[102] But while the vast majority of the material support prosecutions through the 1994 statute have been against people who materially supported acts of international terrorism, at least three other people involved in domestic terrorism have been charged under this statute.[103]

The first use of the 1994 material support statute in a domestic terrorism prosecution occurred just two years after the statute became law. Seven people associated with the West Virginia Mountaineer Militia had assembled explosives in a plot to blow up a new FBI building. A jury convicted Floyd Raymond Looker, the leader of the group, of conspiracy to manufacture explosives. Following the conviction, he pled guilty to several other charges, including providing material support to terrorism. James R. Rogers, a lieutenant in a local fire department, gave the militia photographs of the blueprints for the facility that his firehouse had on file. He too was charged with a material support violation under the provision banning material support for terrorist acts.[104] In 2019, an Ohio woman pleaded guilty to providing material support for terrorism and interstate transportation of explosives as part of a domestic terrorism plot.[105] Elizabeth Lecron, who prosecutors alleged had sent letters and Nazi literature to Dylann Roof in prison while she planned her own mass casualty attack, received a fifteen-year sentence.[106]

As these cases and many like them demonstrate, the 1994 material support statute and the fifty-one federal crimes of terrorism that apply domestically provide ample authority to prosecute domestic terrorism cases. Federal law also provides many other appropriate alternatives.

FEDERAL HATE CRIMES STATUTES

On the morning of Saturday, October 27, 2018, Robert Bowers, armed with an assault rifle and three semiautomatic pistols, entered

Pittsburgh's Tree of Life Synagogue and shot worshippers at Shabbat services. Eleven people were killed in the attack and six were wounded in what became the most deadly anti-Semitic attack in U.S. history.

Bowers's motive was evident on social media, where he posted frequent racist and anti-Semitic rants on Gab, the social networking site popular with far-right extremists. He closely followed the activities of white supremacist and far-right militant organizations, including the Proud Boys and the alt-right Rise Above Movement, whose members were among those who marched in Charlottesville chanting, "Jews will not replace us." Bowers was also tuned in to debates over "optics" among white supremacists, such as whether they should veil their language and violent intentions online.[107]

Bowers's comments in the weeks before the attack focused on the humanitarian organization HIAS, which one of the congregations was supporting in an upcoming National Refugee Shabbat. He was also preoccupied with the caravans of migrants traveling to the U.S. border. Soon before the attack, he posted: "HIAS likes to bring invaders in that kill our people. I can't sit by and watch my people get slaughtered. Screw your optics, I'm going in."[108]

Like Dylann Roof, Bowers was charged with federal hate crimes. While failing to label hate crimes as "acts of terrorism" can deprioritize a subsequent investigation, hate crimes laws also come with severe penalties and are an important component of the robust statutory framework that may be used to prosecute acts of violence committed by white supremacists.

Five federal laws are designed to combat hate crimes.[109] The Matthew Shepard and James Byrd Jr. Hate Crime Prevention Act, passed in 2009, was named for two young men murdered in 1998: Matthew Shepard was a gay student tortured and beaten to death in Wyoming, and James Byrd Jr. was a Black man killed by white supremacists in a horrific attack in Texas. The Shepard-Byrd Act criminalizes the infliction of bodily injury using a dangerous weapon because of the victim's actual or perceived race, color, religion, national origin, gender, sexual orientation, gender identity, or disability.

The first hate crime law, passed as part of the Civil Rights Act of 1968, criminalizes violent interference with federally protected rights. Subsequent laws added sanctions for additional hate crimes, including interfering with the right to fair housing and obstruction of exercise of religious beliefs. The Shepard-Byrd Act expanded existing hate crime laws, removing the requirement that the target be engaged in a constitutionally protected activity and adding language to include crimes motivated by gender, sexual orientation, and disability.[110]

A hate crime may also be considered an act of domestic terrorism. Indeed, FBI policy demands they be investigated as such. When a suspect in a hate crimes investigation "has a nexus to any type of white supremacist extremist group," FBI policy instructs agents to open a parallel domestic terrorism investigation.[111] This policy likely applied to its investigation of Robert Bowers, due to his online activity, and should have in the case against James Alex Fields, the neo-Nazi who killed Heather Heyer at the 2017 Unite the Right rally in Charlottesville, Virginia. Perhaps that is why Attorney General Jeff Sessions appropriately labeled Fields's Charlottesville attack an act of "domestic terrorism" at the time.[112] It remains unclear why the FBI's investigation of Fields did not expand to implicate the other white supremacists who conspired with him or committed other acts of violence at the rally, however, as it should have if the bureau treated the attack as an act of terrorism.

INTERSTATE TRANSPORTATION TO RIOT

Many of the participants at the violent far-right rallies that left journalists and counterprotesters around the country beaten, stabbed, shot, and even killed, have used social media to promote their intention to commit violence at these events.[113] In October 2017, ProPublica journalists published an article that documented how members of the white nationalist Rise Above Movement advertised their group with YouTube videos promoting their pugilistic training sessions and the violence they committed at far-right rallies in Huntington Beach, San Bernardino, and Berkeley, California, with little law enforcement attention. The journalists identified several Rise Above Movement members, many with criminal records, engaging in violence in California before traveling to Charlottesville, Virginia, where they again attacked counterprotesters at the Unite the Right rally.[114] Federal anti-rioting charges seem tailor-made to address this type of organized group violence.

Federal law criminalizes interstate travel or the use of interstate commerce to incite, organize, promote, encourage, or participate in a riot, or commit, aid, or abet a violent act during a riot.[115] In October 2018, a year after the violence in Charlottesville and two months after PBS's *Frontline* aired a documentary highlighting ProPublica's reporting on the Rise Above Movement, the Justice Department finally charged eight members of the group with rioting and conspiracy, four in Virginia and four in California.[116] Questions remain regarding why the federal government didn't take earlier advantage of the 1968 Anti-Riot Act to investigate and prosecute the far-right militant groups who crossed state lines to commit organized violence at earlier events around the country, and why it charged so few of those who participated in violence at the Unite the Right rally.

The prosecution of the four Rise Above Movement members charged in Virginia in 2018 succeeded, and in 2020, the Fourth Circuit Court of Appeals upheld the convictions even while finding that unrelated parts of the Anti-Riot Act were unconstitutional.[117] The subsequent Anti-Riot Act prosecution of four other Rise Above Movement members for violence committed at far-right rallies in California has taken some bizarre turns over the years and remains unresolved at this writing.

Robert Rundo, who founded the Rise Above Movement, had previously served prison time for a 2009 gang-related stabbing in New York and was arrested in Berkeley, California, in 2017 for punching a police officer, though local prosecutors declined to charge him. Rise Above Movement members Tyler Laube and Robert Boman both reportedly had prior convictions for robbery, among other charges.[118] When the federal Anti-Riot Act indictments were issued against them in 2018, Rundo fled to Central America but was ultimately captured and returned to the United States for trial. Laube pleaded guilty to conspiracy to riot, but Rundo and Boman chose to go to trial.[119] In 2019, U.S. District Court Judge Cormac J. Carney dismissed the charges during pre-trial motions, finding the entire Anti-Riot Act an unconstitutional infringement on First Amendment rights.[120] The judge also allowed Laube to rescind his guilty plea. Once the judge released them, Rundo fled the country once again while the government appealed the dismissal. The Ninth Circuit Court of Appeals reversed the district court's decision in 2021 and reinstated the charges. But it took another two years before Rundo, who had been organizing white supremacist mixed martial arts "Active Clubs" throughout Eastern Europe, was finally arrested by Romanian authorities and extradited back to the United States.[121]

The case once again came before Judge Carney. In the first indication that Carney's approach would remain idiosyncratic, he refused to accept the guilty plea of co-defendant Robert Boman, after Boman disputed facts that had been stipulated in the plea agreement. Judge Carney several times referred to the people Boman assaulted as "Antifa," and declared they were "not sympathetic victims."[122] A month later, in February 2024, Judge Carney again dismissed the charges against Rundo and Boman, adopting the false equivalency of the "both sides" narrative pushed by right-wing media. Judge Carney argued that though the Rise Above Movement members likely committed violence at the rallies, the Justice Department's charges against them amounted to selective prosecution based on their ideology, because it did not bring Anti-Riot Act charges against "far-left extremist groups, such as Antifa," who he asserted committed similar, if not worse, violence at rallies.[123] Carney further ordered Rundo's immediate release, despite his history of fleeing prosecution, which sent prosecutors scrambling to submit an emergency appeal to the Ninth Circuit Court of Appeals.

Perhaps hinting at how they might view Judge Carney's dismissal of the indictment, the Ninth Circuit reinstated the detention order for Rundo, allowing the FBI to rearrest him, and then ordered that any future decision to release him be delayed ninety-six hours so the appeals court could weigh in.[124] At the time of this writing the government's appeal of the dismissal is pending.

The Anti-Riot Act is a broad statute, and it's easy to see how law enforcement officials and prosecutors could abuse it to target disruptive protesters due to bias against their political viewpoint. But when a group of people with violent criminal records trains specifically to commit violence in a coordinated manner, advertises their intent publicly, then repeatedly travels in interstate commerce to engage in gang violence at public events, the Anti-Riot Act seems to be an appropriate law enforcement vehicle. It is likely that the Ninth Circuit will again reinstate the charges in the Rise Above Movement case; but even if it upholds the selective prosecution argument, the operative parts of the statute will remain a viable means to address planned mob violence like that seen at the Unite the Right rally and the January 6, 2021, attack on the Capitol.

CONSPIRACY AND RACKETEERING

Some in federal law enforcement may argue that the consequences of a successful terrorist attack are so dire that new laws are needed to enable prosecutors to pursue members of white supremacist organizations before they can commit a specific hate crime or one of the fifty-one crimes of terrorism that apply to domestic acts. My undercover operations proved that proactive investigations predicated on terrorism charges could be successful in preventing acts of terrorism as well as solving them. But other available statutes, including conspiracy and racketeering, also provide prosecutors ample flexibility to address serious criminal activities that pose a significant danger to human life.

As with the statute prohibiting material support to foreign terrorist organizations, civil libertarians and criminal justice reform advocates have long maintained that these laws give prosecutors overly broad discretion to charge and severely punish people only tangentially involved in serious criminal activity.[125] Nonetheless, the availability of these broad authorities and the Justice Department's reliance on them to prosecute far-right violence undercut any claim that a new domestic terrorism statute is necessary.

The goal of prohibiting material support to foreign terrorist organizations is to denigrate and ultimately destroy these dangerous organizations by starving them of resources. Similarly, the Racketeer Influenced and Corrupt Organizations Act (RICO) enables federal prosecutors to dismantle domestic terrorism organizations by targeting them as corrupt criminal enterprises.[126] RICO increases penalties and expands statutes of limitations to reach the activities of all participants in the criminal organization, and it has proven useful in prosecuting white supremacist groups.

In 2006, the Justice Department used RICO to try to break up the Aryan Brotherhood, the largest and deadliest prison gang in the United States, by charging its members and leaders under RICO.[127] The gang, founded at California's San Quentin Prison in 1964, has over twenty thousand members, both in and out of prison. Inside prisons, the gang is known for gambling, extortion, drug trafficking, and male prostitution rings, along with targeting Black inmates. Outside, the gang engages in organized crime, murder for hire, gunrunning, drug trafficking, and more.[128]

The federal investigation began in 1992, when federal officials successfully recruited several gang members as informants. To protect these self-described "dropouts" from retribution, they housed them in a dedicated cell block known as "H-Units" at the U.S. Penitentiary Administration Maximum, or ADX, in Florence, Colorado.[129]

After a years-long investigation, the Justice Department launched a federal racketeering case to prosecute Aryan Brotherhood leaders including Barry Byron Mills; three of his top lieutenants, Tyler "The Hulk" Bingham, Edgar "The Snail" Hevle, and Christopher Overton Gibson; and dozens of members. Charges included involvement in as many as thirty-two murders and attempted murders in maximum-security prisons. During the trial, the government's witnesses testified that Bingham passed a note, written in invisible ink made from urine, from his cell in Florence, Colorado, where, prosecutors alleged, it was used to incite a race war.[130] The gang leaders were convicted of racketeering, conspiracy, and murder, with Mills and Bingham receiving multiple life terms but avoiding the death penalty.[131] While the prosecution did not succeed in destroying the Aryan Brotherhood, federal authorities have continued to use racketeering statutes to pursue white supremacist prison gangs.

RICO has become a more important tool as white supremacist prison gangs have moved their violent criminal enterprises out of the prison and jail systems and now engage in a multitude of violent crimes that terrorize communities across the country. In 2012, for instance, thirty-four alleged members of the Aryan Brotherhood of Texas were indicted on RICO charges, which included murders, fire-bombings, and kidnapping.[132] In March 2018, eight people tied to Aryan Circle, a multistate white supremacist gang, were charged in Louisiana with racketeering following the murder of a fellow gang member, Clifton Hallmark.[133] Twenty-four more members of Aryan

Circle were arrested in October 2020 for crimes committed across eleven states.[134] Fifty-four members of the New Aryan Empire were arrested in Arkansas in 2019 for racketeering crimes including attempted murders and kidnappings.[135]

These are just a handful of the many racketeering cases brought against white supremacist gangs, which typically are not categorized as domestic terrorism prosecutions despite the racist violence these groups perpetrate. But if policymakers and the public want to understand the impact of white supremacist violence on our society, these cases certainly need to be counted. If any other terrorist movement had tens of thousands of members cycling through the prison system, with uncounted hundreds being released back into society each year, it would be a scandal.

All the necessary tools already exist. What the Justice Department has refused to do thus far, however, is to prioritize these investigations properly by producing a comprehensive national strategy to combat white supremacist and far-right militant violence. Though Congress in the National Defense Authorization Act of 2020 required the FBI to report annual baseline data regarding domestic terrorism incidents, investigations, and prosecutions, the bureau has so far failed to do so. Without this data, it is impossible to measure properly the threats posed by different domestic terrorist groups so that resources can be directed to the most dangerous perpetrators. Accurate data is the missing tool in the federal toolbox, and the most important.

6

A STRATEGY FOR CHANGE

On the evening of January 5, 2021, FBI officials wrapped up work with cautious optimism that the Stop the Steal protest planned for the following day would require little police intervention. Their primary concern was not the assault on the Capitol predicted by a crescendo of intelligence tips in the preceding weeks. Instead, according to a June 2023 Senate report, the FBI warned about potential fighting between protesters and counterprotesters, as in this email sent at 10:11 p.m.:

> Of note for tonight, Metro PD has shut down their [Command Post] so that's a good sign that, largely, the crowds have diminished and remain peaceful. Only notable event tomorrow that could trigger a flashpoint is a planned POTUS rally/speech on the ellipse at 1100EST. It's estimated that 30,000 participants will then march toward the Capital [sic] which will coincide with the 1300EST scheduled Congressional meetings to certify the electoral college vote. Obvious concerns remain if counter-protests ensue and opposing ideologies clash.[1]

How did FBI officials arrive at a threat assessment that proved so tragically wrong? Ample evidence shows it was not for lack of intelligence, despite FBI protestations to the contrary in the days after the attack. A January 5 memo sent from the Norfolk FBI office, first reported by the *Washington Post*, warned of "war" at the Capitol, with conspirators sharing maps of tunnels in the Capitol complex.[2] The same day, the New Orleans FBI office informed agencies across federal law enforcement of online discussion about an armed "quick reaction force" that the Oath Keepers were planning in northern Virginia. Militia members "should bring mace, flash lights, body armor, and head protection," one post advised.[3]

Previous days had brought many other warnings. A December 26 tip informed the FBI that the Proud Boys planned to be in D.C. and "their plan is to literally kill people."[4] The social media company Parler flagged concerning posts, including one sent on January 2, which read: "This is not a rally and it's no longer a protest. This is a final stand where we are drawing the red line at Capitol Hill. [. . .] don't be surprised if we take the #capital building."[5] Another announced, "Everyone is coming with weapons. They may be concealed at first but if congress does the wrong thing expect real chaos because Trump needs us to cause chaos to enact the #insurrectionact"—referencing a chilling idea, cited in Trump's August 2023 indictment, that Trump could deploy the military to seize power.[6]

The Senate committee report concludes that the FBI didn't alert law enforcement to the high volume of reported threats because, as the *Washington Post* put it, "federal officials simply didn't believe what they were being told."[7] Officials viewed the warnings as hyperbole and "suffered from a bias toward discounting intelligence that indicated an unprecedented event." The failure to see the real danger, according to the committee, was akin to the "failure of imagination" that the 9/11 commission had described twenty years before.[8]

While the attack on the Capitol was indeed unprecedented, law enforcement's blindness to threats of white supremacist violence is far too familiar. The FBI's misguided focus on a potential clash of "opposing ideologies" echoes the threat assessment on the eve of the 2017 Unite the Right rally, when law enforcement's passive stance enabled the violence that ensued. And again, the criminal histories of known participants such as the Proud Boys did not trigger appropriate evaluation.

Amid the national shock of the January 6 attacks and the revelations of investigations, the United States has an opportunity to examine and change the way federal law enforcement polices white supremacy. At the Unite the Right rally in Charlottesville four years before, police inaction and implicit endorsement by a sitting president emboldened groups that four years later would self-identify as Trump's "army." After January 6, we must ensure that violent groups receive the opposite message. As our nation grapples with how to tackle white supremacist and far-right violence, it is past time for the Justice Department to commit to a national strategy that explicitly names and focuses on this problem.

A strategy for change must include investigating and addressing the persistence of racism, white supremacy, and far-right militancy in law enforcement. Any doubt that this problem is real was undercut by the sheer number of current and retired police and military personnel arrested for breaching the Capitol: of the more than one thousand alleged rioters arrested as of March 23, 2023, about 15 percent have a reported background in the military or law enforcement.[9] One of the alleged Oath Keepers arrested for criminal activity claimed in court filings to have previously been employed by the FBI, and a reporter given access to Oath Keeper membership records identified applicants claiming to be Immigration and Customs Enforcement officers, one person claiming to be a Secret Service agent, and two claiming to be FBI employees.[10]

Post–January 6 revelations also point to pervasive bias within the FBI. An email sent to a top FBI official, released during the January 6 Committee's ninth public hearing, expressed concern that "a sizable percentage" of employees "felt sympathetic to the group that stormed the Capitol," and viewed the actions as "no different" from the Black Lives Matter protests in the summer of 2020. "I literally had to explain to an agent from a 'blue state' office the difference between opportunists burning and looting during protests that stemmed [from] legitimate grievance to police brutality vs. an insurgent mob whose purpose was to prevent the execution of democratic processes at the behest of a sitting president," recounted the unnamed writer, likely a former agent or FBI contractor. "One is a smattering of criminals, the other is an organized group of domestic terrorists."[11] The email also cited conversations with multiple Black agents who turned down opportunities to join the SWAT team because they did not trust that "every member of their office's SWAT team would protect them in an armed conflict."[12] This assessment of racism within FBI culture, while anecdotal, bears further investigation and public accountability. The FBI has not indicated whether it has made any attempt to address this problem.

Perhaps most disturbing is evidence suggesting that some police may have actively aided far-right militants. Federal prosecutors accused Shane Lamond, who led the Metropolitan Police's intelligence branch, of sharing confidential information with convicted Proud Boys leader Enrique Tarrio. "I can't say it officially, but personally I support you all and don't want to see your group's name or reputation dragged through the mud," Lamond allegedly wrote to Tarrio in a private message on the app Telegram on January 8, 2021.[13] Whether or not these messages were part of Lamond's efforts to gather intelligence, as his lawyer has previously argued, will be examined when Lamond's case goes to trial.

Lamond's case, while striking, is not alone as an example of alleged police affiliation and sympathetic ties with white supremacist and far-right militant groups. It is imperative that the Justice Department confront and resolve the persistent problem of explicit racism in law enforcement, and protect the communities policed by these dangerously compromised law enforcers. An effective approach to preventing far-right violence must include a commitment to policing white supremacy within the ranks.

REJECT THE FBI'S MISLEADING DOMESTIC TERRORISM CATEGORIES

The first step in a national strategy is to change the way the government documents and shares data on racist and far-right violence. Currently, domestic terrorism and hate crime data are incomplete, rife with error, often arbitrary, and based on vague and conflicting categorization schemes. To compel FBI managers and Justice Department prosecutors to focus on white supremacist and far-right militancy they otherwise choose to ignore, Congress must require specificity in the language used to set domestic terrorism strategy, policy, and practices.

Public attention to misleading domestic terrorism categories began when a leaked August 2017 report revealed the FBI's new Black Identity Extremist label, which painted Black activists protesting racist police violence as a violent threat themselves.[14] The FBI report cited the 2014 shooting of Michael Brown in Ferguson, Missouri, as the catalyst for this invented movement and warned, "The FBI assesses it is very likely Black Identity Extremist (BIE) perceptions of police brutality against African Americans spurred an increase in premeditated, retaliatory lethal violence against law enforcement and will very likely serve as justification for such violence."[15] It is ironic that the agency responsible for investigating allegations of police brutality would blame the victims, identifying Black activists' "perceptions" of the excessive police violence in their communities as the catalyst for retaliatory violence rather than the police brutality itself.

The revelation of the Black Identity Extremism category drew immediate criticism, with many correctly observing that the label was a political ploy to manufacture an equivalent threat to white supremacists, and put a law enforcement target on the backs of Black activists protesting police violence and racism. Congress took note. Amid attention to emboldened white supremacists after the Unite the Right rally, Democratic senators began to seek transparency in how the FBI allocated its domestic terrorism resources. The controversy over the Black Identity Extremism assessment added public pressure to the effort.

In May 2017, Sen. Richard Durbin (D-IL) introduced the Domestic Terrorism Prevention Act, which sought data documenting the number of attempted and completed incidents the FBI categorized as domestic terrorism, and their corresponding fatalities.[16] The bill also required the FBI to enumerate investigations and prosecutions for each of its eleven domestic terrorism categories, which included white supremacists, anarchists, environmentalists, far-right militants, Black separatists (a category later revealed to have been changed to Black Identity Extremists), and others. By getting both sides of the ledger—that is, knowing how many domestic terrorism incidents resulting in fatalities occur for each category, how many investigations are initiated, and then the number of successful prosecutions that result—the data would allow Congress to determine if the FBI was properly allocating resources to the correct categories based on the level and seriousness of the crimes committed. If one hundred domestic terrorism incidents resulted in fatalities in a particular category but only fifty investigations took place, that would represent an underallocation of resources. Likewise, if ten attacks with no fatalities occurred in another category, fifty investigations would be an overallocation of resources. On the other side of the ledger, if the FBI started fifty investigations targeting people in one category but few of them resulted in successful prosecutions, that would indicate a misuse of resources in improperly targeting people who fit that ideological category without sufficient evidence of criminal wrongdoing.

Though the bill had not yet passed, Sen. Durbin requested an FBI briefing on the matter for members of the Senate Judiciary Committee, who are responsible for conducting oversight of the FBI and the Justice Department. The briefing that the FBI finally provided in April 2019 revealed that the bureau had collapsed the white supremacist and Black Identity Extremist categories into a new "Racially Motivated Violent Extremist" (RMVE) category. The far-right militia and the anarchist categories had similarly been merged into a single "Anti-Government and Anti-Authority Violent Extremist" (AGAAVE) category. An "Abortion-Related Violent Extremist" category now included extremists "with ideological agendas in support of pro-life *or pro-choice beliefs*" [emphasis added], despite the lack of deadly violence perpetrated by pro-choice activists.

These groupings make little operational sense. Subjects of an investigation of white supremacists would rarely overlap or work together with subjects of an investigation into Black Identity Extremists, and likewise for militias and anarchists. The intelligence base and informant recruitment needed to target white supremacists would be of little help in investigating so-called Black RMVEs. White supremacists and far-right militant groups have significant overlap, however. White supremacists are often active in militia groups, and the two groups regularly engage in violence and other crimes together, in common cause. Keeping these groups in separate categories dilutes the perception of the threat they pose together and sows confusion about how to investigate individuals and groups that fit both ideological categories. Some Proud Boys chapters are openly white supremacist, for instance, while others disavow racism, making it unclear whether the various FBI field offices categorize cases involving the same group differently.[17]

What the FBI's misguided new groupings appeared to accomplish, as Sen. Durbin suggested in a 2019 letter to the Justice Department, is to obscure the comparative data his bill sought.[18] The groupings allow the FBI to disguise which groups within the combined categories are committing violence and which are receiving the most investigative attention, enabling FBI agents to focus on less violent groups they disfavor due to individual or institutional biases, or political pressure from above. The relatively high rate of violence committed by white supremacists, for example, could be used to justify resources for more investigations targeting the RMVE category, resources that could then be used to investigate less active and less violent Black extremists. Likewise, the relatively high rate of violence from far-right militants could be used to direct resources to the AGAAVE category, which could then be used to investigate less-violent anarchists.

Congress ultimately passed this data-reporting requirement in the National Defense Authorization Act of 2020. This act commanded the FBI and DHS to issue annual reports containing the number of domestic terrorism incidents, fatalities, indictments, and prosecutions broken down by each of the FBI's new categories, thereby providing accountability in how the bureau disburses resources within its misguided categorization scheme. So far, the FBI has simply refused to fully comply with the requirements of the law.[19] In reports filed in May 2021, October 2022, and June 2023, the FBI stated that it could not provide comprehensive domestic terrorism incident data because "there is no mandatory incident reporting requirement" for state and local law enforcement agencies, seemingly ignoring that the National Defense Authorization Act places the reporting requirement on the FBI, not state and local law enforcement.[20]

The FBI instead provided a selective number of "significant domestic terrorism incidents," depriving Congress of the data needed to understand whether these selected incidents are representative of the totality. As Sen. Durbin warned would happen back in 2019, the FBI's 2021 report obscured rather than clarified the relative threat from different groups. It broke down the data regarding its investigations by its new categories, so the number of investigations for white RMVEs versus Black RMVEs, and militia AGAAVE groups versus anarchist AGAAVE groups, remains hidden.[21] Finally, the FBI also said it was unable to provide the prosecution data Congress requested, explaining that "the number of federal charges with a nexus to [domestic terrorism] is not currently maintained by the FBI or DOJ in a comprehensive manner."[22]

It would be reasonable to assume that an agency that calls counterterrorism its number one priority would want to keep an accurate count of how many domestic terrorist incidents occur in the United States each year, and know who commits them. Further, an agency that operates two hundred Joint Terrorism Task Forces and employs thousands of investigators and analysts across the country presumably has the capability to catalog these incidents and document its successful prosecutions. So why doesn't it?

A clue was revealed at a Homeland Security and Government Affairs Committee hearing in November 2022.[23] When Sen. Rick Scott (R-FL) asked what the FBI was doing about reports of violence targeting anti-abortion activists, FBI director Christopher Wray responded that since the Supreme Court's June decision to overturn *Roe v. Wade*, "probably in the neighborhood of 70 percent of our abortion-related violence cases or threats cases are cases . . . where the victims are pro-life organizations."[24]

This answer likely assuaged Scott's concern, but on its own, it is a meaningless statistic. The evidentiary threshold for opening FBI investigations is extremely low, so agents can open as many investigations as they desire.[25] Without knowing the number of incidents and the number of resulting convictions within different categories of terrorism cases, a release of data regarding the number of investigations the FBI is pursuing can give a misleading impression of the prevalence of different types of terrorist activity. More problematically, it can hide the fact that FBI resources are not being allocated toward the greatest threats.

Wray's response highlights how the lack of data regarding domestic terrorism incidents and convictions allows the FBI to use domestic terrorism investigations as a political tool, wielded to satisfy the demands of politicians or driven by the biases of agents. While recent reports of arsons targeting anti-abortion facilities deserve investigation, abortion-related violence resulting in death or serious bodily injury has historically been committed predominantly, if not exclusively, by anti-abortion militants. That trend has only increased in recent years, bringing into question whether devoting 70 percent of abortion-related terrorism investigations to violence and threats *against* anti-abortion activists is an appropriate distribution of FBI resources.[26]

What the FBI reports do reveal, however, is that the bureau significantly undercounts white supremacist homicides as compared to public reports by academic researchers and advocacy groups. Comparing the data from the FBI reports to domestic terrorism incident and fatality numbers published by just one advocacy organization, the Anti-Defamation League, demonstrates that the bureau significantly undercounts white supremacist violence.

For instance, in its May 2021 report, the FBI claimed there were five domestic terrorism incidents in 2017 resulting in eight deaths, including two fatalities caused by white supremacists and five by Black RMVEs.[27] The ADL, however, identifies thirty-four murders committed by domestic extremists in 2017, including eighteen by white supremacists, two by right-wing militants, and five by Black extremists.[28] In 2018, the FBI reported six lethal domestic terrorism incidents resulting in seventeen deaths, with sixteen of the killings committed by white supremacists and one by a far-right militant. The ADL documented fifty fatalities, forty-nine of which were committed by what it characterized as "right-wing extremists," including thirty-nine by white supremacists.[29] In 2019, the FBI said there were five attacks resulting in thirty-two deaths, including twenty-four fatalities caused by white supremacists. The ADL reports seventeen incidents involving forty-two murders, thirty-eight of which were by right-wing extremists, including thirty-four by white supremacists and two by individuals claiming to be "sovereign citizens."[30] In its October 2022 report, the FBI said there were no fatalities caused by white "racially motivated violent extremists" in 2020.[31] The ADL identified nine killings by white supremacists that year.[32] The FBI's 2023 report identified just one deadly white supremacist attack in the United States in 2022, which resulted in ten fatalities.[33] The ADL identified twenty-five fatalities resulting from right-wing extremists in 2022, including eighteen murders committed by white supremacists.[34] These data make clear the FBI systematically undercounts fatal incidents committed by right-wing extremists, particularly white supremacists. Given that the ADL and other advocacy or academic organizations that collect their data from public records routinely publish the incident details so that they can be fact-checked, it is striking that the FBI continues to release much lower white supremacist homicide counts without any attempt to reconcile the disparities. At a minimum, this conspicuous failure indicates the FBI's lack of interest in accurately tracking violent acts committed by white supremacists and far-right militants.

Of course, the Justice Department prosecutes the FBI's domestic terrorism cases, so it too could be a source of data Congress could rely on to understand whether counterterrorism resources are used appropriately. The Justice Department regularly releases domestic terrorism prosecution data when it promotes statistical accomplishments to Congress in budgeting requests. But when it releases these cases to the public, the Justice Department redacts the cases' docket numbers, making it impossible to cross-check claimed counterterrorism successes against case records. The Brennan Center sued the Justice Department under the Freedom of Information Act to obtain the docket numbers in these reported terrorism prosecutions so that the public could understand how the government uses its counterterrorism authorities.[35] Though the Justice Department acknowledged that it uses the data in congressional reporting, in litigation it argued the docket numbers need to remain secret because some of the defendants convicted in cases it reported as domestic terrorism prosecutions may not be terrorists. In contrast, the department routinely releases identifying data on cases that it considers to be international terrorism, even where the crimes charged bear no relation to terrorism. The judge hearing the case wrote that "the public has an interest in knowing that the [Justice Department's prosecutions] database contains inaccuracies and that those inaccuracies may have resulted in erroneous public reporting from the Department."[36]

Through litigation, my Brennan Center colleagues were able to obtain a sample of these docket numbers and examine the cases. In contrast to the eighty-five "significant" domestic terrorism cases the FBI selectively highlighted in its 2021 report, which mostly included RMVEs and AGAAVEs, almost 60 percent of the prosecutions the Justice Department produced case information for were tagged as animal rights and environmental extremists.[37]

As far-right militants have increasingly threatened election workers, school administrators, and even members of Congress with violence, it is important to know which threats draw FBI scrutiny and which do not.[38] Congress can determine whether the FBI is using its domestic terrorism authorities appropriately and without bias only if it has the data to demonstrate it.

BIDEN'S NATIONAL STRATEGY ON COUNTERING DOMESTIC TERRORISM IS HELPFUL BUT INSUFFICIENT

When Joe Biden announced his candidacy for the 2020 election, his video message described the events at the Charlottesville Unite the Right rally as his inspiration, citing the violence instigated by "Klansmen and white supremacists and neo-Nazis," and Trump's notorious response that there were "some very fine people on both sides."[39] Soon after Biden took office in 2021, his administration launched a National Strategy on Countering Domestic Terrorism, which calls domestic terrorism "the most urgent terrorism threat the United States faces today."[40]

The Biden administration's strategy is a positive step toward reform, but it is hampered by the FBI's improper categorization scheme. The strategy highlights the fact that white supremacist and far-right militant violence are the most prevalent and most deadly of the domestic terrorism categories, but it had to wrestle with the FBI's language to make its intent clear. It uses the FBI's language identifying "racially and ethnically motivated violent extremists" but then adds a parenthetical: "(principally those who promote superiority of the white race)." This additional language is needed to make clear that it intends the focus of cases in this category to be white supremacists rather than so-called Black Identity Extremists, which go unmentioned.[41] A similar caveat is embedded when citing the intelligence community's assessment of the domestic terrorism threat, clarifying that "[racially and ethnically mo- tivated violent extremists] who promote the superiority of the white race" are the most serious transnational threat among other so-called RMVEs. When it describes the most lethal threats, the strategy docu- ment uses "racially and ethnically motivated violent extremists (RMVEs) and militia violent extremists (MVEs)," adopting the FBI's revised category that includes groups other than white supremacists, but abandoning the use of the Anti-Government and Anti-Authority Violent Extremist (AGAAVE) category to focus on one element within it.[42] These tortured addendums and reductions inject unnecessary con- fusion that could have been avoided if the FBI had not awkwardly com- bined dissimilar groups into a single category.

The Biden administration's domestic terrorism strategy also refer- ences other "ideologies" that may motivate domestic terrorism and specifically mentions animal rights and environmental activism. This reinforces the perception that domestic terrorism investigators and prosecutors should pursue cases targeting these groups despite the lack of deadly violence attributed to them.[43] The persistence of an entire FBI domestic terrorism category focused on animal rights and environ- mental activists creates a false equivalency with the white supremacists and far-right militants that the strategy attempts to recognize as the most deadly threat.

ACCURATE DATA ARE NEEDED TO ENACT SOUND POLICIES

What's needed, and what the Justice Department has so far refused to produce, is a comprehensive national strategy specifically designed to address white supremacist and far-right militant violence, beginning with the collection of accurate data about these attacks across all its programs. Absent such an approach, the FBI will continue to fail to prioritize domestic terrorism resources properly.

Ironically, the multiple pathways Congress has provided to prosecute white supremacist and far-right militant violence inadvertently have given the Justice Department another way to obscure the true nature of the threat. If a white supremacist murdered someone, the FBI could consider the crime an act of domestic terrorism, a hate crime, or simply a violent crime. All of these charges may carry severe penalties, but if the act is not labeled as "domestic terrorism," it will not appear in FBI statistics, nor will it receive the kind of robust investigative attention that the FBI devotes to terrorism cases, its number one priority.

Many acts of violence targeting minority groups or LGBTQ+ people are prosecuted as hate crimes, which fall into the fifth-ranked priority as civil rights violations. But federal hate crime prosecutions are very rare compared to the numbers reported by state and local police, or collected in victim surveys.[44] This is the result of the Justice Department's long-standing policy of referring investigations of hate crimes to state and local law enforcement, even though some states don't have hate crime laws and many more rarely use them.

The Biden domestic terrorism strategy recognizes the need for collaboration between federal domestic terrorism prosecutors and federal hate crimes prosecutors, since crimes committed by white supremacists and far-right militants could often fit either category. The FBI had created fusion cells, teaming agents assigned to domestic terrorism with agents assigned to hate crimes investigations, long before the January 6 attack, for this same reason.[45] But the Justice Department has still not changed its policy of deferring hate crimes investigations to local authorities, so it is unlikely that the FBI's fusion cells see the vast majority of reported hate crimes. It is also unclear whether the Biden domestic terrorism strategy will require the Justice Department to account for hate crimes it defers to state and local authorities for prosecution. And, of course, it is impossible to count cases that are not reported to law enforcement, or not investigated or charged as hate crimes because of a lack of law enforcement interest rather than lack of evidence.[46] So even if better federal coordination occurs, the Justice Department may still not be able to provide comprehensive national hate crime data to Congress, as required.

Clearly not all the hundreds of thousands of annual violent hate crimes recorded in victim surveys or the thousands documented by state and local law enforcement agencies each year would necessarily fit the federal definition of domestic terrorism or be fairly attributed to white supremacists or far-right militants. But many undoubtedly would. The FBI should treat all cases in which white supremacist and far-right militants engaged in deadly violence among its top investigative priorities, whether currently classified as domestic terrorism, hate crimes, or violent crimes, rather than deferring these investigations and prosecutions to state and local law enforcement officials uninterested in pursuing them. This accounting for white supremacist crimes, regardless of the label, will enable federal authorities to understand the scope and nature of this violence. It will also ensure that citizens of states without robust civil rights legislation receive equal protection, which is the reason Congress assigned responsibility for protecting civil rights to the federal government.

Without a national strategy, cases involving violent white supremacists and far-right militants will continue to fall through the cracks. Recent examples of far-right violence that appear to have met the statutory definition of domestic terrorism but resulted in no federal charges include the 2018 slaying of a gay Jewish man in California by a member of the violent neo-Nazi group Atomwaffen Division; the 2017 murder of a Black man in New York City by a white supremacist intent on starting a race war; and the 2016 vehicular homicide of a Black man in Oregon by a member of European Kindred, a white supremacist prison gang.[47] State and local prosecutors charged perpetrators in California and Oregon with hate crimes and, in the New York City case, with violating a state terrorism statute. While state charges may have been an appropriate choice in these cases, the Justice Department must still properly account for them in threat assessments that inform a national strategy. Failing to trace possible connections between individual violent actors and organized white supremacist and far-right militant groups forfeits intelligence that could be used to prepare for and perhaps prevent future attacks.

In addition, a significant percentage of Justice Department prosecutions of violent white supremacists are products not of Joint Terrorism Task Force investigations or civil rights cases but of federal violent crimes task force investigations. These investigations are sometimes led by the Bureau of Alcohol, Tobacco, and Firearms or the Drug Enforcement Agency rather than the FBI. These cases receive surprisingly little attention, even though serious violent crimes are often alleged, including murders, and dozens of white supremacist gang members are arrested at a time in multiagency raids. Twenty-four members of Aryan Circle were arrested in Texas in October 2020, for instance, and fifty-four members of the New Aryan Empire were arrested in Arkansas in 2019.[48] The 2018 arrests of forty members and associates of the United Aryan Brotherhood in Florida recovered 110 illegal firearms, including two pipe bombs and a rocket launcher.[49] These cases probably do not appear in Justice Department domestic terrorism statistics, but certainly Congress needs this data to understand the full scope of white supremacist violence in the United States in order to establish effective policies to address it. This balkanization of white supremacist violence into separate investigative categories also risks impairing intelligence collection and analysis, where FBI agents assigned to Joint Terrorism Task Forces investigating white RMVE groups may be completely unaware of a white supremacist gang investigation conducted by ATF agents in the same locality.

To be clear, these federal organized crime and violent crime prosecutions are effective tools the Justice Department can and should use to prosecute violent white supremacist and far-right militant groups. Indeed, this methodology could be effective in addressing violent crimes committed by organized groups like the Proud Boys. But the Justice Department needs to capture the data from these prosecutions, and the FBI needs the intelligence collected during these investigations, to develop a comprehensive national strategy to address this violence. The goal of effectively combating white supremacist and far-right militant violence can be accomplished only with a comprehensive strategy that utilizes all available criminal enforcement tools in a coordinated fashion, so the true scope and nature of the threat from white supremacist militants can be recognized, their tactics understood, and their crimes more effectively combated.

BANK ROBBERY DATA: A POSSIBLE MODEL

The lack of data about violations of domestic terrorism and hate crimes statutes contrasts greatly with other programs, such as bank robberies. Each year, the FBI publishes a detailed report of violations of the federal bank robbery statutes.[50] The 2016 report, for example, outlined information regarding 4,251 violations of the "Federal Bank Robbery and Incidental Crimes" statute, which punishes theft of under $1,000 from banks.[51] It also lists thirty-six violations of the statute criminalizing "interference with Commerce by threats or violence."[52] For each violation of the two statutes, the report broke down the number, race, and sex of the perpetrators, the occurrences by day of week and time of day, the modus operandi used, injuries, deaths, and hostages taken, among other factors.[53] The high level of detail in the assessed factors suggests that the FBI has an intimate understanding of each statutory violation, from petty thefts to violent heists.

Just as the bank robbery data used indicators that are relevant to that particular crime, Congress should standardize the metrics that must be collected in each instance of domestic terrorism or hate crimes.

This data could include information about the defendants and their affiliations as well as the victims, information about the plot, and the federal, state, and local agencies that were involved, among other factors. Congress should require federal law enforcement to revamp its data collection policies and practices and ensure that the various government entities that investigate white supremacist crimes collect data using similar metrics and definitions, as they do for bank robberies.

Requiring the Justice Department to produce detailed reports on all potential violations of the federal domestic terrorism and hate crimes statutes, whether prosecuted by federal, state, or local authorities, would force the FBI to become sufficiently familiar with each incident and develop relevant details about both the perpetrator and the victim of each crime. These reports would provide invaluable data for calibrating counterterrorism and law enforcement resources and would assist in developing appropriate responses designed to protect all American communities from violence.

7

FOCUSING THE FBI

During a June 2021 Capitol insurrection hearing on "unexplained delays and unanswered questions," Rep. Alexandria Ocasio-Cortez (D-NY) focused her questions for FBI director Christopher Wray on the role of social media. Given that "we now know that the attacks were planned out in the open on popular social media platforms like Parler and Telegram," she asked, "Does the FBI regularly include social media monitoring as part of its efforts to combat violent extremism?"[1]

In his response, Wray echoed earlier inaccurate claims by FBI assistant director for counterterrorism Jill Sanborn, who told senators that gathering information from publicly available, First Amendment–protected online activity was outside the FBI's authorities.[2] "What we can't do on social media," Wray asserted, is monitor "without proper predication and an authorized purpose." He then suggested a remedy: "Now, if the policies should be changed to reflect that, that might be one of the important lessons learned coming out of this whole experience."[3]

The FBI's authorities are a matter of public record. Contrary to Sanborn's and Wray's claims, current rules allow agents to monitor publicly available information even when there is no authorized purpose, allegation, or information suggesting that criminal activity may occur—and agents and contractors in fact conducted this kind of monitoring before the attack on the Capitol. A U.S. Government Accountability Office investigation confirmed that prior to January 6 the FBI obtained threat information posted on social media through manual online searches; from other federal, state, and local law enforcement agencies; directly from the companies running social media platforms; and through open-source analysis tools that search across platforms.[4]

Misinformation about the scope of the FBI's powers to investigate domestic terrorism has confused the policy debate about "lessons learned" from the January 6 failures. In the wake of the attack, the Justice Department has used imagined gaps in authorities to justify seeking new statutory powers and resources. This has included revival of the efforts to create a federal domestic terrorism statute that began after the 2015 attack on Mother Emanuel Church in Charleston.[5] The FBI has also sought additional funding in the aftermath of the attack, including a 2021 request for $1.8 million for data collection and $4.4 million for operational expenses.[6]

The January 6 attacks renewed public calls for greater attention to domestic terrorism. But in light of the FBI's misleading and inaccurate claims, Congress must proceed with caution in the face of proposals to expand the bureau's investigative authorities. To prevent far-right violence effectively, the FBI needs narrower powers, not broader ones. And the American public needs a clear understanding of how the federal government's chief investigative agency uses and abuses its powers.

ABUSE AND REFORM OF FBI INVESTIGATIVE AUTHORITIES

In 1908, President Theodore Roosevelt and Attorney General Charles Bonaparte hired thirty-four agents to form the Justice Department's first detective force. Attorney General Bonaparte promised a resistant Congress that the new investigative bureau would never be used for political spying, and pledged to develop a system of internal controls to prevent abuse.[7]

For close to seventy years, the bureau had no consolidated formal guidelines or external controls governing its authorities. Operating outside the rule of law, the FBI used its ample investigative powers to inhibit the speech and association rights of groups whose politics it found threatening, most notoriously targeting left-wing and Black activists. In October 1919, for example, a young J. Edgar Hoover, then director of the Bureau of Investigation's General Intelligence Division, justified pursuing Black nationalist Marcus Garvey because of his alleged association with "radical elements" that were "agitating the Negro movement."[8] Hoover admitted Garvey had violated no federal laws. But the bureau, the precursor organization to the FBI, infiltrated Garvey's Universal Negro Improvement Association and used informant provocateurs and undercover agents to stir up conflict and search for any justification for deporting him. In 1923, the Justice Department ultimately won a conviction against Garvey on a dubious mail fraud charge.[9]

The FBI's lawlessness faced a public reckoning in the 1970s, when a Senate committee led by Sentor Frank Church brought public attention to the covert COINTELPRO operations, which aimed to "disrupt," "discredit," and "neutralize" leaders of the civil rights and anti-war movements of the 1960s.[10] Methods included informant-driven disinformation campaigns designed to spark conflict within groups, discourage donors and supporters, and even break up marriages. The FBI's COINTELPRO program targeting civil rights leaders including the Rev. Dr. Martin Luther King Jr. and Stokely Carmichael was specifically designed to "prevent the rise of a 'messiah' who could unify and electrify the militant black nationalist movement" rather than to prevent any violent acts they might perpetrate.[11]

COINTELPRO's nominal goal was to prevent violence by specific, named groups, which first included the Communist Party USA, the Socialist Workers Party, Black nationalist hate groups, and the New Left. When three civil rights workers were killed by Ku Klux Klan members in 1964, President Lyndon Johnson pressured the FBI to add a COINTELPRO targeting "white hate" groups.[12] In contrast to the other programs, the Church Committee found that the "white hate" COINTELPRO used fewer techniques that "carried a risk of serious physical emotional, or economic damage to the targets."[13] And while the other categories cast a wide net to target nonviolent civil rights, anti-war, and feminist organizations, the "white hate" category focused on specific, named suspects and did not broaden to cover nonviolent right-wing organizations—the likely reason that the "white hate" COINTELPRO was considered most successful in actually preventing violence.

An era of reform began in 1976, when the Church Committee released its findings on the COINTELPRO programs and other FBI abuses. In the aftermath of these revelations, Attorney General Edward Levi published the first version of guidelines governing the FBI, the "Attorney General's Guidelines for Domestic FBI Operations."[14] The Levi Guidelines refocused the FBI on crime detection and prevention by imposing important limitations on the bureau's investigative activities. Most significantly, they required FBI agents to establish a reasonable factual indication of criminal activity before intrusive investigations could be launched.

By the Justice Department's own measures, these restraints effectively ensured that the FBI directed resources toward investigating unlawful activities rather than monitoring the First Amendment–protected speech of disfavored political activists. In congressional testimony in 1979, Attorney General Benjamin Civiletti stated that the three years of experience with the Levi Guidelines "has demonstrated that guidelines can be drawn that are well understood by Bureau personnel and by the public and which can be extensively and productively reviewed by the appropriate congressional committees."[15]

Subsequent attorneys general modified and added to these guidelines over the years, but the greatest expansion of FBI authorities came after the al Qaeda attacks of September 11, 2001. To protect the nation from attackers they feared would strike again, Congress, the White

House, and attorneys general gave the FBI enhanced investigative and surveillance authorities, in theory to empower the bureau to identify and mitigate terrorist threats before they materialized.[16] Under this post-9/11 terrorism prevention lens, the reforms established in response to the Church Committee findings were eroded or eliminated, increasing the risk of abuse not just in terrorism cases but in all investigative matters under federal jurisdiction.

In 2002, President George W. Bush's first attorney general, John Ashcroft, issued new Attorney General's Guidelines, which included rules allowing FBI agents to attend First Amendment–protected gatherings such as religious events and political meetings without having any basis to suspect that criminal activity would take place. They also permitted the FBI to "conduct online search activity and access online sites and forums on the same terms and conditions as members of the public generally."[17] Faced with concern that the FBI would abuse its expanded authority to target activity protected by the First Amendment, Bush's newly installed FBI director, Robert Mueller, explicitly stated that the FBI had no plans to infiltrate mosques.[18] But in disturbing echoes of the COINTELPRO programs, journalists and civil rights organizations documented a sharp post-9/11 increase in the FBI's controversial use of informants to stir up trouble and instigate plots in mosques and other Muslim community organizations.[19]

CURRENT FBI AUTHORITIES: UNDERSTANDING "ASSESSMENTS"

In 2008, President George W. Bush's third attorney general, Michael Mukasey, expanded the FBI's authorities once again, creating the guidelines that still govern the FBI. Mukasey's guidelines cemented the FBI's transformation from a law enforcement agency to a domestic intelligence agency, most significantly by authorizing a new category of investigations called "assessments."

To open a thirty-day assessment, agents are not required to suspect that the target of the investigation may be involved in criminal activity. Agents must state only that they believe they have an "authorized purpose"—namely, to prevent federal crimes or threats to national security, or to collect foreign intelligence. During assessments, which may be renewed for an unlimited number of thirty-day extensions, agents are allowed to employ a broad array of intrusive investigative methods that include recruiting and tasking informants, conducting covert and overt interviews, and obtaining grand jury subpoenas for telephone or electronic mail subscriber information.[20]

Three months after the Mukasey guidelines took effect in 2008, the FBI issued the *Domestic Investigations and Operations Guide*, a regularly updated instruction manual for conducting investigations. This manual, which purported to clarify and limit FBI powers, interpreted these new assessment authorities to allow agents to use census data to map American communities by race and ethnicity, as well as to identify and monitor ethnic "facilities" and "behaviors."[21] A 2009 memo from the Atlanta FBI, for example, cited fears of a "Black Separatist" terrorism threat to justify opening an assessment that documented the growth of the Black population in Georgia.[22] And after the fatal 2014 shooting of unarmed teenager Michael Brown in Ferguson, Missouri, the FBI used its assessment authority to conduct months-long investigations of Black Lives Matter protesters. One report obtained by civil rights groups included an activist's plans to travel from New York for a protest at a Ferguson facility of the agrochemical corporation Monsanto, including details about funds raised for bail and protest materials, but no facts pointing to potential violence.[23]

In 2011, the FBI updated the *Operations Guide* to grant its agents additional investigative authorities that go even beyond the scope of the Mukasey guidelines.[24] The revision expanded the tactics available during assessments to include searching an individual's trash for compromising information that could be used to compel them to become an informant. It also included a new authority, called a "pre-assessment," that allows agents to search publicly available records, online resources, subscription-based commercial databases, and government databases without documentation stating the nature or purpose of these searches, and without even opening an assessment. FBI agents are instructed to retain information from a pre-assessment only if it is used to open an assessment or broader investigation, leaving little record of these searches.

"PRELIMINARY" AND "FULL" INVESTIGATIONS

After assessments, the next level of investigation under the Mukasey guidelines is a "preliminary investigation," a renamed and expanded version of the "preliminary inquiry" that was part of FBI investigative authorities when I worked undercover in the 1990s. A preliminary investigation lasts for six months and may be extended twice, for a total of eighteen months. It permits agents to use the legal process to compel evidence production; to conduct mail covers (which allow the FBI to record data on the outside of a mailed envelope or package); to execute undercover operations; and to engage in consensual monitoring of communications, with at least one party agreeing to the recording, as federal law requires. To open a preliminary investigation, agents need only have "information or an allegation" suggesting a crime or national security threat might take place, and the approval of a frontline supervisor. The allegation may be speculative, and it can be based on sources that include other government agencies, informants, or news reports. A 2010 Inspector General's Office audit of FBI investigations targeting domestic advocacy groups found that bureau agents often made the allegations necessary to satisfy this requirement themselves, based on speculation about who might commit crimes in the future.[25]

Despite this low threshold, being subjected to a preliminary investigation into domestic or international terrorism carries real consequences for those targeted. FBI policy requires that subjects of terrorism-related preliminary investigations be placed on the Terrorist Screening Database, commonly known as the terrorist watch list. The watch list is accessible to customs, border, and immigration authorities as well as federal, state, and local law enforcement agencies, private contractors, and many foreign governments.[26] Placement on the watch list will likely lead to travel restrictions, prolonged detentions, and increased risk to these subjects, as routine interactions with law enforcement could be treated with heightened alarm.[27]

Only "full investigations," during which agents may employ all legal investigative methods, require articulable facts establishing a reasonable indication that criminal activity or threat to national security has occurred, is occurring, or may occur in the future. This "reasonable indication" standard is still a low evidentiary bar, similar to the "reasonable suspicion" standard police use to "stop, question, and frisk" people on the street for investigative purposes.[28] During a full investigation, agents may pursue judicially authorized search warrants and nonconsensual electronic monitoring once they obtain sufficient evidence showing "probable cause," which is a higher evidentiary bar than "reasonable suspicion."[29]

ILLUSORY PROTECTIONS AGAINST BIAS-BASED INVESTIGATIONS

Given the FBI's history of using its authority to target minority communities and suppress First Amendment–protected activities, the Attorney General's Guidelines and the FBI's *Operations Guide* include provisions that claim to restrict abuse, as do other Justice Department policies. But these protections are weak and provide little protection in practice.

The Justice Department's 2023 Guidance for Federal Law Enforcement Agencies Regarding the Use of Race, Ethnicity, Gender, National Origin, Religion, Sexual Orientation, Gender Identity, and

Disability Status, for example, prohibits federal law enforcement from using these attributes "unless specific conditions are present." [30] But the "specific conditions" under which these attributes can be used under the new policy remain overly broad and subjective. For instance, the new rules give agents discretion to use these characteristics whenever they have "trustworthy" information linking a person to a particular "criminal incident, scheme, or organization" and they reasonably believe it is "merited under the totality of the circumstances." [31] The new guidelines also allow the FBI to continue mapping American communities by race and ethnicity. And while FBI policy forbids conducting investigative activity based "solely" on the race, ethnicity, or gender of the subjects, agents need only an authorized purpose to justify using a range of investigative methods based on these characteristics. [32]

These fluid guidelines have facilitated, rather than prevented, systematic racial profiling and stereotyping of marginalized communities. For instance, the Black Identity Extremism category of domestic terrorism was used to justify a nationwide operation called Iron Fist, in which FBI agents engaged in enhanced surveillance and investigations of Black activists. [33] In 2018 the Justice Department also launched a China Initiative, in a misguided effort to combat economic espionage. This program used race and national origin (often referred to as a "nexus" to China) to justify investigating Chinese and Chinese American scientists and technologists and encouraging academic institutions to monitor Asian students and faculty closely. [34]

While Assistant Attorney General Matt Olsen has acknowledged the public national security harms the program inflicted, the Justice Department has not fully acknowledged the role of anti-Asian bias in the China Initiative investigations. The "othering" of Asians was clearly articulated in FBI counterintelligence training materials obtained by the American Civil Liberties Union in 2011, which included a slide that warned agents to "never attempt to shake hands with an Asian" and "never stare at an Asian."[35] While the Justice Department formally ended the program in February 2022, the heated anti-China rhetoric and enduring anti-Asian bias continue to drive abusive investigations.

Supervisory approval is in itself an illusory guard against bias. The Attorney General's Guidelines identify several "sensitive investigative matters," which are subject to approvals from higher-level officials. These include corruption or national security investigations targeting public officials; investigations of religious or political organizations, or prominent leaders of them; investigations with an academic nexus; and investigations of members of the news media. But the same institutional and individual biases that might drive an agent's decision to open an improper investigation can influence the higher-level officials' approval. For example, two of the San Francisco FBI's top executives, the chief division counsel and the special agent in charge, approved an investigation of the anti-racist group By Any Means Necessary, whose members were among those stabbed by white supremacists while protesting a far-right rally, based on the claim that By Any Means Necessary potentially violated the civil rights of the Ku Klux Klan. The opening memo signed off on by these executives described the Klan as a group "that some perceived to be supportive of a white supremacist agenda." The FBI agent's highly misleading description of the Klan and the approval of the investigation by these high-level executives were made only more egregious by the fact that the Klan was not one of the white supremacist groups at the event, which a simple Google search would have revealed.[36]

Moreover, internal FBI records show that agents routinely fail to comply with the requirements regarding sensitive investigative matters. As part of a 2019 audit, the FBI's Inspection Division examined a sample of 353 cases involving sensitive matters and identified 747 compliance errors, many of which involved failing to make the proper notifications and obtain the required approvals.[37]

SOCIAL MEDIA MONITORING AND INFORMATION OVERLOAD

The Ashcroft and Mukasey guidelines and the FBI's *Operations Guide* do not specifically mention social media monitoring. Content posted on public-facing social media platforms is treated as publicly available information, which, thanks to the pre-assessment authority, agents may search without opening an investigation or articulating any basis to suspect criminal activity. It is this authority that Wray and Sanborn misrepresented in their post-9/11 testimony.

FBI agents have even broader authority to monitor social media once they have initiated formal investigations. During assessments, which require no factual predicate suggesting wrongdoing, agents can search, view, and save public social media postings and maintain them in intelligence databases. Further, agents determine that less intrusive methods will be ineffective for achieving the assessment's "authorized purpose," they may also task informants to obtain nonpublic information.[38]

During a preliminary investigation, agents may monitor and consensually record private online conversations in real time, using an informant as the required consenting party.[39] With supervisory approval, an agent may also create a false identity on social media and work undercover to obtain the necessary access to consensually monitor online conversations and chat rooms.[40] Once agents initiate a full investigation, which requires reasonable indication of criminal activity, they may seek probable-cause warrants for surreptitious searches and wiretapping of electronic communications online or over phones.

These broad permissions for social media monitoring rest on a very low or nonexistent evidentiary bar. The only bright-line limit the FBI places on its agents is the prohibition against conducting investigative activity based *solely* on First Amendment–protected activities. The term "solely" is thin protection, as an agent's mere assertion of an authorizing purpose can justify an assessment of any person or organization. The speculative possibility that a person or group may pose a threat in the future, which is true of everyone, has proven sufficient to get an agent over this limitation in investigations targeting domestic advocacy groups.[41]

The massive volume of public information available online has proven irresistible to intelligence agencies, which after 9/11 envisioned achieving "total information awareness."[42] The FBI has permitted agents to search online platforms at will, and has even awarded multimillion-dollar contracts to private companies to conduct social media monitoring services on its behalf.[43] But too much information is as serious an impediment to effective intelligence analysis as too little, particularly when the information sources contain factual errors, satire, hyperbole, and intentional disinformation, as social media often does.[44] Social media can also be misleading and difficult to interpret, and has led law enforcement officials to spread misinformation and divert security resources where no genuine threat exists.

Agents can and should act on fact-based threats that appear in public social media posts, just as agents may find evidence of criminal activity in published written materials or mainstream media broadcasts. But employing a team of FBI agents to scour every book, newspaper, magazine, and interview for vague indicators of wrongdoing would not be an effective way to prevent crime or terrorism, and the same holds true for social media. To imagine that datamining algorithms and artificial intelligence can effectively sort such massive datasets and accurately predict rare events like a terrorist attack defies statistical and mathematical realities.[45] Rather than trying to analyze millions of social media postings to guess which might lead to the commission of a crime, law enforcement should start where there is evidence of criminal activity and follow reasonable leads to their logical conclusions.

SOCIAL MEDIA MONITORING BEFORE JANUARY 6

Federal agencies' lack of preparation for the violent attack on the Capitol is just the latest instance where information overload blunted response. As noted earlier, FBI officials initially claimed they had no warnings of the attack, but a January 5, 2021, memo from the FBI's Norfolk office that was leaked to the *Washington Post* reported intelligence gleaned from social media:

> An online thread discussed specific calls for violence to include stating "Be ready to fight. Congress needs to hear glass breaking, doors being kicked in, and blood from their BLM and Pantifa [*sic*] slave soldiers being spilled. Get violent. Stop calling this a march, or rally, or a protest. Go there ready for war. We get our President or we die. NOTHING else will achieve this goal."[46]

The Norfolk memo was shared broadly throughout the FBI and with other relevant law enforcement agencies, but it prompted no response, likely because this type of fiery rhetoric on social media is commonplace. Similar warnings regularly flood law enforcement intelligence reporting streams, and the vast majority do not come to fruition.[47] Without specific intelligence about the individuals or groups involved, it is extremely difficult to discern who among the millions of people engaging in hyperbolic and offensive language online might actually present a real threat.[48]

The Norfolk memo failed as an intelligence warning, not because the information it presented was inaccurate—it wasn't—but because the methodology of conducting broad-scale social media monitoring untethered from evidence of criminal activity is unsound. The FBI obviously can't (and shouldn't) react to every social media post in which an anonymous person advocates for "war." Instead, it should focus on actual crimes, such as the relatively unpoliced assaults, stabbings, and shootings that had become commonplace at far-right rallies across the country in the years, months, and weeks before the attack on the Capitol.[49] Far-right militants, reportedly including three individuals who later participated in the Capitol breach, had attacked the Oregon State Legislature just two weeks earlier, breaking windows, assaulting police officers, and beating journalists.[50] The previous Proud Boy violence and the attack on the Oregon legislature should have triggered FBI investigations that included monitoring relevant social media accounts. These investigations, in turn, could have put the warnings in the Norfolk memo in a more useful context.

The low thresholds for initiating FBI social media monitoring increase the risk that individual or organizational bias, rather than evidence of wrongdoing, will drive decisions about who will be scrutinized.[51] Law enforcement has traditionally viewed individuals and groups agitating for social change, even when using nonviolent means, as inherently dangerous. Bias-based monitoring of advocacy groups' social media can drive inappropriate and overly aggressive policing of protest activities. For example, a Minnesota FBI Joint Terrorism Task Force officer used an informant to monitor Facebook messages of a local group planning Black Lives Matter protests, reporting the date and times of these events to local police without any reasonable indication of criminal activity, much less terrorism.[52]

Of course, public social media posts that express specific and credible threats can, when brought to the FBI's attention, be the evidence necessary to justify opening a preliminary or full investigation. Likewise, once the FBI opens a properly predicated investigation, agents may logically conclude that monitoring and recording public or private social media posts would be a fruitful investigative step to gather the evidence necessary for a prosecution. The question isn't whether the FBI can ever monitor social media, but rather how and when these law enforcement resources should be used.

A key lesson learned from January 6 is that Congress should limit, not expand, the FBI's authority to monitor social media. New technologies have not changed the need for the commonsense restraints that proved effective in reining in the abuses of the Hoover years. The attorney general should prohibit the FBI from collecting data from social media unless agents cite specific and articulable facts indicating its relevance to an ongoing criminal investigation. Before a public event, FBI agents should be permitted to monitor social media only in order to determine what resources are necessary to keep participants and the public safe, and no social media data should be retained unless it reasonably pertains to criminal conduct. New guidelines should also raise the bar protecting First Amendment rights and prohibit social media monitoring when the justification is based to a substantial degree on race, religion, ethnicity, immigration status, or any other category protected by law. These are the kinds of changes the FBI needs to fulfill its mandate to protect Americans from terrorism and to safeguard constitutional rights.

THE CASE FOR NARROWING THE FBI AUTHORITIES

More than twenty years have passed since 9/11, and U.S. national security policies are overdue for a reckoning. Streamlining the FBI's governing authorities should be a central part of the conversation.

The guidelines governing the post-9/11 FBI have not served their aim of providing a system of internal controls. In addition to the Attorney General's Guidelines, current authorities are explained in a complicated proliferation of policy documents, which, in addition to the FBI's *Operations Guide* and racial profiling guidance, include confidential informant guidelines, undercover guidelines, and consensual monitoring guidelines. Audits by the Justice Department inspector general in 2005 and 2019 revealed substantial violations of these policies, including in more than eight out of ten of the confidential informant files examined.[53] In 2010, numerous FBI officials were caught cheating on tests designed to ensure understanding of the bureau's authorities under the newly adopted Mukasey guidelines.[54] Such high rates of noncompliance indicate that internal guidelines often do not provide the intended safeguards on FBI operations without aggressive independent oversight.

Even when the FBI follows internal policy, the usefulness of its expanded authority is dubious. The scant publicly available data on assessments show that the vast majority yield no criminal activity justifying further investigation. In 2011, data obtained by the *New York Times* showed that over the prior two years, the FBI "opened 82,325 assessments of people and groups in search for signs of wrongdoing."[55] Of these, barely 4 percent were turned into preliminary investigations, which require only "information or an allegation" that a crime might occur.[56] Instead of gathering evidence of dangerous crimes, the FBI has used this overly broad investigative net to collect volumes of personal information about innocent persons and groups and disproportionately to target marginalized communities, including communities of color, Muslim communities, and political activists.[57]

As the amount of personal information available online has skyrocketed over recent decades, expanding FBI authorities has not helped the FBI to identify or prevent credible threats.[58] On the contrary, it has resulted in abusive investigations targeting nonviolent domestic advocacy groups and tens of thousands of assessments that led nowhere.[59] On the flip side, some of the most serious acts of mass violence since 9/11 were perpetrated by individuals previously reported to the FBI as potential threats. Due to the sheer volume of threat reporting, the FBI fails to investigate some of these warnings, such as those regarding Nikolas Cruz, who later conducted a mass shooting at Marjory Stoneman Douglas High School in Parkland, Florida.[60] But even when the FBI does investigate these warnings, the mass of data it has collected does not help to predict the future and, in some cases, actually hinders the ability to interdict attacks.

Information failures were at the heart of the 2009 Fort Hood, Texas, mass shooting, where U.S. Army psychiatrist Nidal Hasan killed thirteen Department of Defense employees and wounded over thirty more. A congressional investigation found that the FBI and Defense Department "collectively had sufficient information" to recognize the potential threat Hasan posed, including communications Hasan had sent to an associate who was the subject of an existing international terrorism full investigation.[61] The Webster Commission, which evaluated the FBI's performance in the Hasan investigation, blamed the FBI's failure to investigate Hasan in part on the "crushing volume" of information that deluged the FBI in its shift to a counterterrorism-centric mission after 9/11. This "data explosion" within the FBI undermined the agents' ability to identify key pieces of evidence already in their possession, the commission determined, which could have justified a more effective response.[62]

Similar revelations emerged from congressional investigations following the Boston Marathon bombing in 2013, when two brothers set off homemade bombs that killed three and injured hundreds of others. Two years prior to the bombing, the Russian Federal Security Services sent a letter informing the FBI that one brother, Tamerlan Tsarnaev, was planning to travel to Russia to join a terrorist group.[63] Tsarnaev had a previous arrest for domestic violence, since dismissed, and his name had come up in two previous FBI investigations that had been closed before receipt of the Russian letter.[64]

After receiving the letter from Russia, an FBI agent conducted an assessment of Tsarnaev but failed to inquire about Tsarnaev's alleged travel plans or contacts with the Russian terrorist suspects. The assessment seemed to be treated as an intelligence-gathering opportunity rather than an investigation into the potentially criminal activity alleged in the Russian letter.[65] The agent closed the assessment, determining Tsarnaev was not a terrorist threat, but, oddly, placed him on the terrorist watch list, which indicated a continuing concern. While it is unclear why the Tsarnaev investigation was cut short, a likely explanation is the "crushing volume" of work caused by the low evidentiary threshold for starting assessments: the Tsarnaev investigation was just one of approximately a thousand assessments the Boston Joint Terrorism Task Force conducted that year alone.[66]

Notably, after receiving an identical letter from the Russian security service, the CIA placed Tsarnaev on the terrorist watch list too. In an indication of the serious nature of the allegations in the Russian letter, the CIA's watch list entry included a mandatory detention requirement if Tsarnaev attempted to leave or reenter the United States.[67] The watch list alerted when Tsarnaev arrived at the airport to fly to Russia, but U.S. officials took no action, later explaining that too many other watch-listed individuals were traveling that day. The watch list alerted again when he returned to the United States, but the FBI did not follow up before the bombing.

Even more troubling, the FBI now alleges that, shortly after it closed its assessment of Tsarnaev, he participated in a September 11, 2011, triple homicide in Waltham, Massachusetts, in which the victims were nearly decapitated. Family members reportedly told local police at the time of the murders that Tsarnaev was close friends with the victims and might have information about the crime. Tsarnaev was never interviewed, and the FBI did not investigate the murder until after the marathon bombings.[68] Focusing more attention on solving violent crimes rather than on trying to predict who may commit one in the future would be a more effective way to ensure public safety.

The FBI's failure to identify and prepare for the January 6 attack on the U.S. Capitol demonstrates many of the problems associated with authorizing investigations and intelligence collection unmoored from evidentiary criminal predicates. The FBI had access to plenty of objective evidence—including social media posts with specific threats brought to the bureau's attention by various sources, reporting in major newspapers, and dozens of previous acts of violence over several years—to establish more than a sufficient basis to conduct investigations of many individuals and groups involved in the Capitol attack. Members of the

Proud Boys, whose leaders were later charged with planning the January 6 assault, had engaged in violence that resulted in several arrests during two rallies in Washington, D.C., in the previous two months, and at many other events across the country over the past four years.[69] But bureau leaders chose not to prioritize investigations into this criminal activity, leaving them ill-prepared to understand the nature of the threat to the Capitol even after it was detailed in FBI intelligence warnings. The problem was not a lack of authority but the choice to prioritize the broad collection of "intelligence" unconnected to criminal activity over investigations into actual acts of far-right violence.

To prevent future acts of violence, new guidelines should clarify and narrow the FBI's authorities for all levels of investigation. A first step is to eliminate the assessment authority granted in the Mukasey guidelines. Investigations collecting the personal information of tens of thousands of persons not suspected of wrongdoing flood intelligence databases with irrelevant information and waste investigative resources that should be focused on dangerous suspects like Tsarnaev and Hasan. Because supervisors may renew assessments indefinitely, intrusive investigations persist far beyond what should be necessary to determine if information exists to substantiate an allegation.

Updated authorities, then, would begin with preliminary investigations, which should be focused on substantiating facts that would justify further attention. At this stage, agents should be allowed to check leads only through law enforcement databases and public information (including public social media posts where relevant) and by interviewing complainants, victims, or witnesses. To ensure agents understand that the purpose of this first stage of investigation is to establish quickly the evidence necessary to justify a full investigation, the FBI should revert to its previous terminology, "preliminary inquiry," and shorten these inquiries to ninety days, as previous versions of the guidelines allowed. The purpose of this narrowed authority is to focus investigative resources where there is reasonable evidence of wrongdoing, as opposed to open-ended intelligence gathering regarding imagined threats. In extraordinary circumstances, the U.S. attorney and special agent in charge could authorize a one-time ninety-day extension.

To proceed to a full investigation, guidelines must insist agents document the articulable facts that establish a reasonable indication that criminal activity has occurred, is occurring, or will occur in the near future. Full investigations should be subjected to regular inspector general audits to ensure they comply with all laws, guidelines, and regulations.

The Justice Department's updated racial profiling guidance failed to close fully the broad loopholes that allow abuse to continue. Congress should step in and pass the Ending Racial and Religious Profiling Act, which was originally introduced in 2019. If passed, this bill would ban all federal, state, and local law enforcement agencies from profiling based on actual or perceived race, ethnicity, religion, national origin, gender, gender identity, or sexual orientation.[70] The 2019 bill should be expanded to protect disability status, and specifically to ban the FBI's racial and ethnic mapping program, which is a form of neighborhood-based profiling that treats one community differently than another based on protected characteristics.

It is time for the FBI to reverse its shift toward broad intelligence collection about innocent Americans and to refocus investigations where facts establish reasonable indications of violence and criminality. Significant changes can and must be made, even during times of unrest, to ensure that FBI resources are focused on real threats. The period in which the Church Committee conducted its investigation, for example, was far from peaceful: the Abu Nadal organization bombed a flight from Tel Aviv to JFK and killed eighty-eight people, CIA station chief Richard Welch was assassinated in Greece, and Croatian nationalists planted bombs at LaGuardia Airport that killed eleven, to name just a few events.[71] Reform is possible now—and indeed essential—to prevent further harm.

With more widespread recognition and fear of white supremacist violence in the aftermath of January 6, Congress and the American public must resist new calls to expand FBI authority. Just as new powers after 9/11 disproportionately targeted Muslim and Arab American communities, any expansion would likely be used to target marginalized communities and political activism. Recent FBI investigations that targeted peace activists, environmentalists, anti-fascists, and Black Lives Matter protesters strongly suggest that the bureau would use any new authorities to engage in similar abuses.[72]

8

A NEW APPROACH TO POLICING HATE CRIMES

Through the years of Donald Trump's 2016 election to the presidency and its aftermath, I have sometimes been asked to comment on a reported rise in hate crimes. In my responses, I have to point out that, while Trump's rhetoric has undoubtedly emboldened far-right attackers, nobody can say for sure how many attacks happened from one year to the next, or whether they increased, because the Department of Justice has long failed in its requirement to collect accurate data on hate crimes. While journalists and civic organizations attempt to fill gaps, statistics are wildly inconsistent, variously based on news reports, victim surveys, and prosecutions. Hate crimes that victims don't report to the authorities, of course, are not counted.

The January 6 spotlight on far-right attacks must extend to illuminate the vast numbers of hate crimes—crimes motivated by prejudice against individuals as representatives of marginalized groups—that go unreported and unprosecuted around the country. These crimes, when unaddressed, tear at the social fabric and undermine public trust in equal protection under the law. When authorities do not respond to attacks quickly and deliberately, perpetrators interpret inaction as official sanction and become emboldened, while the victim communities lose confidence that the law will protect them.

To mitigate harm and build trust, efforts to improve hate crimes enforcement must be coupled with broader police reform initiatives. The same communities targeted by far-right attacks are often underserved by law enforcement as crime victims, even as they are aggressively overpoliced as crime suspects. Half of the violent crimes committed in the United States go unsolved, including in recent years almost 50 percent of the murders.[1] Minority communities are disproportionately victims in these unsolved crimes. It is because of this fraught relationship with law enforcement, studies indicate, that most victims do not report hate crimes to the police.[2]

The federal government has the mandate, and the authority, to address hate crimes properly. Since 1968, Congress has passed five statutes criminalizing hate crimes, which are defined at the federal level as crimes "motivated by bias based on race, religion, national origin, gender, sexual orientation, gender identity, or disability."[3] In addition, the Hate Crimes Statistics Act of 1990 requires the Justice Department to track and document accurately the number of bias crimes throughout the United States.[4] The statute was last modified in 2009 by the Matthew Shepard and James Byrd Jr. Hate Crimes Prevention Act, which added the protected categories of gender and gender identity, and required reporting for every calendar year indefinitely.

The Justice Department abdicates its responsibility to enforce these laws, however, by deferring investigation and prosecution of the vast majority of hate crimes—and the mandated national accounting of this threat—to state and local law enforcement. This deprives U.S. policymakers of intelligence about the nature, scope, and impact of racist violence and leaves victims and their communities without justice or protection from further attacks. It also reinforces the perception that straight white Christian men can assert their social dominance over communities of color, religious minorities, women, and LGBTQ+ people through threats and violence without consequence.

Forging a new approach to hate crimes should mean understanding the organized nature of white supremacist violence and collecting data that allows federal agents to track its spread and influence, so that effective enforcement strategies can be developed. While the federal government cannot and should not be expected to investigate and prosecute all hate crimes around the country, it must recognize that state and local law enforcement are often not willing or able to respond adequately to what is a national and even international crime problem.

Increasing federal attention to hate crimes does not mean that every teenager who scrawls a hateful symbol on a school wall should become the subject of an intrusive FBI investigation or receive draconian punishment. On the contrary, improved data collection and oversight will highlight where problems are emerging, so national resources can be directed to assist local jurisdictions in creating appropriately scaled responses to redress the communal harm that hate crimes inflict.

FEDERAL ATTENTION IS NEEDED TO ENFORCE HATE CRIMES LAWS

State and local hate crime laws differ significantly in whom they protect, their methods and standards for proving bias, and when and how they are applied. Some, like Connecticut's Intimidation Based on Bigotry statute, establish stand-alone crimes.[5] Others authorize penalty enhancements for existing crimes when motivated by bias, such as New Hampshire's law authorizing extended terms of imprisonment when a jury finds the crime was committed "because of hostility towards the victim's religion, race, creed, sexual orientation . . . national origin, sex, or gender identity."[6] Additional statutes criminalize cross-burning, noose-hanging, desecrating or destroying a religious place of worship, and other symbolic acts. Most state laws of this type are not necessarily called "hate crimes" statutes, but the acts themselves would widely be considered hate crimes. A Florida statute "makes it a misdemeanor to place a burning cross on public property or the property of another without express written consent," for instance.[7]

Inconsistent hate crime laws result in widely disparate outcomes for similar crimes. The laws themselves are also vulnerable to challenge, particularly because proving bias often rests on a defendant's constitutionally protected speech and association.[8] One New Jersey hate crime statute, for example, required only a victim's perception that the crime was motivated by bias to obtain a conviction, rather than the more common requirement of proving the biased intent of the attacker.[9] A state appeals court overturned a conviction based on this law in 2013, remanding it for retrial with the added requirement that the defendant's state of mind be proven.[10] The New Jersey Supreme Court rejected the appellate court's rewriting of the statute, however, and deemed that provision of the law unconstitutional in 2015.[11]

A Georgia hate crimes statute that increased sentencing for someone who "intentionally selected any victim or any property of the victim as the object of the offense because of bias or prejudice" was struck down in 2004 as "unconstitutionally vague." Advocates for the Georgia law had initially tried to pass a more specific bill but met resistance over inclusion of sexual orientation as a protected category along with race, religion, gender, and national origin.[12] After three white men chased down and killed Ahmaud Arbery, a Black man who was jogging through their neighborhood, the Georgia legislature passed a new law increasing penalties when the judge or jury finds the defendant selected the victim(s) based on "actual or perceived race, color, religion, national origin, sex, sexual orientation, gender, mental disability, or physical disability."[13]

As of this writing, two states—South Carolina and Wyoming—don't have hate crime laws or penalty enhancements.[14] Several states that have laws on the books rarely if ever prosecute them, and typically less than 15 percent of state and local law enforcement agencies acknowledge that hate crimes occur within their jurisdiction in federal reporting.[15] More than thirty years after Congress passed the Hate Crimes Statistics Act, policymakers still don't know how many of these crimes occur, or where.

This patchwork of unreliably enforced state and local hate crime laws requires sustained federal attention. Federal hate crimes training programs, sometimes proposed as a solution, are impractical: what might be effective advice in one jurisdiction is simply inapplicable in another. Instead, the Justice Department should abandon its policy of automatically deferring hate crimes to state and local law enforcement, and should collect data about these crimes itself. When serious crime involving violence dangerous to human life occurs in a state or district lacking effective hate crimes enforcement, the Justice Department should consider federal prosecutions.

The FBI should also adhere to its own guidelines that require opening a domestic terrorism investigation when the subject of a federal hate crime investigation has a nexus to a white supremacist group, and extend this policy to state hate crimes investigations.[16] Clearly, not all hate crimes could be properly considered terrorism, but illegal acts that are "dangerous to human life" and "intended to intimidate or coerce a civilian population" fit the definition of domestic terrorism that Congress codified. Treating these incidents as potential acts of terrorism makes them the bureau's number one investigative priority, as compared with civil rights violations such as hate crimes, which are ranked fifth. Federal attention to these investigations would provide invaluable data to help the Justice Department understand the scope of far-right violence and ensure that law enforcement resources are allocated appropriately.

Many hate crimes cases, and likely even most, could still be left to state and local police and prosecutors when the facts and circumstances suggest these agencies could provide a better forum, particularly cases involving juveniles. Federal law enforcement need not and should not prosecute every minor assault, property crime, or act of vandalism that does not pose a threat to human life. But involving federal law enforcement in the initial evaluation of bias-based criminal acts would improve the Justice Department's intelligence base, enhancing its understanding of the scope and nature of the threat from racist, white supremacist, and far-right militant violence. Federal attention to these crimes within jurisdictions lacking effective hate crimes statutes may encourage state legislatures to enact appropriate laws and inspire police and prosecutors to enforce them more aggressively.

OBSTACLES TO COUNTING HATE CRIMES

The Justice Department must also take responsibility for accurately documenting hate crimes, as the law requires. Congress passed the Hate Crimes Statistics Act of 1990, requiring the Justice Department to acquire national data about crimes motivated by prejudice. But the Justice Department does not conduct its own investigations and data collection activities. Instead, it relies on state and local law enforcement agencies to report hate crimes voluntarily through the FBI's Uniform Crime Reporting system, which collects data from more than eighteen thousand federal, state, tribal, county, city, and university law enforcement agencies.[17] The problem is that not all police agencies submit data to the federal system, and the vast majority of those that do report data report zero hate crimes.[18]

The Hate Crimes Statistics Act has faced compliance and clarity problems since it was first passed in 1990. In 1998, 83 percent of the 10,730 participating agencies reported no hate crimes. The number of law enforcement agencies participating in uniform crime reporting went up over time, but so has the percentage of agencies reporting zero hate crimes: in 2019, 15,588 agencies participated, but 86 percent of them reported no hate crimes occurring within their jurisdictions.[19] The total of 7,314 incidents reported in the 2019 data are broken down to include 1,158 aggravated assaults, 51 murders, and 30 rapes.[20] But the more than 2,152 property crimes involving destruction, damage, or vandalism are aggregated, making it impossible to distinguish between a potential terrorist act, such as a bombing, and racist graffiti scribbled on a bathroom wall.[21]

These numbers, produced annually, are often reported as rising or falling in comparison to previous years, but this can be highly misleading, as the percentage of law enforcement agencies reporting varies each year. Moreover, the numbers are widely seen as a severe undercount. National Crime Victimization Surveys analyzed by the Justice Department's Bureau of Justice Statistics from 2010 to 2019, for example, indicated that an average of 243,770 hate crimes occur each year, many multiples greater than reported through the Uniform Crime Reporting system. In 2019 alone, the victimization surveys reported 268,910 violent hate crimes that were nonfatal, and 32,540 property crimes.[22] More than 41 percent of the survivors of violent hate crimes did not report them to law enforcement, nor did more than 68 percent of property crime victims.[23]

In January 2021, the FBI transitioned from using the Uniform Crime Reporting system for hate crime statistics to having agencies submit data through a new system called the National Incident-Based Reporting System. The rationale for this change was to provide "more detailed and complete crime statistics to law enforcement, the public, and community leaders."[24] The change, however, reduced participation even further, and the bureau backpedaled, later adding supplemental statistics from the original Uniform Crime Reporting system. With this addition, the FBI's 2021 data include 10,840 incidents as reported by 14,859 agencies, a significant rise from the 8,263 incidents reported in 2020.[25] Hate crimes data for 2022, reported through the National Incident-Based Reporting System and published in October 2023, showed an increase in the number of hate crimes, topping a record-high 11,600 incidents, despite a lower percentage of law enforcement agencies participating in the program.[26] But the true number of hate crimes committed against Americans, and the damage this violence inflicts on American communities, remains unmeasured.

Why does the government persistently fail to count hate crimes properly, when other crimes, like bank robberies, are methodically recorded? Ten years after passage of the Hate Crimes Statistics Act, the Justice Department funded a Northeastern University study to find ways to improve the accuracy of hate crimes reporting. This study, published in 2000, described two barriers: disincentives for state and local police and prosecutors to investigate, prosecute, and document hate crimes; and social conditions inhibiting victims and witnesses from reporting these crimes to law enforcement.[27]

In the decades since the study, factors contributing to these obstacles have been well documented, yet they persist. In 2018, Deputy Attorney General Rod Rosenstein conceded that just "because hate crimes are not reported does not mean they are not happening."[28] But most reforms, including establishing a new website and a "one-stop" portal for police and the public to report hate crimes, reproduce a failed methodology. They ignore the disincentives for state and local law enforcement to address racist and reactionary violence effectively and to report their numbers to the federal government.

No governor, mayor, or police chief wants their state or locality to be known for having a high rate of hate crimes.[29] And even where local politicians encourage hate crimes enforcement, police officers and district attorneys may find that pursuing these charges complicates what might otherwise be a straightforward investigation and prosecution of a violent crime that would receive a significant sentence even without a hate crime enhancement. ProPublica examined 981 hate crimes reported in Texas from 2010 to 2015 and found that only eight were successfully prosecuted using hate crimes statutes.[30] Northeastern University's study compared investigative practices between jurisdictions that reported zero hate crimes and those that reported one or more. Its survey suggested that agencies that did not report hate crimes may be more likely to look for indicators that a crime was not motivated by bias during an investigation rather than factors that would verify bias.[31]

But more than law enforcement's resistance, the fundamental hurdle preventing adequate prosecution of hate crimes at the state and local levels is the steep underreporting of hate crimes by victims and witnesses. The Northeastern University study determined that the most critical factor inhibiting such reporting "appears to be the interaction between police and victim communities."[32] Where an already stigmatized community's tensions with law enforcement are high, victims of hate crimes must consider the costs of subjecting themselves to a potentially negative police interaction.[33]

OVERPOLICED AND UNDERSERVED

The same communities that are often victimized by far-right violence have historically been subjected to high rates of police abuse, violence, and discrimination. Biased police violence has been well documented long before George Floyd's murder brought a surge of attention to the issue. In 2018, 1,166 people in the United States were killed by police, and most of those deaths resulted from stops for nonviolent offenses.[34] A study of fatal interactions with police from January 2012 through February 2018 showed that Black men were 3.2 to 3.5 times more likely to be killed by police than white men, and Latino men were 1.4 to 1.7 times more likely to be killed by police than white men.[35]

A separate study by *The Guardian* using 2015 data found that 62.7 percent of unarmed people killed by police were nonwhite, though minorities make up only 38 percent of the population.[36] Black people were more than twice as likely as white people to be unarmed when killed by police. Native Americans represent just 0.9 percent of the population but account for 2.2 percent of all police killings.[37] Police killings hit a record high in 2022. Again Black people were overrepresented in this data, making up 24 percent of those killed, while constituting less than 15 percent of the U.S. population.[38]

Beyond police killings, these same communities are often subjected to humiliating and discriminatory treatment by law enforcement. For example, the landmark stop-and-frisk case *Floyd v. City of New York* revealed that the New York City Police Department had stopped

4.4 million people between 2004 and 2012, 83 percent of whom were Black or Latinx.[39] NYPD records showed that police stopped, frisked, and used force against Black and Latinx people at much higher rates, even though stops of white people were significantly more likely to result in weapons seizures—the ostensible justification for the stops.[40] Eighty-eight percent of all stops found no evidence of criminality or weapons.[41] Similar racial disparities in police stops have been found in Chicago, Baltimore, Philadelphia, Los Angeles, and elsewhere.[42] Though the NYPD's stop-and-frisk program was curtailed by a court settlement, New York City police officers increased sharply the number of criminal summonses they issued in 2023, more than 90 percent of which were issued to Black and Latinx people.[43]

National data compiled by the Justice Department also indicate that police threaten or use force against people of color more than twice as often as against white people.[44] Law enforcement disproportionately uses militarized units such as SWAT teams in neighborhoods with high populations of African Americans. These tactics inflame community tensions, but research suggests they do not reduce violent crime rates or improve officer safety.[45] Black people, especially women and LGBTQ+-identified individuals, are also more highly vulnerable to sexual violence during police stops than their white counterparts, ranging from invasive searches to "sexual extortion to rape."[46]

Community concerns over the racial disparities evident in police violence and abuse are heightened by a lack of accountability. The Justice Department has jurisdiction over civil rights violations committed under color of law and other police misconduct, but it prosecutes few cases each year.[47] Even as the FBI has warned its agents about white supremacists and other far-right groups infiltrating police departments, the bureau does not appear to have taken significant measures to protect communities of color from this threat.[48] A *Pittsburgh Tribune-Review* analysis of Justice Department records from 1995 to 2015 showed that federal prosecutors declined to pursue charges against law enforcement officials in 96 percent of the civil rights cases referred to them from federal law enforcement agencies.[49] A federal hate crime charge levied against a New Jersey police chief for an on-duty assault of a Black teenager in 2018 was the first such prosecution brought in more than a decade.[50] The police chief was convicted of lying to FBI agents during the investigation, but two separate juries failed to reach a verdict on the hate crime charge, resulting in mistrials.

The aggressive policing these communities face does not keep them safe. Though the U.S. homicide rate has dropped significantly since its peak in 1980, so has the rate at which these crimes are solved—or "cleared," in the parlance used in the Uniform Crime Reports.[51] "Cleared" does not necessarily mean a subject was charged or an arrest was made, just that the responsible law enforcement agency believes it knows who committed the crime. The subject may have died, fled, or been arrested on other charges, or prosecutors may have felt there simply was not enough admissible evidence to charge the case. In 1980, the deadliest year on record, the national homicide clearance rate was 72 percent.[52] By 2016, the clearance rate fell to 59.4 percent, then a record low, despite far fewer homicides to solve.

The problem was considerably worse in many cities. In Detroit, the 2016 clearance rate was less than 15 percent, while in Chicago it was about 26 percent and in New Orleans 28 percent.[53] Though the national clearance rate crept up to 61.6 percent in 2017, more than six thousand murders reported to the Uniform Crime Reporting system remained without charges or arrests.[54] And when homicides spiked during the pandemic of 2020, the clearance rate fell to another record low: just over 50 percent of these crimes were solved.[55]

Homicide clearance rates differ considerably depending on the race of the victim. According to a *Washington Post* study of fifty-two of the largest U.S. cities, over 70 percent of unsolved homicide cases have Black victims.[56] The *Post* found that 63 percent of killings of white victims led to an arrest, while only 47 percent of homicides with Black victims resulted in arrests.[57] The New York *Daily News* found similar results in a study of the New York Police Department's 2013 homicide clearance rates.[58] The NYPD performed significantly better than the national average, solving approximately 70 percent of the homicides in New York City. But when the figures are disaggregated by race, a more complex story is revealed. The clearance rate for homicides involving white victims was 86.2 percent, but the rate dropped to 80 percent for Asian victims, 55.6 percent for Hispanic victims, and 45.4 percent for Black victims.[59] Law enforcement officials often blame uncooperative witnesses for this disparity, highlighting how abusive police tactics ultimately undermine public safety. In Houston, where homicide solve rates for Hispanic victims are lowest, police chief Art Acevedo cited the fear of deportation as a deterrent to cooperation with police investigations.[60]

Nondeadly violence appears to be even less of a priority. The Gun Violence Archive documents an annual average of over 55,000 shooting incidents resulting in roughly 14,000 fatalities, leaving about 41,000 nonfatal shootings each year.[61] A 2019 study of data from twenty-two U.S. cities found that only 21 percent of nonfatal shootings of Black or Latino victims are solved, a rate 16 percent lower than shootings involving white victims.[62]

Sex crimes are also underenforced. According to data from Uniform Crime Reports, the number of reported rapes in the United States has risen steadily over the past five years, topping out at 135,755 in 2017.[63] Law enforcement agencies solve just over one-third of these crimes.[64] Yet rape kit evidence that could identify sex offenders often sits on the shelves of police crime labs untested for months and even years. Estimates suggest that a backlog of hundreds of thousands of untested rape kits still remain, despite several state and federal efforts to address this deficiency.[65]

The decision to pursue investigations and charges has been found to deprioritize cases involving victims of color, with several studies showing that prosecutors are more likely to bring sexual assault charges when victims are white rather than nonwhite.[66] For example, though Native Americans experience the highest rates of sexual violence and rape, a study from 2010 found that the U.S. attorney's office declined to prosecute 67 percent of the sexual assault cases referred for prosecution by tribal law enforcement, the FBI, or the investigative branch of the Bureau of Indian Affairs.[67] In Detroit, Wayne County prosecutor Kym Worthy attributed police failure to test decades of backlogged rape kits in part to racism, noting that 86 percent of the untested kits belonged to victims of color.[68] She also noted that the police reports attached to many of the kits revealed officer bias against the victims, including "writing very disparaging things about our victims—not believing them, dismissing their cases, not bothering to work on them."[69] Worthy's efforts to test 11,000 kits from the Wayne County backlog identified over eight hundred serial rapists and solved other major crimes, including murders, touching thirty-nine states. Worthy raised the funds for this initiative from private donations.

The overpolicing of minority communities as suspects and the unequal justice they receive as crime victims undermines trust in law enforcement. It isn't surprising, given the disparities noted above, that violent hate crimes are 18 percent less likely to result in arrests than non-bias-based violent crimes.[70] Only 4 percent of violent hate crimes result in arrest, according to the victim surveys analyzed by the Justice Department.

Within communities that are overpoliced and underserved, process-oriented reforms, such as a federal hate crimes web portal, will do little to improve hate crimes reporting. But increasing penalties for hate crimes has also proven ineffective as a strategy for reducing these attacks. Without a comprehensive approach to improving police relations with marginalized communities, more severe hate crimes enforcement could heighten tensions rather than reduce them.

A LESS PENAL APPROACH TO HATE CRIMES

Hate crime laws are intended to deter bias-motivated violence, officially condemn prejudice, and express public support for targeted communities. But most hate crimes statutes work by expanding criminal liabilities and/or increasing existing penalties for otherwise prosecutable offenses. This penal approach to hate crimes conflicts with research, corroborated by the Justice Department's National Institute of Justice, that demonstrates that even draconian penalties have not proven effective deterrents to crime.[71] The number of bias offenses reported in victim surveys is remarkably consistent over decades and arguably even increasing in recent years, despite the enactment of new hate crimes laws.[72]

For the most egregious cases involving violent crimes, including murder, aggravated assault, and rape, the hate crime enhancement may not significantly increase the sentences imposed.[73] The racist, anti-Semitic, and xenophobic premeditated murders committed by Dylann Roof, Robert Bowers, Adam Purinton, and Ryan Palmeter all occurred in death penalty states: South Carolina, Pennsylvania, Kansas, and Florida, respectively. In less serious cases involving property crimes, responsible prosecutors may determine that a minor act of vandalism does not justify the increased punishments contemplated in the statutory scheme or serve long-term security benefits.

Particularly for young defendants, imprisonment may harden racist beliefs rather than rehabilitate them. Prisons are often sites of extreme racial violence and segregation, and according to criminology scholar Neil Chakraborti, they "can be 'hotbeds' for prejudice" and recruitment by white supremacist gangs.[74] In a 2022 report, the Anti-Defamation League identified more than seventy-five different white supremacist gangs operating within prison systems in at least thirty-eight states and throughout the facilities operated by the Federal Bureau of Prisons.[75] The report emphasized that these gangs have increasingly expanded their criminal activities outside of the prison systems. Gang members' illegal activities have included numerous murders, violent hate crimes, and charges related to the January 6, 2021, attack on the U.S. Capitol.

Increasing hate crimes enforcement while increasing punishments for perpetrators may reinforce and deepen these existing pathologies in the criminal justice system. Given the number of hate crimes reported in victim surveys, an effort to enforce hate crimes laws more rigorously could aggravate the mass incarceration problem. Perhaps more surprisingly, more severe hate crime laws could also reinforce existing racial disparities in criminal prosecutions.

Preventing racist violence against white people was not the stated motivation for enacting hate crimes laws. But anti-white bias cases represented more than one-fifth of the hate crimes that law enforcement reported under the "racial/ethnic/ancestry bias" category between 2013 and 2017.[76] In 2019, 15.8 percent of the 4,784 offenses that law enforcement agencies documented as motivated by racial/ethnic/ancestry bias involved anti-white bias.[77] That figure was higher than the percentage of reported hate crimes based on anti-Hispanic/Latino, anti-Asian, anti–Pacific Islander, and anti-Arab bias combined (17 percent).[78] As mentioned, hate crimes data for 2021 and 2022 were reported using a different system, but the numbers remained consistent. The 2,042 anti-white hate crimes reported over those two years made up over 15.4 percent of hate crimes involving racial or ethnic bias.[79] Though African Americans make up only about 12.1 percent of the U.S. population, according to the 2020 Census, law enforcement agencies identified them as *offenders* in 19.2 percent of the hate crimes they reported in 2021 and 2022.[80] While there is no doubt that Black people can and do commit racist attacks against white people or others, it is ironic that the pronounced racial disparities seen in criminal prosecutions generally would also be reflected in the enforcement of laws specifically designed to protect minority groups.

The prevalence of young offenders and mentally ill people among the population committing hate crimes also suggests that penalty enhancements for hate crime offenses are not necessarily an appropriate response. Although scholarly research on the subject is sparse, studies have estimated that one in four prosecuted hate crimes are committed by minors (those under eighteen years of age).[81] In 2022, law enforcement reporting through the National Incident-Based Reporting System indicated, of hate crime offenders whose age was known, 19.3 percent were under eighteen.[82] Most states deal with minor offenders in one of two ways: by trying them as juveniles and increasing their sentences, or by trying them as adults and increasing their sentences.[83]

There is also some evidence that a significant number of those charged with hate crimes offenses show evidence of mental illness.[84] In the days following the 2018 Pittsburgh synagogue shooting, the inside of a Brooklyn synagogue was vandalized with hateful and threatening graffiti.[85] The offender, James Polite, was apprehended after setting a fire in the coatroom of another synagogue.[86] Polite, an LGBTQ+ Black man in his mid-twenties, had a documented history of abuse and neglect as a child and spent years in the foster care system.[87] He eventually found a stable home with a Jewish foster family, served an internship at New York's City Hall working on hate crime and domestic violence reduction, and graduated from Brandeis University.[88] He was also reportedly diagnosed with bipolar disorder while going through drug abuse rehabilitation, and received medication.[89]

Leading up to the vandalism, Polite had apparently been experiencing delusions, telling people he believed the FBI, CIA, and DHS had taken over the homeless shelter he was living in.[90] He was also posting anti-Black messages under an online alter ego.[91] Upon his arrest, Polite was transported to Woodhull Hospital for an extended psychiatric evaluation.[92] He was charged with criminal mischief, arson, and reckless endangerment as hate crimes.[93]

There is no doubt the crimes committed by juvenile offenders and those suffering from mental illness like Polite can be as serious and harmful as those perpetrated by rational adults. But increased prison sentences through hate crime enhancements may not be the most effective method to serve the interests of justice, nor to remedy the injury inflicted on the victimized communities and restore social harmony.

THE USE OF RESTORATIVE JUSTICE TO ADDRESS COMMUNAL INJURIES

The use of hate crimes laws is intended to recognize the wide effects of bias-based crimes: according to the Justice Department's website, hate crime victims "include not only the crime's immediate target but also others like them," and "affect families, communities, and at times, the entire nation."[94] Broad harms from hate crimes, including feelings of increased isolation, vulnerability, and psychological stress, have been shown to have long-lasting traumatizing effects, especially where the victims already lack political, economic, or social standing.[95]

Yet for all of the evidence of grave community harms, only a few states attempt to address communal injuries of hate crimes in their statutes.[96] For instance, in 2005, the Illinois Commission on Discrimination and Hate Crimes Act established a commission "to work in partnership with community leaders, educators, religious leaders, social service agencies, elected officials, and the public to identify and uproot sources of discrimination and bias at the source."[97] The commission is additionally tasked with enlisting law enforcement agencies, educators, and community leaders in training and educating the public on issues of discrimination and hate, teaching acceptance, and making the state's hate crime protections broadly known.[98]

Unfortunately, the governor of Illinois failed to appoint members to the commission, with all twenty-one seats remaining vacant for nearly two years.[99] The commission was revived in 2021 under Governor J. B.

Pritzker and issued its first set of recommendations to the Illinois legislature in 2022. Its recommendations include establishing a non-law-enforcement hate crime and bias incident helpline to connect callers to local support services; a grant program for community-based social services; research programs; and developing a strategic community and organizational partner outreach plan.[100] The commission's mandate is a worthwhile example of how hate crimes legislation can be more responsive to the full spectrum of harms created by such attacks.

Similar proposals were made by the New York City Commission on Human Rights in a report examining the rise of hate crimes around the 2016 presidential election.[101] The commission found that police interventions were stymied by underreporting, with only 18.4 percent of victims of physical assault reporting to the police.[102] The commission recommended alternative means for preventing hate crimes, including developing educational tools for vulnerable communities, holding bystander intervention trainings, and engaging in proactive outreach.[103]

Mounting evidence suggests that both victims and communities harmed by hate crimes prefer educational programs and restorative approaches that challenge underlying prejudice instead of enhanced penalties and incarceration.[104] Restorative justice is a different model than rehabilitative justice, which primarily focuses on offenders and is often inconsiderate of the needs of crime victims.[105] A comprehensive restorative response to crime engages the community as a resource for reconciliation of victims and offenders and as a resource for monitoring standards of behavior. There are many different restorative justice approaches, from victim-offender mediations and family and community counseling, to truth and reconciliation commissions.

In the United Kingdom, the University of Sussex used studies, experiments, and interviews with more than one thousand Muslim and two thousand LGBTQ+ people to investigate the indirect effects of hate crimes.[106] They found that the most common individual response to a hate crime within their community was anger, anxiety, and feelings of vulnerability. Sixty-one percent of the Muslim and LGBTQ+ people who took part in the study said that they preferred restorative justice—in which victims communicate with the perpetrators to explain the impact of their crime and agree on a form of reparation—over enhanced prison sentences.[107] The participants in the study believed that restorative justice was better able to address the harm caused by hate and prejudice.

As part of a new strategy to address far-right terrorism and hate crimes, Congress should study restorative justice approaches and develop a plan to fund and implement these methods. For some offenses and offenders, these alternative approaches may significantly reduce the costs of pretrial detention, trial, and incarceration. One study on the economic benefits of restorative approaches in the United Kingdom estimated that a recommended pre-court restorative justice program would pay for itself within the first year and would save the government £1 billion over ten years.[108]

Restorative approaches are designed to build community, facilitate healing, and strengthen social cohesion. For this reason, they are an appropriate match for addressing far-right violence and hate crimes. Too often throughout history, the government sacrificed the security of some communities in the name of protecting others, through neglectful, violent, or intrusive policing. Creating community-based restorative justice alternatives to the criminal justice system is particularly necessary with hate crimes, since they are so frequently not reported to law enforcement. It is time to redefine our notions of public safety and national security to encompass the protection and well-being of all Americans.

9

POLICING THE POLICE

The cruelty of the police murder of George Floyd, captured in viral videos depicting the impassive face of Officer Derek Chauvin as he knelt on the neck of the handcuffed Black man until he was dead, demanded a reckoning. People of all races poured into the streets across the country demanding an end to police violence and racism, and even the abolishment of police altogether. It reminded me of an earlier viral video that had a direct impact on my law enforcement career.

The 1991 Los Angeles police beating of Black motorist Rodney King drew national attention, not because it was an uncommon law enforcement response to noncompliance but because it was one of the first times such abuse was captured on tape. The outpouring of public condemnation led to criminal investigations of the four LAPD officers involved in the beating and broad agreement among law enforcement leaders that police brutality was a national problem that needed to be addressed.[1] Los Angeles mayor Tom Bradley, a former police officer, established the Independent Commission on the Los Angeles Police Department, known as the Christopher Commission, to examine the department's structure and operations to determine what led to excessive uses of force.

Local white supremacists had a different idea. After the four LAPD officers were acquitted by a mostly white jury in suburban Simi Valley, public anger at the verdicts erupted into five days of arsons, looting, and shootings throughout Los Angeles that left sixty-two people dead, including ten people killed by LAPD officers and National Guardsmen.[2] In the aftermath of the rioting, white supremacists began manufacturing firearms and explosives and plotting attacks designed to provoke a wider race war.

The federal government swung into action on two fronts. The Justice Department charged the LAPD officers with federal civil rights violations, attempting to redress what was widely seen as a miscarriage of justice in their state court acquittals. At the same time, the FBI authorized an undercover operation targeting weapons trafficking by neo-Nazi skinheads. I was asked to be the undercover agent.

The white supremacists I was embedded with kept close watch on news reports about the ongoing civil rights case against the officers, hoping to take advantage of another riot if the federal trial resulted in additional acquittals, as they expected. They started devising spectacular racist attacks that they thought could trigger broad anti-white violence in reaction, which would force all white people to join the fight. Their rooting for acquittals could not be mistaken as affection for the police officers, however. One of the proposed plots involved assassinating white police officers and framing Black people as the culprits, to drive more anti-Black sentiment among nonracist white people.

Fortunately, the LAPD officers were convicted in the federal court trial, frustrating the white supremacists' plans, but not deterring them from plotting further violence. Ultimately, my undercover operation uncovered sufficient evidence to bring a number of neo-Nazis and their arms suppliers to trial on both federal and state charges. We solved a series of racist bombings, recovered dozens of illegal firearms and explosives, and disrupted a conspiracy to terrorize the Black and Jewish communities in Southern California.

The LAPD officers' federal conviction on civil charges and my undercover case did more than just solve the discrete crimes charged in the indictments. They began the process of reestablishing a bond with historically underserved communities victimized by racially motivated crimes. The success of these investigations demonstrated to an embattled community, where distrust of the police ran high, that law enforcement was fully capable of addressing racist violence, both in response to an incident and proactively, when it chose to apply the necessary resources. The chairman of the First African Methodist Episcopal Church in Los Angeles, which was on the skinheads' target list, told the *Los Angeles Times*: "The gratitude is very deep. . . . It has given us the beginnings of a new relationship with the current administration of the FBI."[3]

In the wake of the King beating, the Christopher Commission also called for additional steps to address systemic and institutional racism. The commission's investigative report on the LAPD was blunt in its assessment that a significant number of officers regularly engaged in excessive force in defiance of written policies, and that persistent racism and ethnic bias often drove this violence. But it didn't just blame these bad apples. It placed the responsibility squarely on deficient LAPD leadership. The commission found that "senior and rank-and-file officers generally stated that a significant number of officers tended to use force excessively, that these problem officers were well-known in their divisions, that the Department's efforts to control and discipline those officers were inadequate, and that their supervisors were not held accountable for excessive use of force by officers in their command."[4] It complained of a police culture of aggression and confrontation that treated the public with "resentment and hostility," rather than courtesy and respect.[5]

The commission reported that supervisors failed to discipline officers who made racist remarks in LAPD communications systems, and frequently used offensive language themselves.[6] It made comprehensive recommendations seeking to establish more accountable police department leadership and increased community oversight. These recommendations included calls for LAPD to improve screening for recruits, intensify supervision of officers with serious complaint histories, upgrade promotional and disciplinary procedures, and implement new

training programs that emphasized communications, community relations, and cultural awareness. The Christopher Commission also recommended that the city create an independent inspector general to
investigate misconduct.

The commission warned that these reforms could be subverted by
inaction, in a statement that recognizes that what police departments
say to the public often differs from what they do:

> We urge that the leadership of the LAPD go beyond rhetoric in carrying out
> its existing policies against excessive force. From the Chief of Police on down
> to the sergeants, this means taking a firm stand against the "bad guys" on the
> force and employing all the instruments available—training, discipline, as-
> signments, and promotion. It also means monitoring and auditing all avail-
> able data—patrol car transmissions, use of force reports, and citizen
> complaints—and then acting on the data. We urge a comparable effort to
> monitor and root out the manifestations of racism and bias.[7]

In parallel with the Christopher Commission's local efforts, the federal government advanced national measures to address racist police
misconduct. To address the institutional failings of law enforcement
agencies, Congress passed legislation in 1994 authorizing the Department of Justice to file lawsuits against police departments that engage
in a pattern or practice of violating people's constitutional rights. The
new legislation also provided funds to establish the Community Oriented Policing Services office (aptly referred to as COPS) within the
Justice Department, which provides training and research in community policing practices to state and local law enforcement.[8]

These reform efforts were all well conceived, and some of them, like
the establishment of an LAPD inspector general and the COPS office,
are still producing tangible benefits in regard to public accountability
and community relations. But law enforcement was slow to implement
others, particularly around accurate data collection, and the reform

agenda was ultimately overtaken by other events. The 1994 law that gave the Justice Department the authority to sue police departments that systematically abused civil rights also empowered law enforcement in dangerous ways. It provided funds to hire 100,000 more police officers across the country, expanded anti-gang laws, encouraged harsher mandatory sentencing, and funded a prison-building boom that contributed to mass incarceration, which continues disproportionately to impact people of color.[9]

When the government expands law enforcement powers before cementing effective methods to stem police violence and racism, it puts marginalized communities and democracy itself in mortal danger. The 1995 white supremacist bombing of the Alfred P. Murrah Federal Building, followed by the 9/11 al Qaeda attacks, ushered in an era of aggressive and militarized counterterrorism policing. The concept of crime prevention morphed from funding the midnight basketball tournaments and drug abuse reduction education programs of the 1990s to the mass surveillance, racial and ethnic mapping, and predictive algorithms of the 2000s and 2010s.

"US VERSUS THEM" POLICING

The growing militarization of policing has increased the alienation of law enforcement from the communities they were sworn to serve. Police militarization that began with the development of Special Weapons and Tactics (SWAT) teams in the 1980s and 1990s was hypercharged by the war on terrorism. "Warrior cop" training materials and seminars became popular among officers. Police training encouraged police officers to view American communities as battlefields on which the police are under constant mortal threat.[10] Federal programs made surplus military gear originally designed for fighting wars abroad available to state and local police at low or no cost. It became normal to see regular officers on patrol outfitted with assault rifles and military-style uniforms. Combined with acquisitions of armored personnel carriers sent directly from foreign battlefields, local police took on the appearance of occupying armies. Community policing strategies that the Christopher Commission recommended in the 1990s were largely abandoned in favor of surveillance-oriented, intelligence-led policing, in which entire communities were viewed as the suspect pool rather than constituents.

The 2014 police killing of Michael Brown in Ferguson, Missouri, highlighted and intensified this divide. Street protests followed the killing, raising the profile of the Black Lives Matter movement—a decentralized network of grassroots organizers and activists opposing police violence and racism. Police officers with sniper rifles, riot gear, and armored personnel carriers set up barricades that would soon become a common sight.

The original narrative that drove the protests' "Hands Up, Don't Shoot" messaging—that Brown was surrendering when shot—was later contradicted by multiple witnesses, but the community's distrust of law enforcement was well earned from a history of racialized abuse. While one Justice Department investigation cleared the officer who shot Brown of criminal wrongdoing, a broader investigation of the Ferguson Police Department found it had engaged in a pattern and practice of unconstitutional stops and arrests of Black residents, driven by racial bias, that were conducted primarily for the purpose of generating revenue through fines and fees.[11]

Regardless, a Blue Lives Matter movement rose in opposition, arguing that police officers' lives were threatened by the Black Lives Matter narrative that police were racist and targeted unarmed Black people with unjust and excessive force.[12] Blue Lives Matter advocates pointed to ambush murders of police officers by Black men in New York City, Dallas, and Baton Rouge as evidence, though none of the perpetrators responsible for those crimes had direct ties with the Black Lives Matter movement. Since assaults on police officers already carried stiff penalties and rarely went uninvestigated or unpunished, many saw the Blue Lives Matter movement as a means to antagonize Black Lives Matter activists and oppose calls for police reform.[13] White supremacists and far-right militants quickly adopted the slogan in an effort to legitimize their opposition to anti-racism protesters and joined Blue Lives Matter events to cozy up to law enforcement.

Following the demonstrations in Ferguson, the Obama administration established a Task Force on 21st Century Policing, charged with developing "recommendations to the President on how policing practices can promote effective crime reduction while building public trust."[14] The task force's recommendations were familiar. They included pleas for law enforcement to change its culture from a warrior mindset to a guardian mindset, acknowledge law enforcement's role in past and present injustices, embrace transparency and accountability, gather and publish data, establish better community relations, increase diversity, employ de-escalation tactics, improve communications with the public, and modernize training.[15]

In a sign of how politically sensitive accusations of racism in law enforcement had become over the twenty-three years since the Christopher Commission addressed the issue head-on, the 2014 executive order establishing the task force made no mention of it. The task force's final report, issued in 2015, never used the word "racism," and instead focused on implicit bias and the need for training to mitigate it. The report mentioned explicit bias only in passing, stating that "common sense" revealed how damaging it is to police-community relations. But then it pivoted back to implicit bias, which it said was equally harmful.[16] No recommendations to address explicit bias in law enforcement were proposed.

Even the relatively modest Obama-era police reform efforts, sanitized of any discussion of racism, were abandoned under the Trump administration. Law enforcement bias became much more overt, both in minimizing the threat from white supremacist and far-right militant groups and in actively collaborating with them, often in public.[17] The FBI stopped using the term "white supremacist" in its counterterrorism program in favor of "racially motivated violent extremist," a term designed to obscure. Racist murders and police killings of unarmed Black people continued apace.

There was universal recognition, even among prominent law enforcement leaders, that Officer Chauvin's murder of George Floyd demanded condemnation and a reevaluation of police practices. Yet police around the country met the Black Lives Matter protests with excessive and often arbitrary violence, at times in tandem with far-right militants. These aggressive protest policing tactics had been discredited through research conducted decades earlier and abandoned in favor of a negotiated management methodology that was shown to be less likely to provoke a riotous response.[18] It seemed to me that the police responding to the 2020 protests knew exactly what they were doing: exploiting the opportunity to physically punish their political enemies—anti-fascist protesters and journalists—who just happened to be President Trump's explicitly designated enemies as well.

But the renewed calls for reform were again overcome by the forces of reaction. Many police leaders blamed an uptick in murders during the 2020 pandemic on anti-racist protesters' calls to defund the police, ignoring the fact that no police departments were defunded and that modest cuts to police budgets in a number of cities were often later restored.[19] Most law enforcement agencies obtained funding increases after the 2020 protests.[20] Chiefly overlooked in the debate over rising crime was that homicide clearance rates had been declining for decades, reaching a record low in 2020 and begging the question of whether police solve serious crimes in the first place.[21] Studies of crime data suggest they don't.[22]

An unsanctioned NYPD work slowdown in late 2014 into early 2015 provided some evidence to support the theory that less policing could produce a safer society. In reaction to protests following the failure to charge an NYPD officer in the strangulation killing of Eric Garner, and to the assassination of two police officers by a Black assailant in retaliation, NYPD officers engaged in a work slowdown, which lasted seven weeks. So-called proactive police practices, including issuance of summonses, stop-and-frisks, and minor crime arrests, dropped precipitously. A later analysis of NYPD data showed that during this slowdown period, civilian complaints of major crimes—murder, rape, robbery, felony assault, burglary, grand theft, and grand theft auto—dropped 3 to 6 percent, totaling approximately 2,100 fewer major crime complaints than normal. Once the police work slowdown was ended, the rate of major crime complaints gradually returned to pre-slowdown numbers.[23]

Unfortunately, the political will did not materialize to challenge the tough-on-crime narrative, evaluate these studies, and experiment with alternative public safety practices that reduce the law enforcement footprint. Even in Minneapolis, where the defund-the-police model had the most traction following George Floyd's murder, a referendum to replace the police with a new public-health-oriented safety agency failed, and the city council then increased the police budget.[24] Law enforcement fearmongering about increasing crime, amplified in right-wing media, inflamed public fears and cowed politicians from challenging the deceptive narrative that giving law enforcement more resources reduces crime.[25]

The urgent need for police reform was about to get even clearer. On January 6, 2021, for the first time in U.S. history, a mob of white supremacists and far-right militants attacked the Capitol as part of a multifaceted conspiracy to overturn a presidential election. Law enforcement, Homeland Security, and military officials charged with protecting the nation from just such a threat were among the insurrectionists. Leaders of these agencies received timely and prescient warnings but chose to ignore them. Current and former Justice Department attorneys allegedly conspired with the defeated president to remain in power illegally.

The actions of just a handful of individuals may literally have prevented the government from falling into chaos: Vice President Mike Pence's refusal to bend to President Trump's demands that he illegally reject the electoral votes and throw the election to state legislators; Capitol Police officer Eugene Goodman's clever maneuver to lead the rioters away from the Senate chamber so that the senators could escape; a couple of White House lawyers who stopped the president from ordering the military to seize voting machines. Far too many members of law enforcement and the military were willing to help in the coup attempt by a defeated president.

In the aftermath of January 6, Congress has forfeited important opportunities to reform federal law enforcement deficiencies. Rep. Liz Cheney (R-WY), one of two Republican members of the January 6 Committee, reportedly suppressed the committee staff's research into the roots of white supremacy and its continuing influence over our government institutions and demanded that the findings regarding pre-attack intelligence failures at the FBI and DHS be omitted from the public report.[26] FBI officials testifying in congressional inquiries after January 6 repeatedly misstated their authorities, attempting to divert blame for their personal and institutional failures, without consequence. Many Republican government officials and right-wing media figures began sowing confusion about the nature of the January 6 insurrection, claiming it was just a rowdy protest or an FBI-staged plot to justify an anti-conservative crackdown. Rep. Jim Jordan (R-OH) chaired a select subcommittee to study the "weaponization of government," deceitfully accusing the FBI of initiating investigations against the rioters and insurrectionists based on bias against conservatives—a charge that FBI director Christopher Wray, a lifelong Republican, member of the Federalist Society, and appointee of Presidents Trump and Bush, called "somewhat insane."[27]

Regardless of Wray's incredulity, millions of Americans believe that white Christian conservatives are being victimized, and that government institutions are either incompetent to protect them or actively targeting them. Even FBI agents have embraced these conspiracy theories. A group of agents calling themselves "the suspendables" wrote a letter to Wray complaining about diversity, equity, and inclusion training and discrimination against "unvaccinated conservative/ Christian men" in the FBI. The letter included dozens of questions regarding an array of FBI-related conspiracies promulgated on far-right social media.[28] Far-right militants, citing similar conspiracies and their support for Trump, have threatened FBI agents and attacked bureau offices.[29]

EMPOWERING REFORMERS TO POWER REFORM

We can't expect law enforcement to fight white supremacist and far-right violence effectively if law enforcement leaders don't have the will to take on racism and far-right militancy within the profession. Increased efforts to root out white supremacists and far-right militants within law enforcement after January 6 gradually slowed and faltered. Proposed reforms have focused on empowering law enforcement agencies to conduct more thorough background investigations, polygraphs, and social media monitoring to identify police recruits and officers who embrace a racist ideology, raising concerns about infringement of First Amendment rights.[30] But these solutions misidentify the problem. Police officers who hold hate in their hearts aren't so secretive and difficult to identify that law enforcement agencies would need to probe their innermost thoughts and monitor their off-duty activities to uncover them. If they were so well hidden and careful in masking their bias while on duty, there would be much less of a problem with racist policing. The truth is that police officers know who the racists within their departments are, as do many of the supervisors. They know which officers routinely engage in excessive force or other misconduct. And so do the victims of their abuse.

The problem that must be solved is that racist, violent officers who are known within their departments are too often not punished but rather rewarded. Minneapolis officer Derek Chauvin was the subject of more than a dozen complaints from community members, including allegations of racism and excessive force, long before he killed George Floyd.[31] That Chauvin remained on the force couldn't be surprising to anyone who knew how ineffective internal police investigations of community complaints are in disciplining wayward officers. But the more troubling fact is that Minneapolis police leaders selected Chauvin to be a training officer, instructing young police academy graduates in how policing is performed out on the streets. It is inconceivable that they did not know his history, especially since two complaints reportedly resulted in disciplinary action.[32]

Law enforcement leaders too often see citizen complaints as allegations to defend against, rather than opportunities to identify problem officers. This defensive impulse is even more troubling when a department employee raises an accusation or discrimination complaint against a fellow officer or supervisor. The department has an equal duty to protect both employees, so there is no institutional reason to defend the person alleged to have committed the misconduct rather than support the complainant. But today, in far too many law enforcement agencies, reporting a fellow officer's racist misconduct is more threatening to a police officer's career than actually engaging in racist misconduct.

Part of the answer is in establishing or strengthening whistleblower protections, which often fail to provide sufficient legal protection for employees who see misconduct on the job to allow them to feel comfortable reporting it. This is especially true in law enforcement, which has a strong tradition of enforcing a blue wall of silence. This culture can be defeated by imposing an affirmative duty on officers to report racist misbehavior and excessive force they witness, with penalties for failing to intervene.

In a case with striking parallels to Chauvin's murder of George Floyd, in 2006, a Buffalo, New York, police officer punched and then started choking a handcuffed Black man after an arrest. Officer Cariol Horne saw the victim was in distress and intervened, pulling the offending officer's arm away from the man's neck. Horne, a Black female officer, was sanctioned by her department, reassigned, and ultimately fired, while the other officer was promoted. He was later charged in another assault against handcuffed Black teenagers and sentenced to prison.[33] Officer Horne ultimately took legal action and received compensation fifteen years after the events took place. In October 2020, the Buffalo mayor signed into effect "Cariol's Law," which imposed a duty on police officers to intervene and report excessive force used by other officers.[34] Failing to do so could result in criminal penalties.

All localities should impose similar obligations on law enforcement officials. But breaking a tradition is also a matter of leadership. Law enforcement leaders must make it clear to all personnel that racist misconduct of any kind will not be permitted. In one example of positive action, after a Houston police officer was charged for crimes related to the January 6 attack, Chief Art Acevedo addressed his police academy cadets, as recounted by the *New York Times*:

"Is there room for hate?"

"No, sir!"

"Is there room for discrimination?"

"No, sir!"

"Is there room for a militia in this department or any other police department?"

"No, sir!"

Chief Acevedo then made them repeat four times that they understood they were required to report officers with extremist affiliations. A cadet who allegedly claimed membership in the Aryan Brotherhood, a criminal gang, was reportedly dismissed.[35]

All police departments should have clear written policies banning racist speech and behavior, as well as a ban on active affiliation with racist, white supremacist, and far-right militant groups. These policies should be properly vetted to ensure they comply with all contractual, legal, and constitutional requirements and include effective due process protections.

Where police officers are found to be involved in white supremacist or far-right militant activities, racist violence, or related misconduct, police departments should initiate mitigation plans designed to ensure public safety and uphold institutional integrity. Mitigation plans should include referrals to prosecutors for possible criminal charges, dismissals, and decertification.

Where an officer's misconduct does not merit criminal charges, dismissal, or decertification, other disciplinary actions should be pursued. The law enforcement agency should report the misconduct to prosecutors, so that they may independently review previous cases in which the officer provided evidence to determine if bias tainted the prosecution. Going forward, the law enforcement agency should consider limitations on that officer's assignments to reduce potentially problematic contact with the public, retraining, intensified supervision, and auditing. Law enforcement officials and prosecutors have an obligation to provide defendants with exculpating information in their possession, including information about police witnesses' misconduct that may reasonably impeach their testimony. Prosecutors should include officers known to have engaged in overtly racist behavior on Brady lists, so that defendants have an opportunity to challenge the reliability of their testimony at trial.[36]

WHO HAS RESPONSIBILITY TO POLICE THE POLICE?

Of course, racism, white supremacy, and far-right militancy in law enforcement are national problems that require more than just the efforts of individual police departments and localities to resolve. The Justice

Department has acknowledged that law enforcement involvement in white supremacist and far-right militia organizations poses an ongoing threat, but it has not produced a national strategy specifically focused on addressing it. Efforts to address the problem so far have been bogged down by treating it as an effort to eradicate "extremism" in law enforcement rather than misconduct, which misdirects the inquiry from examining what police do to probing what they think.

First of all, "extremism in law enforcement" is an overly broad description of the current problem. I am not aware of public concerns that Marxist police officers are profiling and using excessive force against corporate executives across the country. I haven't seen police officers being arrested for breaking into mink farms and liberating caged animals. Racism, however, has been a consistent and persistent issue in law enforcement for decades, and it isn't just a problem of a few "extremist" officers on the margins. Police chiefs have been implicated in racist misbehavior and white supremacy as well as officers and department members at every position in between.[37] Racism is a systemic, institutional, and explicit problem in law enforcement. It is demonstrated in the pervasive use of racist language in law enforcement agencies' official communications channels all across the country and at all levels, federal, state, and local. It is also measurable in persistent racial disparities in police stops, searches, uses of force, arrests, sentences, citizen complaints, and racial discrimination lawsuits brought by law enforcement employees.

Second, treating the problem as one of "extremism" justifies misguided solutions. Giving police managers—who may harbor biased views themselves—expanded powers to delve into the beliefs and private behavior of employees is likely to result in more official misconduct than it uncovers. Police agencies are notorious for retaliating against whistleblowers who report internal mismanagement, misconduct, and abuse, and have often been found liable for discriminating against employees based on race, gender, and sexual orientation. Based on available evidence, supporting the Black Lives Matter movement or other civil rights organizations would be more likely to draw negative scrutiny to an applicant or officer than active involvement in gun clubs that include Three Percenters militia members. Trying to scrutinize associational activity with ideological groups and movements would be a fraught exercise.

Instead, law enforcement screening must focus on misbehavior. Federal law, most state laws, and law enforcement regulations already ban discrimination based on race, ethnicity, gender, and sexual orientation. Most law enforcement agencies have policies barring public association with known criminals.[38] Simply taking complaints seriously and enforcing existing laws and policies with regard to racist misconduct is all that's necessary. Unfortunately, there has been no comprehensive national effort to document police misconduct that can be used to hold law enforcement agencies accountable and prevent officers dismissed from one agency from just moving to the next. The lack of comprehensive data on police misconduct makes it more difficult for policymakers to understand the problems and tailor effective solutions.

The Justice Department has only recently begun collecting national data regarding use of force by law enforcement officials. It must accelerate this effort by requiring the FBI actively to collect data, rather than waiting for state and local agencies to report it.[39] The Justice Department has also periodically provided funding to a private nonprofit group, the International Association of Directors of Law Enforcement Standards and Training, which collects data regarding the most severe form of punishment for a police officer: decertification. States regulate police officer certification requirements through Police Standards and Training offices. In 2000, the group began collecting the names of officers decertified by their state standards and training offices, and started alerting departments seeking applicants to officers who have had their certifications revoked in another jurisdiction. The Justice Department provided grants to the nonprofit at its inception, and again in 2005 and

2020. But the database is not public, not every state participates, and it reportedly isn't well known within law enforcement, so it often goes unchecked when police departments hire officers.[40]

The Biden administration's 2022 executive order required the Justice Department to establish a federal law enforcement accountability database, which it launched in December 2023. The database will include misconduct records only of federal law enforcement officers, and can be used only by federal law enforcement agencies for making hiring decisions. This National Law Enforcement Accountability database should be expanded to include misconduct records for state and local law enforcement officers, and it should be accessible to federal, state, and local prosecutors who might otherwise rely on these officers' testimony in court proceedings. The national database should absorb the decertification data regarding state and local law enforcement that is now held by the International Association of Directors of Law Enforcement Standards and Training. All law enforcement agencies should be required to contribute misconduct records to this unified database as a condition of receiving federal funds. Congress should ensure the effort is properly funded and includes appropriate due process and independent auditing for fairness and accuracy. Any derogatory information collected regarding racist misconduct and moral turpitude should be deemed Brady material that must be disclosed to defense attorneys when the officer provides evidence in a prosecution.

In addition, the Justice Department should establish a working group to examine law enforcement associations with white supremacist and other far-right militant groups, and to assess the scope and nature of the problem in a report to Congress. The working group should use this review to develop an evidence-based national strategy designed to protect the security and civil liberties of communities policed by law enforcement officers who are active in white supremacist or far-right militant organizations. A national strategy will ensure that U.S. attorneys and FBI offices across the country properly prioritize civil rights and police misconduct investigations and harmonize their tactics to guarantee equal justice for all. The national strategy should include publishing data and metrics to evaluate the effectiveness of the methodologies it employs.

Part of this strategy should be working with Congress to amend the evidentiary standard for civil rights violations by members of law enforcement. Court decisions interpreting the current requirement to prove that police officers "willfully" violated constitutional rights have proven an impediment to prosecutions of racist violence by law enforcement. Reducing the requirement to a "knowingly or recklessly" standard would allow Justice Department prosecutors to hold more police officers accountable for civil rights violations resulting from intentional uses of excessive force.[41]

The Justice Department should also require the FBI to review its investigations of white supremacists and other overtly racist or fascist militant groups in order to document and report all indications of active links between these groups and law enforcement officials. This intelligence would both inform the department's assessment and national strategy and, where evidence of potential civil rights violations or other criminal activities by these law enforcement officers exists, allow investigations to be initiated. The FBI should be required to determine whether any law enforcement officials it investigates for civil rights violations or other criminal matters have connections to violent white supremacist organizations or other far-right militant groups, have a record of discriminatory behavior, or have a history of posting explicitly racist commentary in public or on social media platforms. This information should be provided to FBI agents assigned to domestic terrorism matters for investigative and intelligence purposes, and to federal, state, and local prosecutors to consider their inclusion on Brady lists.

Of course, the alleged involvement of at least one Justice Department official and an FBI agent in supporting the former president's attempt to overthrow the 2020 election demands an independent internal review of events leading up to and following the January 6 insurrection. The lack of a public accounting has ceded ground to right-wing conspiracy theorists who allege the attack on the Capitol was a plot manufactured by FBI agents and informants. Greater government transparency is required to restore public trust in the institutions we rely on to defend our democracy and the rule of law.

THE SCIENCE OF REFORMING RACISM IN LAW ENFORCEMENT

Crafting a holistic set of public safety recommendations to transform how law enforcement is conducted in this country is beyond the scope of this book. But it is obvious that the current system is unsustainable and serves neither the public nor the law enforcement officers and agents who are committed to serving their communities and country properly. An evaluation of legal settlements of police misconduct lawsuits in the fifteen largest cities in the United States revealed that constitutional violations cost taxpayers $2.26 billion from 2010 to 2020.[42]

Fortunately, significant research into policing practices since the 1990s provides a basis for evidence-based reforms. The Christopher Commission recommended greater minority recruiting and hiring, for instance. It remains important that law enforcement agencies reflect the diversity of the communities they serve, and while some agencies, such as the LAPD, have improved, law enforcement across the country remains predominantly white and male.

We also know now that diversifying police departments alone doesn't solve the problem of violently racist policing. The police beating death of Tyre Nichols in Memphis, Tennessee, at the hands of five Black officers highlights what research has shown—that through police training and socialization, Black officers can harbor implicit racial biases and anxieties similar to those of white officers.[43] But a recent study of 1.6 million enforcement events by Chicago police officers from 2012 to 2015 demonstrated that diversity can reduce potentially adverse interactions with the public, particularly in minority communities. The study found that Black and Hispanic officers made fewer stops and arrests for lower-level offenses, particularly against Black civilians. It also found that female officers use force less frequently than male officers.[44] Another study found that female officers conduct fewer searches of cars and drivers when they make police stops, as compared to male officers, but have a higher hit rate for finding contraband. This evidence suggests female officers are less likely to escalate encounters needlessly with drivers they stop.[45]

Other characteristics can inform hiring as well. Though study results vary, some research shows that officers with four-year college degrees receive fewer misconduct complaints. More intriguing, one study found that police departments that screen officers for experience volunteering and performing community service receive one-third fewer sustained excessive force complaints.[46]

The Christopher Commission's most important recommendation, based on evidence, was that police managers should pay greater attention to officers who receive a significant number of misconduct complaints. Research examining data on fifty thousand complaints filed against Chicago police officers found that the 1 percent of officers with the highest number of complaints were responsible for five times the number of payouts in civil rights litigation and four times the amount of damages. So again, more aggressively addressing the misconduct of a relatively small number of officers is likely to reduce civil rights complaints and ensuing costs to taxpayers significantly.[47] Rather than blaming activists protesting police misconduct for poor morale and recruiting, law enforcement officials should focus their ire on the small number of problem officers who bring disrepute to the profession.

Finally, both the Christopher Commission and the Task Force on 21st Century Policing recommended more effective law enforcement training that emphasized communications, community relations, and cultural awareness. The scholars who developed the Extremist Crime Database, which is one of the most comprehensive datasets capturing both ideological and nonideological crimes committed by white supremacists and far-right militants, documented the need for specialized training to deal with this threat. They said this training should "provide a better understanding of the contours of the far right; discuss the unique geographic, crime-incident, and structural characteristics of the far right; and describe the need to examine all ideologically motivated crimes, regardless of whether they are also defined as terrorist." [48]

These are appropriate recommendations, and it is easy for policymakers to approve additional training for law enforcement officers. But there is little supervision of the actual training they receive. For years the FBI, DHS, and Defense Department provided law enforcement and military officials with bigoted counterterrorism training materials that presented Muslims and Arabs as backward and inherently violent. [49] A 2022 Reuters investigation revealed that instructors with ties to far-right militant organizations and right-wing conspiracy movements, including the Proud Boys and Oath Keepers, have trained hundreds of law enforcement officers across the country, some of whom have cast doubt on the validity of the 2020 presidential election. [50] In at least thirty states, police training has been provided by the Constitutional Sheriffs and Peace Officers Association, a far-right group that promotes the view that sheriffs are the highest independent authority for interpreting the Constitution and can lawfully resist federal law enforcement efforts they deem unconstitutional, by force if necessary. Researchers have identified sixty-nine active sheriffs who are members or supporters of the Constitutional Sheriffs and Peace Officers Association. [51]

Without national standards and independent oversight, law enforcement reforms requiring more training can increase police bias rather than cure it. Police training is often provided by private for-profit companies, which receive little independent vetting regarding the qualifications of the instructors or the content of the tactics they promote. In a rare divergence from this norm, the New Jersey Comptroller's Office audited a six-day conference in 2021 provided by a New Jersey company called Street Cop Training attended by 990 police officers from around the country. The comptroller's report, published in December 2023, found that during the conference Street Cop instructors promoted unconstitutional practices in police stops, glorified police violence, and "espoused views and tactics that would undermine almost a decade of police reform efforts in New Jersey."[52] The investigation documented "over 100 discriminatory and harassing remarks by speakers and instructors, with repeated references to speakers' genitalia, lewd gestures, and demeaning quips about women and minorities." In addition to the $75,000 in direct costs to New Jersey taxpayers for 240 officers from across the state to attend the conference, the comptroller's report identified additional costs in excessive force, discrimination, and harassment lawsuits; the expense of retraining the officers who attended the conference; as well as the suffering of communities subjected to unconstitutional police practices promoted there. At least fifty unregulated private companies provide police training in New Jersey alone, and many more across the country, exponentially increasing these costs.

GETTING BEYOND RHETORIC

Police representatives who acknowledge racism in law enforcement as a serious concern, or who appear to sympathize with anti-racism activists or the Black Lives Matter movement, are often ostracized. Congressman Matt Gaetz (R-FL) demanded the identification of FBI agents who "took a knee" in response to requests from participants in a 2020 Black Lives Matter march in Washington, D.C., singling one out by name for public condemnation that spread on right-wing media.[53] An NYPD officer wrote an apology to his colleagues for kneeling at another rally, saying the action went "against every principle and value that I stand for."[54] A Massachusetts police officer was fired for posting a picture of her niece at a Black Lives Matter rally on her personal social media page. Her colleagues complained that signs visible in the photograph criticized law enforcement and could have been interpreted as threatening. The mayor who demanded the officer's dismissal absurdly compared the matter to an earlier firing of a police officer who forwarded a story about the murder of Heather Heyer at the Unite the Right rally in Charlottesville, with the social media post "Hahahaha love this. Maybe people shouldn't block roadways."[55]

Richmond, California, police chief Chris Magnus was criticized by his department's union for holding up a Black Lives Matter sign at a 2014 protest.[56] Magnus weathered this criticism in large part because the community policing reforms he brought to the minority-majority city won public support for his leadership and reduced violent crimes.[57] In 2020, Chief Magnus, then leading the Tucson, Arizona, Police Department, participated in a discussion about racism in law enforcement organized by the *New York Times* after the murder of George Floyd. Magnus explained that many police officers

> take it very personally when someone says police are racist or when they even hear the term "systemic racism." But part of the problem is they haven't gotten any education about the history of policing. And they don't realize what the role of police were, going back as oppressors, and how that carries over even into the modern day.[58]

A reluctance to acknowledge and address explicit racism in law enforcement influences police training. The Justice Department offers civil rights and implicit bias training to law enforcement and often mandates it in consent decrees following pattern-and-practice lawsuits. While this training may be important to help sensitize law enforcement to unconscious bias, it fails to address overt racism, and its effectiveness in curbing police bias remains unproven.[59] A 2019 study suggested that police officers' fears of being stereotyped as racists threaten their self-esteem and make them more likely to support the use of aggressive and coercive tactics.[60] It's a vicious catch-22, in which the people most in need of education regarding police racism are the least receptive to it.

The authorities responsible for providing equal justice under the law cannot abandon this obligation simply to avoid offending the racists among them. The reticence to call out police racism directly makes it that much more difficult to eradicate—or, worse, reinforces it. Correctly and clearly identifying the problem is the only way to craft an effective solution.

CONCLUSION: LAW ENFORCEMENT'S ROLE IN RESISTING WHITE SUPREMACY

White supremacy—the belief that white people should dominate others within a system of racial hierarchy—was enshrined in our nation's founding documents and enforced in law for more than two hundred years. While our laws have been reformed, racial inequality remains a serious problem. The U.S. Treasury Department, the agency responsible for managing the nation's economy and fiscal policy, has recognized that an uneven distribution of resources, political power, and economic opportunity contributes to enduring racial disparities in "wealth, education, employment, housing, mobility, health, rates of incarceration, and more."[1] For decades, these disparities have been measured, documented, and discussed in congressional hearing rooms, state legislatures, city halls, corporate boardrooms, academic institutions, and mass media, yet they persist.

In a pluralistic country that professes to provide equal opportunity and justice to all, theories of unconscious bias have been developed as a way to explain the persistence of racial inequality. What these theories don't explain, however, is why once unconscious forms of bias are recognized and the resulting racial disparities demonstrated, there remains such stiff resistance to reform. At some point we must acknowledge that the resistance to correcting the uneven distribution of power and resources represents an *explicit* form of bias. People with the power to change the system that produces these inequities— politicians, their wealthy donors, and corporate titans—are the ones who benefit most from it. It is in their self-interest to defend and entrench the systems that enabled their wealth and power.

This dynamic explains why even during the administration of the first Black president, Barack Obama, challenges to status quo power structures by activist movements such as Occupy Wall Street, Standing Rock water protectors, and Black Lives Matter were treated as national security threats that required suppression with FBI and Homeland Security surveillance and police violence.[2] Racist violence that tends to reinforce existing power structures, on the other hand, has not been treated as a national threat requiring a similarly ferocious police response since President Ulysses S. Grant sent federal troops to put down the first iteration of the Ku Klux Klan. This is the foundational, systemic aspect of white supremacy—the desire among people in power to keep the existing system and the privileges it bestows. It is overt but too often denied or ignored.

Would-be authoritarians sell a different story to the public about who is hoarding power. A 2020 Pew poll found that 70 percent of Americans believe politicians, corporations, and the wealthy are too powerful and that the economic system is unfair.[3] The discontent reflected in this poll might drive a popular movement to restrain corporate power and tackle government corruption and self-dealing, but it is also fertile ground for reviving ancient hatreds and instigating social division. Forty years of bipartisan political support for neoliberal economic policies granting massive tax cuts to the wealthy, while gutting social services for the middle and working classes, has brought about unprecedented levels of wealth inequality, wage stagnation, and increased economic anxiety. White supremacist theories appeal to this anxiety by blaming a shadowy elite—international bankers, socialists, globalists, Jews—that is secretly rigging the system and conspiring to replace white Americans with people of color and nonwhite immigrants.

Bigotry and racial resentments are not new, but they have bubbled back to the surface as people in authority have made it more acceptable to express such views in public. Resurgent white supremacy is visible today in racist, nativist, anti-Semitic, anti-immigrant, and Islamophobic rhetoric that is increasingly voiced by elected officials and media personalities in public discourse and over hate-filled social media channels. It drives the reactionary backlash to the latest mass movement for civil rights, represented by Black Lives Matter protesters' demands for full and equal protection of the law. The multifaceted counterattack has included legal assaults on voting rights and affirmative action, and a well-funded campaign, disguised as a "parents' rights" movement, to ban books from school libraries and prevent teachers from discussing America's history of racial oppression.

Better law enforcement will not cure the political, economic, and social ills that have contributed to the resurgence of overt white supremacy. Indeed, part of the problem in law enforcement today is that police have been increasingly tasked with addressing social problems such as homelessness, drug addiction, school disciplinary matters, and mental health emergencies for which they are not properly trained or equipped. This expansion of responsibilities has contributed to soaring law enforcement budgets, mass incarceration, unnecessary police violence, and increasing public distrust.[4] Foundationally, the spread of white supremacist beliefs is better countered through public education rather than government suppression, which is why public libraries, school curricula, and the news media are among the reactionaries' primary targets.

Where law enforcement *can* address systemic white supremacy is by prioritizing white supremacist violence as a serious national security threat. We need a national strategy that directs police at federal, state, and local levels to prosecute far-right crimes consistently and to fulfill their responsibility to collect and share accurate data about the scope and nature of white supremacist violence. Data is knowledge, and a government entity withholding data steals power from those who could use that knowledge in ways that such a government entity can't control.

Suppressing data on white supremacist violence means silencing the stories of those it harms. Efforts to prevent children from learning about racist violence of the past run parallel with the FBI's refusal to enumerate attacks by white supremacists completely and accurately.

Public pressure is needed to insist that the FBI account for how it uses its domestic terrorism resources. The FBI of course knows how many criminal incidents it considers domestic terrorism. It could easily pull the information together from investigations and intelligence reporting. Likewise, the FBI and Justice Department know how many cases in each of their domestic terrorism categories have been prosecuted. The FBI tracks agent work hours by case captions, and it rates agent performance by specific statistical accomplishments including indictments, arrests, and convictions.

The information on hate crimes that Congress requires the Justice Department and FBI to provide annually is also collectible and producible. The Justice Department could make better use of its victim surveys, and could task researchers from its Bureau of Justice Statistics, National Institute of Justice, and Bureau of Justice Assistance to work with federal, state, and local law enforcement to get accurate data about white supremacist crimes. But federal law enforcement does not want to be held accountable for how it uses the domestic terrorism resources Congress provides.

An informed public is crucial to a healthy democracy. A 2017 Congressional Research Service report outlined why a "regular public accounting" on domestic terrorism is needed.[5] It explained that such reporting would allow policymakers and the public to compare domestic terrorist threats, "assess the effectiveness of the government's response," and inform the "allocation of resources to specific federal counterterrorism efforts."[6] This public knowledge would also make it more difficult for political leaders to mislead their constituents about who is committing political violence. Depriving policymakers of relevant data allows law enforcement to continue prioritizing the suppression of protest movements it opposes. It also enables individual or institutional biases, rather than evidence of harm, to shape priorities. Collective denial about the scope of white supremacist violence is essential to maintaining the status quo.

Law enforcement has an extremely limited but crucial role to play in resisting systemic white supremacy: by accurately accounting for and aggressively addressing its criminal forms. Accurate and comprehensive data is essential to creating an effective national strategy to address this violence. There are also other steps law enforcement can and should take now.

More than enough laws already exist to allow federal, state, and local police to respond to racist, white supremacist, and far-right militant violence more aggressively and strategically. Data and details about these crimes should be compiled, analyzed, shared, and cross-referenced, so that law enforcement can understand how the networks and organized groups conspire and cooperate to pursue their criminal agendas. This information is true criminal intelligence: concrete details about crimes and those who are committing them, not the wholesale monitoring of hateful musings of anonymous individuals on obscure social media platforms.

Militant white supremacists, while more numerous than any other movement the FBI categorizes as domestic terrorists, are relatively small in number compared to those embracing racist ideologies. Properly responding to and prosecuting the crimes these militants commit will whittle their numbers, check their progression to more dangerous crimes, and deter like-minded individuals from committing similar crimes. Tracking actual crimes, rather than broadly monitoring social media or profiling ideologies, properly focuses law enforcement attention on illicit activity rather than speech or association.

The criminal law enforcement approach will also yield indirect benefits. A sustained period of effective enforcement will create heightened apprehension within the militant movement about informants, making it more difficult for militants to trust one another enough to risk engaging in a broad or complex criminal conspiracy. Sustained enforcement will make it more dangerous for the militants to commit acts of public violence or promote their violence on social media, as doing so will provide law enforcement with evidence to prosecute them. Regularly prosecuting the crimes of white supremacist militants will also make it riskier for establishment figures to associate with them, for fear of enmeshing themselves in criminal conspiracies and tarnishing their reputations. Effective and sustained enforcement activity will help clarify the line between ideologues and militants.

To be clear, law enforcement has no role in policing ideology or shaming politicians who promote odious viewpoints. If law enforcement officials are doing their jobs properly, however, they have a duty to provide the public with accurate, unbiased, and complete information about criminal activities and those who commit them. With accurate and objective crime data, policymakers and the public can educate themselves, establish priorities, and hold law enforcement accountable. Unfortunately, counterterrorism policing as practiced over the last three decades has been the opposite of transparent and unbiased. Law enforcement officials withhold or manipulate crime data, selectively release information from investigations to create deceptive narratives, and politicize threat assessments.

Law enforcement needs to be limited to its primary responsibility of enforcing the criminal laws in a fair, equal, and transparent manner. We know what needs to be done because the Christopher Commission drew up the blueprint more than thirty years ago. It isn't more complicated than directing law enforcement officials to focus their tools on investigating and prosecuting white supremacists' violent crimes. As the Christopher Commission advised, this requires law enforcement's sustained attention and political will. To restore public confidence, law enforcement must act in the public's interest and not just its own. It must cede authority and resources to other government services and community organizations more capable of solving social problems, public health emergencies, and educational needs with less risk of violence.

Redressing the harmful effects of white supremacy is a challenge that all of society must commit to rectifying. Rather than relying primarily on law enforcement solutions, we must devote resources to empowering communities to develop individualized responses that seek to restore social cohesion and public safety. We need greater investments in education, public health, civic engagement, social services, and anti-corruption. A healthy democracy is more resilient to fascist or authoritarian threats. Law enforcement has a role to play in reducing political violence, including police violence, but it can be successful only if it responds in a timely, transparent, properly focused, and constitutionally sound manner.

My experience working undercover in the white supremacist movement sensitized me to the signs of fascist organizing, both at the street level among militants vying for attention and recognition, and among government officials who employ rhetoric and execute policies that scapegoat minority groups and champion violence and vigilantism. As the racism infusing right-wing populist politics has become more overt—in policies restricting voting rights and immigration, barring racial justice education, and attacking affirmative action and diversity, inclusion, and equity programs—a frustrating reluctance remains to call it out for what it is: white supremacy, fascism, a mortal threat to democracy.

It would be easy to place the blame for the rise of white supremacy entirely at the feet of former president Trump, as Representative Cheney attempted to do in her role on the January 6 Committee. But Trump was just the latest vehicle for white identity politics that an element within the Republican Party has championed since the days of Pat Buchanan and Lee Atwater. Today, it isn't unusual for Republican governors, members of Congress, state legislators, and presidential candidates openly to promote white grievances and to make direct appeals for violence against their political enemies.[7] And a sizable audience remains receptive to this messaging and professes a willingness to use force against anyone challenging their vision for society.

Former president Trump's coup attempt failed, largely because many in law enforcement and the military did their duty that day, engaging in brutal hand-to-hand combat with a mob that included their current and former colleagues, to protect the official certification of a presidential election and, in a literal way, democracy itself. But the malignancy in the heart of our political system has not been cured. While the Justice Department has charged over 1,200 insurrectionists with crimes related to the attack on the Capitol, most of these charges were misdemeanors, and they represent less than half of the 2,500 to 3,000 people estimated to have engaged in criminal acts that day.[8] Federal and state prosecutors have charged former president Trump and many of his cronies with dozens of felonies relating to his business dealings, retention of national security material, and the conspiracy to remain in power illegally.[9] A New York City jury convicted Trump of thirty four counts of fraud relating to hush money payments he made to an adult film actress before the 2016 election.[10] The six Republican-appointed justices of the U.S. Supreme Court later issued a ruling granting the former president broad immunity from criminal prosecution, however, imperiling those convictions and throwing the remaining indictments into question.[11] Despite his alleged crimes and the tumultuous ending of his first term in office, at this writing, Trump remains his party's nominee in the 2024 presidential race. During his campaign, Trump has promised to pardon the January 6 insurrectionists, conduct a political purge of the federal workforce, investigate prosecutors "for their illegal, racist-in-reverse enforcement of the law," immunize police officers from prosecution, and indemnify them for lawsuits.[12]

The positive steps the Biden administration has taken to better account for and address the impact of white supremacist and far-right militant violence have been too hesitant and ineffectual. Should Trump win the election, these efforts will likely be scuttled. Justice Department prosecutors and FBI agents will still have an obligation to fulfill their constitutional duties to enforce the laws in a fair and equal manner, but the lack of effective whistleblower protections will make it difficult to resist and report illegal orders or violations of civil rights. With federal enforcement lacking, greater responsibility will fall to governors and other elected and appointed officials at the state and local levels. These authorities should work together to support pro-democracy and civil rights advocacy organizations and community members who mobilize to resist racist, fascist, and far-right militant organizing.

Even if Trump loses the election, however, the threat remains. Many of his Republican colleagues have embraced his belligerent, racist, and authoritarian attitudes to compete for the role of heir apparent. Most threatening for the future, many people still in power in Congress, the courts, state legislatures, county offices, and city councils—and in law enforcement—continue to support the January 6 insurrection and will be better prepared for the next opportunity.

Our government's continued unwillingness to prioritize investigating and prosecuting white supremacist violence as the most persistent and deadly form of domestic terrorism, and to identify and root out racists, white supremacists, and far-right militants from law enforcement and the military—the institutions we depend on to protect us all—leaves the future of our democracy in peril.

ACKNOWLEDGMENTS

I have many people to thank for helping me with this book. *Policing White Supremacy* was developed from a series of reports, white papers, and congressional testimonies I produced with the Brennan Center for Justice after the racist riot at the 2017 Unite the Right rally in Charlottesville, Virginia, urging the federal government to prioritize the investigation and prosecution of white supremacist and far-right militant violence. I want to thank the Brennan Center staff that assisted me in researching, drafting, and editing those materials and testimonies, especially Sara Robinson, Emanuel Mauleón, and Kaylana Mueller-Hsia, who each co-authored one of the reports, as well as Kirstin Dunham, who ensured they landed on the right desks in Congress. And my deep appreciation goes to Faiza Patel, Liza Goitein, Rachel Levinson-Waldman, John F. Kowal, and Michael Waldman, who provided the platform for me to do this work and the organizational leadership that made the Brennan Center's Liberty & National Security program a trusted commodity among national policymakers. Thanks also to Rep. Mike Levin and his director of constituent services, Shannon Bradley, who helped to speed up the FBI's review process. I also need to thank Diane Wachtell, executive director of The New Press, for convincing me that this seed material could be expanded, updated, and adapted into a complete and cohesive book, and then encouraging me to do it. Diane gave me an additional gift by introducing me to my co-author, Beth Zasloff, who partnered with me to conceive a clear narrative, and wove the varied arguments from my previous writings, along with new content, into a coherent whole. Beth was always in good humor, despite the nature of the material, and her writing and editing skills made the book eminently more readable. Finally, I'd also like to thank Rachel Vega-DeCesario, Sharon Swados, and Maury Botton, the staff at The New Press who helped put it all together.

NOTES

Introduction: Democracy in Danger

1. Amy Sherman, "A Timeline of What Trump Said Before Jan. 6 Capitol Riot," Politifact, January 11, 2021, www.politifact.com/article/2021/jan/11/timeline-what-trump-said-jan-6-capitol-riot/.

2. Steve Schmidt (@SteveSchmidtSes), "It appears to me on the basis of video evidence that the US Capitol Police have been infiltrated and compromised. There is a fifth column within their ranks. They have surrendered the US Capitol to insurrectionists without a shot fired. It may be the greatest law enforcement," Twitter, January 6, 2021, 6:57 p.m., twitter.com/steveschmidtses/status/1346969162585944064?s=11.

3. Jackie Kucinich, "Anti-war Protesters Spray Paint Capitol Building," *The Hill*, January 28, 2007, web.archive.org/web/20070203050051/http:/www.thehill.com/thehill/export/TheHill/News/Frontpage/012507/protesters.html/.

4. "Identifying Far-Right Symbols That Appeared at the U.S. Capitol riot," *Washington Post*, January 15, 2021.

5. Associated Press, "Rioter Who Wore 'Camp Auschwitz' Sweatshirt Gets Jail Term," National Public Radio, September 16, 2022.

6. Devlin Bartlett et al., "Dozens of People on FBI Terrorist Watch List Came to D.C. the Day of the Capitol Riot," *Washington Post*, January 14, 2021.

7. Ryan J. Reilly, "Florida Man Charged with Setting Off Explosive Device in Capitol Tunnel During Jan. 6 Riot," NBC News, May 2, 2023.

8. Zoe Tillman, "Here's Every Weapon the Capitol Rioters Are Accused of Having on Jan. 6," Yahoo News, November 9, 2021, news.yahoo.com/guns-knives-flagpoles-skateboard-guide-174530861.html.

9. Pierre Thomas, Victor Ordonez, and Eliana Larramendia, "Capitol Police Officer Recounts Jan. 6 Attack: Exclusive," ABC News, abcnews.go.com/Politics/capitol-police-officer-recounts-jan-attack-exclusive/story?id=76036587.

10. Mike Maciag, "Which Cities Have the Biggest Police Presence?," Governing, May 7, 2014, www.governing.com/archive/gov-cities-with-the-greatest-police-presence-most-officers-per-capita.html.

11. Craig Timberg and Drew Harwell, "Pro-Trump Forums Erupt with Violent Threats Ahead of Wednesday's Rally Against the 2020 Election," *Washington Post*, January 5, 2021.

12. Rachel Kurzius, "Hotel Harrington and Harry's Bar, Proud Boys Rendezvous, to Close During MAGA March," National Public Radio, January 4, 2021.

13. Dina Temple-Raston, "Why Didn't the FBI and DHS Produce a Threat Report Ahead of the Capitol Insurrection?," National Public Radio, January 13, 2021.

14. Ben Mathis-Lilley, "The Long List of Killings by White Extremists Since the Oklahoma City Bombing," *Slate*, August 14, 2017.

15. Joshua Freilich et al., "Extremist Crime Database (ECDB), 1990–2010," National Consortium for the Study of Terrorism and Responses to Terrorism, 2010, www.start.umd.edu/research-projects/united-states-extremist-crime-data base-ecdb-1990-2010.

16. Arlie Perliger, "Challengers from the Sidelines: Understanding America's Violent Far-Right," Combating Terrorism Center at West Point, November 2012, 100, https://ctc.westpoint.edu/wp-content/uploads/2013/01/ChallengersFromtheSide lines.pdf.

17. Center for Extremism, "Murder and Extremism in the United States in 2022: Including an In-Depth Analysis of Extremist Mass Killings," Anti-Defamation League, February 22, 2023, 2; Center on Extremism, "A Report from ADL Center on Extremism: Murder and Extremism in the United States 2021," Anti-Defamation League, February 10, 2022, 6; Center on Extremism, "A Report from the Center on Extremism: Murder and Extremism in the United States in 2020," Anti-Defamation League, February 2021, 8; Center on Extremism, "A Report from the Center on Extremism: Murder and Extremism in the United States in 2019," Anti-Defamation League, February 2020, 18; Center on Extremism, "A Report from the Center on Extremism: Murder and Extremism in the United States in 2018," Anti-Defamation League, January 2019, 9; Center on Extremism, "Murder and Extremism in the United States in 2017: An ADL Center on Extremism Report," Anti-Defamation League, January 12, 2018, 7.

18. Lauren Leatherby and Richard A. Oppel Jr., "Which Police Departments Are as Diverse as Their Communities?," *New York Times*, September 23, 2020; Jeremy Ashkenas and Haeyoun Park, "The Race Gap in America's Police Departments," *New York Times*, April 8, 2015; U.S. Department of Justice Office of Justice Programs, "Local Police Departments Personnel, 2020," 2020.

19. Kelli Weill, "Whistleblower: DHS Hyped 'Antifa,' Soft-Pedaled White Supremacist Threat," *Daily Beast*, September 9. 2020, www.thedailybeast.com/whis tleblower-dhs-hyped-antifa-soft-pedaled-white-supremacist-threat.

20. U.S. House of Representatives., Committee on Government Oversight, Subcommittee on Civil Rights and Civil Liberties, "Confronting White Supremacy (Part

IV): White Supremacists in Blue—The Infiltration of Local Police Departments," September 29, 2020, www.congress.gov/116/chrg/CHRG-116hhrg41981/CHRG-116hhr g41981.pdf.

21. Allana Durkin Richer and Michael Kunzelman, "Hundreds of Convictions, But a Major Mystery Is Still Unsolved After the Jan. 6 Capitol Riot," Associated Press, January 5, 2023, https://apnews.com/article/capitol-riot-jan-6-criminal-cases-anni versary-bf436efe760751b1356f937e55bedaa5.

22. Judy Woodruff, et al., "How Citizen Investigators Are Helping the FBI Track Down Jan. 6 Rioters," *PBS NewsHour*, January 3, 2024, www.pbs.org/newshour/show /how-citizen-investigators-are-helping-the-fbi-track-down-jan-6-rioters; Laura Italiano, "The Proud Boys Seditious Conspiracy Trial Is Underway. But the New Leadership Has Moved On from the 2020 Election to LGBTQ Issues," *Business Insider*, February 14, 2023, www.businessinsider.com/proud-boys-2022-break-records-anti -lgbtq-protests-extremism-watchdog-2023-1?op=1.

23. Sam Levi, " 'It Never Stops': Killings by Police Reach Record High," *Guardian*, January 6, 2023; N'dea Yancey-Bragg, "2023 Was the Deadliest Year for Killings by Police in the U.S. Experts Say This is Why," *USA Today*, January 17, 2024, www.usatoday.com/story/news/nation/2024/01/17/police-killings-record-2023/721 74081007/.

1. Uniting the Right

1. Jason Wilson, "Charlottesville: Far-Right Crowd with Torches Encircles Counter-Protest Group," *Guardian*, August 12, 2017.

2. "Report: UVa Police Had Intelligence of Torch Rally Days in Advance," *Daily Progress*, November 21, 2017, dailyprogress.com/news/local/report-uva-police-had -intelligence-of-torch-rally-days-in-advance/article_1af5d13c-cf01-11e7-9744-83ab 950de3a3.html.

3. Ruth Serven Smith, "Heaphy Report: UVa Police's Lack of Response to Torch-Lit Rally on Grounds Allowed Aug. 11–12 Events to Escalate," *Daily Progress*, December 1, 2017, dailyprogress.com/news/local/heaphy-report-uva-police-s-lack-of-re sponse-to-torch-lit-rally-on-grounds-allowed/article_2424ced4-d6f4-11e7-b4b4 -1be4c2571c57.html.

4. Hunton & Williams, "Independent Review of the 2017 Protest Events in Charlottesville, Virginia," 2017, 98, 122.

5. The Heaphy report referenced only one incident in which an officer left the barricades to interrupt a fight, which resulted in no arrests. Ibid., 128.

6. Frances Robles, "As White Nationalist in Charlottesville Fired, Police 'Never Moved,' " *New York Times*, August 25, 2017.

7. CBS News, "3 Arrested on Connection to Violence at Charlottesville White

Nationalist Rally, Police Say," CBS News, August 12, 2017; Hate Watch Staff, "Florida League of the South Involved in Arrest, Beating at Charlottesville Rally: Update," Southern Poverty Law Center, August 17, 2017, www.splcenter.org/hatewatch /2017/08/17/florida-league-south-involved-arrest-beating-charlottesville-rally-up date; Joseph A. Wulfsohn, "Man Arrested in Charlottesville Was Counter-Protestor Who Punched Female Reporter," Mediaite, August 13, 2017, www.mediaite.com/on line/one-of-the-men-arrested-in-charlottesville-was-a-counter-protestor-who -punched-a-female-reporter/; and Alana LaFlore, "Friend Says Chattanooga Man Arrested in Charlottesville Was a Counter-protester," News Channel 9, newschannel9 .com/news/local/chattanooga-man-arrested-in-charlottesville-was-a-counter-protestor.

8. Sam Adler-Bell, "With Last Charges Against J20 Protesters Dropped, Defendants Seek Accountability for Prosecutors," *The Intercept*, July 13, 2018, theintercept .com/2018/07/13/j20-charges-dropped-prosecutorial-misconduct/.

9. Hunton & Williams, "Independent Review," 152.

10. Ibid., 96.

11. Ibid., 152.

12. International Association of Chiefs of Police, "Virginia's Response to the Unite the Right Rally: After-Action Review," 2017, 10–11.

13. Smith, "Heaphy Report."

14. International Association of Chiefs of Police, "Virginia's Response to the Unite the Right Rally."

15. See, for example, Von Uwe Klußmann, "The Ruthless Rise of the Nazis in Berlin," *Der Spiegel*, November 29, 2012, www.spiegel.de/international/germany /how-the-nazis-succeeded-in-taking-power-in-red-berlin-a-866793.html.

16. See Emil Julius Gumbel, "Four Years of Political Murder" (1922), reprinted in Anton Kaes et al., eds., *The Weimar Republic Sourcebook* (Berkeley: University of California Press, 1994); Barbara Manthe, "Terror from the Far-Right in the Weimar Republic," Open Democracy, November 21, 2019, www.opendemocracy.net/en/can -europe-make-it/terror-from-far-right-in-weimar-republic/.

17. Brian E. Crim, "Terror from the Right: Revolutionary Terrorism and the Failure of the Weimar Republic," *Journal of Conflict Studies* 27, no. 2 (Winter 2007), available at www.erudit.org/en/journals/jcs/2002-v22-n1-jcs_27_2/jcs27_2art04/.

18. This fascist tactic was so common that we included a violent Klan rally scene in a screenplay I co-wrote with director Daniel Ragussis, which became the feature film *Imperium*, starring Daniel Radcliffe. Eerily, the riot scene was filmed in 2015 in Hopewell, Virginia, less than two hours from Charlottesville.

19. See, for example, Spencer Ackerman, "FBI Teaches Agents: 'Mainstream' Muslims Are 'Violent, Radical,'" *Wired*, September 14, 2011, www.wired.com /2011/09/fbi-muslims-radical/; Noah Shachtman and Spencer Ackerman, "U.S.

Military Taught Officers: Use 'Hiroshima' Tactics for 'Total War' on Islam," *Wired*, May 10, 2012, www.wired.com/2012/05/total-war-islam/.

20. Christopher Bail, "The Fringe Effect: Civil Society Organizations and the Evolution of Media Discourse About Islam Since the September 11th Attacks," *American Sociological Review* 77, no. 6 (December 1, 2012): 856, doi.org/10.1177/000312241 2465743.

21. Oliver Laughland, Jon Swaine, and Joanna Walters, "White Militiamen Roam Ferguson with Rifles While Black Men Wrongly Arrested: Oath Keepers Group Say Police Allowed Their Weapons at Protests, While Group of Young Black Men Found to Be Unarmed After Arrest on Suspicion of Carrying Guns," *Guardian*, August 12, 2015.

22. See "Oath Keepers," Anti-Defamation League, June 26, 2017, www.adl.org /resources/backgrounder/oath-keepers; "Oath Keepers," Southern Poverty Law Center, www.splcenter.org/fighting-hate/extremist-files/group/oath-keepers.

23. Sarah Childress, "The Battle over Bunkerville: The Bundys, the Federal Government and the New Militia Movement," PBS, May 16, 2017; Sarah Fowler, "Ferguson Unrest: Who Are the Mysterious 'Oath Keepers'?," BBC, August 12, 2015.

24. Jesse Bogan, "Police Shut Down Mysterious 'Oath Keepers' Guarding Rooftops in Downtown Ferguson," *St. Louis Post-Dispatch*, November 30, 2014, www.stltoday .com/news/local/crime-and-courts/police-shut-down-mysterious-oath-keepers-guard ing-rooftops-in-downtown/article_f90b6edd-acf8-52e3-a020-3a78db286194.html.

25. Laughland, Swaine, and Walters, "White Militiamen Roam Ferguson."

26. Jeff German, "Suspected Boogaloo Trio Indicted Twice, Accused of Terrorism and Violence," *Las Vegas Review-Journal*, June 17, 2020, www.reviewjournal.com /crime/courts/suspected-boogaloo-trio-indicted-twice-accused-of-terrorism-and-vi olence-2055101/; Matt Sepic, "Texas Man, 24, Admits Shooting at Minneapolis Police Station During Riot," *MPR News*, September 30, 2021, www.mprnews.org/story /2021/09/30/texas-man-24-admits-shooting-at-minneapolis-police-station-during -riot; "California Militia Grizzly Scouts Plotted 'War' Against Police, Feds Say," KCRA 3, June 7, 2021, www.kcra.com/article/california-militia-grizzly-scouts-boo galoo-steven-carrillo-court-documents/36652091.

27. Lois Beckett, "US Police Three Times as Likely to Use Force Against Leftwing Protesters, Data Finds," *Guardian*, January 14, 2021.

28. Matt Coker, "7 Charged in Anaheim KKK Melee—But Stabby Klanner Not One of Them," *OC Weekly*, July 1, 2016, www.ocweekly.com/7-charged-in-anaheim -kkk-melee-but-stabby-klanner-not-one-of-them-7305812-2/; James Queally, "Ku Klux Klan Rally in Anaheim Erupts in Violence; 3 Are Stabbed and 13 Arrested," *Los Angeles Times*, February 26, 2016, http://www.latimes.com/local/lanow/la-me-ln -klan-rally-in-anaheim-erupts-in-violence-one-man-stabbed-20160227-story.html.

29. Frank John Tristan, "Rise Above, Unmasked: A Former *Weekly* Intern Recalls How His Surf City Assault Became an FBI Criminal Probe into an Alt-Right Group," *OC Weekly*, November 8, 2018, www.ocweekly.com/rise-above-unmasked-a-former -weekly-intern-recalls-how-his-surf-city-assault-became-an-fbi-criminal-probe-in to-an-alt-right-group/.

30. R. Scott Moxley, "DA Whitewashed Neo-Nazi in Assault Trial from 2017 Trump MAGA Rally," *OC Weekly*, August 21, 2019, www.ocweekly.com/white-su premacist-antifa-trump/#.XV4Die-38AR.twitter.

31. Raheem F. Husseini, "White (Nationalist) Privilege," *Sacramento News and Review*, March 14, 2019, www.newsreview.com/sacramento/content/white-nationalist-priv ilege/27838335/; Sam Levin, "California Police Worked with Neo-Nazis to Pursue 'Anti-Racist' Activists, Documents Show," *Guardian*, February 9, 2018, www.theguard ian.com/world/2018/feb/09/california-police-white-supremacists-counter-protest; Sam Levin, "Stabbed at a Neo-Nazi Rally, Called a Criminal: How Police Targeted a Black Activist," *Guardian*, May 25, 2018; Sam Levin, "How a California Officer Protected Neo-Nazis and Targeted Their Victims," *Guardian*, January 25, 2019.

32. Lois Beckett, "Three Men Charged After Protesters Shot at Following Richard Spencer Sheet," *Guardian*, October 20, 2017; Ernest Owens, "ICYMI, Philly Police Made Sure to Defend the Free Speech of White Supremacists," *Philadelphia Magazine*, July 14, 2021, www.phillymag.com/news/2021/07/14/white-supremacist -patriot-front-march/; Christopher Mathias, "After Fights and Arrests, Richard Spencer Speaks to Tiny Crowd at Michigan State," *HuffPost*, March 5, 2018, www.huffpost .com/entry/richard-spencer-michigan-state_n_5a9d8eafe4b0479c0255e2b6; Janet Reitman, "U.S. Law Enforcement Failed to See the Threat of White Nationalism. Now They Don't Know How to Stop It," *New York Times*, November 3, 2018, www.nytimes .com/2018/11/03/magazine/FBI-charlottesville-white-nationalism-far-right.html; Amy Goodman and Tina-Desiree Berg, "Proud Boys and Far-Right Groups Tied to Jan. 6 Attack Reporters and Others at Anti-Mask, Anti-Vax," *Democracy Now!*, August 23, 2021, www.democracynow.org/2021/8/23/anti_vaccine_protest_los_angeles; National Consortium for the Study of Terrorism and Responses to Terrorism, "Proud Boys Crimes and Characteristics," 2022.

33. Meryl Kornfield, Austin R. Ramsey, Jacob Wallace, Christopher Casey, and Verônica Del Valle, "Swept Up by Police: Analysis of Arrests in 15 Cities Reveals Most George Floyd Protesters Were Charged with Misdemeanors and Lived within the Metro Area Where They Were Arrested," *Washington Post,* October 23, 2020.

34. "More than 300 Facing Federal Charges for Crimes Committed During Nationwide Demonstrations," press release, United Sates Attorney's Office, Eastern District of Missouri, September 24, 2020, www.justice.gov/usao-edmo/pr/more-300 -facing-federal-charges-crimes-committed-during-nationwide-demonstrations.

35. Katie Way, "Police Violence at Protests Is Undeniable. All the Videos Are Right Here," *Vice*, June 5, 2020, www.vice.com/en/article/7kpbmy/police-violence-at-protests-is-undeniable-all-the-videos-are-right-here; "George Floyd Protest—Police Violence Videos on Twitter," Greg Doucette, creator, and Jason E. Miller, curator, docs.google.com/spreadsheets/u/1/d/1YmZeSxpz52qT-10tkCjWOwOGkQqle7Wd1P7ZM1wMW0E/htmlview?pru=AAABcql6DI8*mIHYeMnoj9XWUp3Svb_KZA#.

36. Charlotte Godart, "Visualizing Police Violence Against Journalists at Protests Across the U.S.," Bellingcat, June 5, 2020, www.bellingcat.com/news/americas/2020/06/05/visualizing-police-violence-against-journalists-at-protests-across-the-us/.

37. Ricardo Torres-Cortez, "The Last Minutes of Protester Jorge Gomez's life," *Las Vegas Sun*, June 7, 2020, lasvegassun.com/news/2020/jun/07/the-last-minutes-of-jorge-gomezs-life/; Billy Kobin, "Ex-Louisville Metro Police Officer Gets Probation in Case Tied to David McAtee's Death," *Louisville Courier Journal*, January 30, 2023, www.courier-journal.com/story/news/crime/2023/01/30/ex-louisville-police-officer-katie-crews-sentenced-in-david-mcatee-case/69795423007/.

38. Meg Kelly, Joyce Sohyun Lee, and Job Swaine, "Partially Blinded by Police," *Washington Post*, July 14, 2020.

39. Gloria Oladipo, "US Cities to Pay Record $80m to People Injured in 2020 Racial Justice Protests," *Guardian*, May 25, 2023.

40. Erica Chenoweth and Jeremy Pressman, "This Summer's Black Lives Matter Protesters Were Overwhelmingly Peaceful, Our Research Finds," *Washington Post*, October 16, 2020.

41. Kim Barker, Mike Baker, and Ali Watkins, "In City After City, Police Mishandled Black Lives Matter Protests," *New York Times*, March 20, 2021.

42. See, for example, Wesley Lowery, " 'Shooting Police Is Not a Civil Rights Tactic': Activists Condemn Killing of Officers," *Washington Post*, July 17, 2016.

43. Libor Jany and David Chanen, "3 Men in Custody, 1 Released in Minneapolis 4th Precinct Protest Shooting," *Star Tribune*, November 25, 2015, www.startribune.com/police-searching-for-suspects-who-fired-into-crowd-at-blm-protest-outside-4th-precinct/353154811/; Alex Baumhardt, Lindsey Bever, and Michael E. Miller, "Two Men Arrested in Shooting of Black Lives Matter Protesters in Minneapolis," *Washington Post*, November 24, 2015; Mihir J. Chaudhary and Joseph Richardson Jr., "Violence Against Black Lives Matter Protesters: A Review," *Current Trauma Reports* 8, no. 3 (May 27, 2022), doi.org/10.1007/s40719-022-00228-2.

44. Azi Paybarah, "K.K.K. Member Who Drove into Protesters Gets More than Three Years in Prison," *New York Times*, February 9, 2021, www.nytimes.com/2021/02/09/us/virginia-kkk-harry-rogers-sentenced.html.

45. "KKK 'Leader' Charged for Attack on Black Lives Matter Protesters," BBC, June 9, 2020; Taylor Romine, Ashley Killough, and Ed Lavandera, "Unsealed

Documents from the Daniel Perry case Show He Made Comments on Social Media About Killing Protesters and Muslims," CNN, April 14, 2023.

46. Sarah Childress, May 16, 2017.

47. Alleen Brown and Naveena Sadasivam, "Pipeline Company Spent Big on Police Gear to Use Against Standing Rock Protesters: TigerSwan Worked with Law Enforcement to Fight an Information War Against the Indigenous-Led Water Protectors," *The Intercept*, May 22, 2023, theintercept.com/2023/05/22/stand ing-rock-energy-transfer-tigerswan/; Joshua Barajas, "Police Deploy Water Hoses, Tear Gas Against Standing Rock Protesters," PBS, November 21, 2016.

48. Will Parrish, "An Activist Stands Accused of Firing a Gun at Standing Rock. It Belonged to Her Lover—An FBI Informant," *The Intercept*, December 11, 2017, theintercept.com/2017/12/11/standing-rock-dakota-access-pipeline-fbi-informant -red-fawn-fallis/.

49. Sam Levin, " 'He's a Political Prisoner': Standing Rock Activists Face Years in Jail," *Guardian*, June 22, 2018.

50. Katie Shepard, "Portland Police Declare a Riot After Right-Wing Marchers Begin Beating Antifascists with Flag Poles: Homeland Security Officers Fired Pepper Balls into a Crowd of Leftist Protesters," *Willamette Week*, June 30, 2018, www .wweek.com/news/2018/06/30/portland-police-declare-a-riot-after-right-wing -marchers-begin-beating-antifascists-with-flag-poles/; Katie Shepard, "Portland Police Saw Right-Wing Protesters as 'Much More Mainstream' than Leftist Ones: Deleted Scenes from a Protest Review May Bolster Activist Suspicions," *Willamette Week*, June 27, 2018, www.wweek.com/news/courts/2018/06/27/portland-police-saw -right-wing-protesters-as-much-more-mainstream-than-leftist-ones/.

51. Arun Gupta, "Playing Cops: Militia Member Aids Police in Arresting Protester at Portland Alt-Right Rally," *The Intercept*, June 8, 2017, theintercept .com/2017/06/08/portland-alt-right-milita-police-dhs-arrest-protester/.

52. Laughland, Swaine, and Walters, "White Militiamen Roam Ferguson"; Edward Helmore, "Kenosha Police Accused of 'Deputizing' Militia Vigilantes During Jacob Blake Protests: Lawsuit Brought by Gaige Grosskreutz, Who Was Wounded by Kyle Rittenhouse During Anti-Police Brutality Protests in August 2020," *Guardian*, October 17, 2021; Ernest Owens, July 14, 2021.

53. Mike Baker, "Police Presentation in Portland Celebrated Violence Against Protesters," *New York Times,* January 14, 2022.

54. Winston Favor, "The Lost Story of the Marcus Garvey Movement in Newport News," Mariners' Museum and Park, February 22, 2023, www.marinersmuseum .org/2023/02/the-lost-story-of-the-marcus-garvey-movement-in-newport-news/; Jonathan Eig and Jeanne Theoharis, "The Man Who Knew Exactly What the F.B.I. Was Doing to Martin Luther King Jr.," *New York Times*, April 12, 2023.

55. Courtney Bublé, "FBI Has Failed to Move the Needle on Diversity over the Past Decade, Despite Efforts of Recent Directors," Government Executive, February 14, 2020, www.govexec.com/workforce/2020/02/fbi-has-failed-move-needle-diversity-over-past-decade-despite-efforts-recent-directors/163127/; Jeff Pegues, Andrew Bast, and Michael Kaplan, "Former Black Special Agents Say FBI's Culture Is 'Not Conducive to Minorities,' " CBS News, October 7, 2020.

56. "Antifa: A Look at the Anti-Fascist Movement Confronting White Supremacists in the Streets," Democracy Now!, August 16, 2017, www.democracynow.org/2017/8/16/antifa_a_look_at_the_antifascist.

57. See, for example, Nigel Copsey and Samuel Merrill, "Violence and Restraint within Antifa: A View from the United States," Perspectives on Terrorism 14, no. 6 (December 2020): 122–38.

58. Silja J. A. Talvi, "Breaking Rank: Former Seattle Police Chief Norm Stamper Takes on the Drug War, Domestic Violence, Community Policing, and the WTO," In These Times, November 1, 2005, inthesetimes.com/article/breaking-rank.

59. Jim Compton, Jan Drago, and Nick Licata, "Report of the WTO Accountability Review Committee Seattle City Council," 2000, 4.

60. Meg Kelly and Elyse Samuels, "Who Caused the Violence at Protests? It Wasn't Antifa," Washington Post, June 22, 2022.

61. Ryan Devereaux, "Leaked Documents Show Police Knew Far-Right Extremists Were the Real Threat at Protests, Not 'Antifa,' " The Intercept, July 15, 2020, theintercept.com/2020/07/15/george-floyd-protests-police-far-right-antifa/.

62. Quinn Myers, "How Facebook Misinformation Turned a White Supremacist Conspiracy into Policy Action," MEL Magazine, 2020, melmagazine.com/en-us/story/how-facebook-misinformation-turned-a-white-supremacist-conspiracy-into-police-action.

63. Jason Wilson, "Intelligence Report Appeared to Endorse View Left Wing Protesters Were 'Terrorists,' " Guardian, April 1, 2019.

64. Daniel Villarreal, "DHS Investigates Alleged Antifa Protesters as Terrorists Trained in Syria," Newsweek, August 3, 2020, www.newsweek.com/dhs-investigates-alleged-antifa-protesters-terrorists-trained-syria-1522544.

65. Tim Cushing, "The FBI Issued Warning to Law Enforcement Agencies After Being Duped by a Satirical 'Paid Protester' Website," Tech Dirt, July 27, 2020, www.techdirt.com/2020/07/27/fbi-issued-warning-to-law-enforcement-agencies-after-being-duped-satirical-paid-protester-website/.

66. International Association of Chiefs of Police, "Virginia's Response to the Unite the Right Rally: After-Action Review," 2017, 9.

67. See, for example, Jack Evans, "Pinellas Police Union Head Pushes Debunked Paid-Protester Theory," Tampa Bay Times, April 2, 2021, www.tampabay.com/news

/st-petersburg/2021/04/02/pinellas-police-union-head-pushes-debunked-paid-pro
tester-theory/.

68. Ali Breland, "How a Dubious Claim of Cement Milkshakes in Portland Became a Right-Wing Meme," *Mother Jones*, July 2, 2019, www.motherjones.com/poli
tics/2019/07/how-a-dubious-claim-of-cement-milkshakes-in-portland-became
-a-right-wing-meme/.

69. "Have Hate, Will Travel: The Demographics of Unite the Right," Anti-
Defamation League, October 8, 2017, www.adl.org/resources/blog/have-hate-will
-travel-demographics-unite-right.

70. Ira Glass, Zoe Chace, and Robyn Semien, "White Haze," *This American Life*,
September 22, 2017, www.thisamericanlife.org/626/transcript.

71. Katja Cresanti, "Jason Kessler Sentenced After Assault Conviction," *Cavalier
Daily*, May 10, 2017, www.cavalierdaily.com/article/2017/05/jason-kessler-sentenced
-after-assault-conviction.

72. "Jason Kessler Pleads Guilty to Misdemeanor Assault," WINA, 2017, wina
.com/news/064460-jason-kessler-pleads-guilty-to-misdemeanor-assault/.

73. "Prosecution Declines to Prosecute Jason Kessler's May Disorderly Conduct
Charge," WINA, 2017, wina.com/news/064460-prosecution-declines-to-prosecute-ja
son-kesslers-may-disorderly-conduct-charge/; *Brandenburg v. Ohio*, 395 U.S. 444 (1969).

74. Joshua Eaton, "Charlottesville Prosecutor Loses Cases Against Hate Rally Organizer for the Dumbest Reason," Think Progress, March 21, 2018, archive.think
progress.org/kessler-perjury-charges-dismissed-b0c8a32c391a/.

75. Hunton & Williams, "Independent Review of the 2017 Protest Events in Charlottesville, Virginia," 112.

76. Christopher Cantwell, "My Path to Radical Celebritarianism," Christopher
Cantwell, February 4, 2015, web.archive.org/web/20150208034907/http://chris
tophercantwell.com/2015/02/04/path-radical-celebritarianism; Rachel Janik, "Christopher Cantwell 'In the Process' of Turning Himself in to Police," Southern Poverty
Law Center, August 23, 2017, www.splcenter.org/hatewatch/2017/08/23/christo
pher-cantwell-process-turning-himself-police.

77. "Charlottesville: Race and Terror," *Vice News Tonight* on HBO, air date August 14, 2017, https://video.vice.com/en_us/video/charlottesville-race-and-terror
-vice-news-tonight-on-hbo/59921b1d2f8d32d808bddfbc; Justin Wm. Moyer, " 'Cry-
ing Nazi' Pleads Guilty to Assault Committed During Charlottesville Rally," *Washington Post*, July 20, 2018.

78. Associated Press, "White Nationalist Sentenced to 4 Years in Prison for California Capitol Melee," *Los Angeles Times*, July 3, 2019.

79. Associated Press, "White Nationalist Leader Pleads Guilty in Trump Rally
Case," CBS News, July 20, 2017.

80. Hunton & Williams, "Independent Review of the 2017 Protest Events in Charlottesville, Virginia," 70.

81. Associated Press, "2 Soldiers and 2 Civilians Arrested in Theft of Huge Weapons Cache," *New York Times*, November 19, 1990; Ronald Smothers, "U.S. Indicts 3 After Searches Find Explosives and Racist Literature," *New York Times*, January 26, 1991, www.nytimes.com/1991/01/26/us/us-indicts-3-after-searches-find-explosives-and-racist-literature.html.

82. "Have Hate, Will Travel," October 8, 2017.

83. "Michael Ralph Tubbs," Southern Poverty Law Center, www.splcenter.org/fighting-hate/extremist-files/individual/michael-ralph-tubbs; Suman Varandani, "Who Is Michael Tubbs? KKK Supporter Accused of Ordering Charlottesville Violence," *International Business Times*, August 14, 2017, www.ibtimes.com/who-michael-tubbs-kkk-supporter-accused-ordering-charlottesville-violence-2578082.

84. Shane Bauer, "I Met the White Nationalist Who 'Falcon Punched' a 95-Pound Female Protester," *Mother Jones*, May 9, 2017, www.motherjones.com/politics/2017/05/nathan-damigo-punching-woman-berkeley-white-nationalism/.

85. Hailey Branson-Potts, "In Diverse California, a Young White Supremacist Seeks to Convert Fellow College Students," *Los Angeles Times,* December 7, 2016.

86. A. C. Thompson, ProPublica, Ali Winston, and Darwin BondGraham, "Racist, Violent, Unpunished: A White Hate Group's Campaign of Menace," ProPublica, October 19, 2017, www.propublica.org/article/white-hate-group-campaign-of-menace-rise-above-movement.

87. Janet Reitman, November 3, 2018.

88. In the Matter of a Search of Facebook User ID Danield B. Borden or Email Funnysters@gmail.com or Instagram Account DanDaamaan88, No. 3:18mj00005-JCH (W.D. Va. Mar. 16, 2018), 4.

89. Ian Shapiro, "Finding the White Supremacists Who Beat a Black Man in Charlottesville," *Washington Post*, August 31, 2017; Maja Bashri and Nazar Zaki, "#Allhandsondeck Shaun King and Unite the Right Rally: Mobilization and the Networked Social Journalist," *Atlantic Journal of Communication* 29, no. 5 (July 5, 2021): 297, doi.org/10.1080/15456870.2021.1947285.

90. Thompson et al., "Racist, Violent, Unpunished."

91. " 'Mostly Peaceful': Countering Left-Wing Organized Violence, Before the House Homeland Security Subcommittee on Oversight, Investigations, and Accountability," 118th Cong., 2023 (statement of Amy Spitalnick, senior adviser on extremism, Human Rights First).

92. *Sines et al v. Kessler et al,* No. 3:17-cv-00072, *Document 557, page 23* (W.D. Va. 2019).

93. "Leaked: Chats of #UniteThe Right Charlottesville Organizers Exposed on

Discord App," Unicorn Riot, August 14, 2017, unicornriot.ninja/2017/white-suprem acists-unitetheright-charlottesville-plans-exposed-discord-app/.

94. *Sines et al. v. Kessler et al.*, No. 3:17-cv-00072, *Document* 1 (W.D. Va. 2017).

95. *Application for Search Warrant in the Matter of Case Number 3:18-mj-00040, Document* 3 (W.D. Va. 2018); Thomas Brewster, "Revealed: FBI Raided Discord Chats of 'Unite the Right' Leader," *Forbes*, January 8, 2020, www.forbes.com/sites/thomas brewster/2020/01/08/revealed-fbi-raided-discord-chats-of-unite-the-right-organizer /?sh=9fa1a2d78ed0.

96. Seamus Hughes and Will Sommer, "FBI Got Warrants for 'Unite the Right' Organizer Jason Kessler, Antifa Activists," *Daily Beast*, January 8, 2020, www.thedaily beast.com/fbi-got-warrants-for-unite-the-right-organizer-jason-kessler-antifa-activists.

97. "Nazi Cop John Joseph Donnelly of Woburn, Massachusetts #BlazerAviators UTR," Ignite the Right, October 14, 2022, ignitetheright.net/profiles/; "Internal Affairs Investigation into Woburn Officer John Donnelly Complete," CBS News, October 21, 2022, www.cbsnews.com/boston/video/internal-affairs-investigation-into -woburn-officer-john-donnelly-complete/.

98. Christopher Mathias, "He Marched at the Nazi Rally in Charlottesville. Then He Went Back to Being a Cop," *HuffPost*, October 13, 2022, www.huffpost.com/entry /john-donnelly-police-officer-charlottesville-white-supremacist-woburn-massachu setts_n_634856a1e4b08e0e60812d63.

99. "Unite the Right's Head of Security Identified: Allison Richard 'Jack' Peirce IV of Indianapolis, Indiana," Anonymous Comrades Collective, November 10, 2021, accollective.noblogs.org/post/2021/11/10/allison-richard-jack-peirce-iv/.

100. Detective Sergeant Anthony Newberry, "Declaration of Detective Sergeant Anthony Newberry," *Kessler v. City of Charlottesville*, 441 F. Supp. 3d 277 (W.D. Va. 2020), 3.

101. Vanessa Ochavillo, "Ex-Woburn Cop Loses Police Certification over Alleged Involvement in 2017 White Supremacist Rally," WBUR, May 9, 2023, www.wbur.org /news/2023/05/09/john-donnelly-woburn-police-officer-decertified.

102. Mark Morales and Steve Almasy, "Jury Finds Unite the Right Defendants Liable for More than $26 Million in Damages," CNN, November 23, 2021, www.cnn .com/2021/11/23/us/charlottesville-unite-the-right-trial-deliberations-tuesday/in dex.html.

103. Colin Daileda, "White Nationalist Caught Assaulting Protester on Viral Videos Blames President Trump in Court," Mashable, April 18, 2017, mashable.com /article/donald-trump-matthew-heimbach-protester-assault-rally-lawsuit.

104. Dan Merica, "Trump Condemns 'Hatred, Bigotry and Violence on Many Sides' in Charlottesville," CNN, August 13, 2017, www.cnn.com/2017/08/12/politics /trump-statement-alt-right-protests/index.html.

105. Dave Boyer, "Donald Trump Denounces White Nationalists After Violence in Charlottesville," *Washington Times*, August 14, 2017, www.washingtontimes.com /news/2017/aug/14/trump-denounces-white-nationalists-after-violence/.

106. Fabiola Cineas, "Donald Trump Is the Accelerant," Vox, January 9, 2021, www.vox.com/21506029/trump-violence-tweets-racist-hate-speech.

2. The Rise of the Proud Boys

1. Leila Fadel, "Trump Appears to Engage Far Right Group During Debate Answer," National Public Radio, September 30, 2020, www.npr.org/2020/09/30/918572904 /trump-appears-to-engage-far-right-group-during-debate-answer.

2. Robert O. Paxton, *The Anatomy of Fascism* (New York: Knopf, 2004), 218.

3. Gary Potter, "The History of Policing in the United States, Part 1," Police Studies Online, Eastern Kentucky University, June 25, 2013, plsonline.eku.edu/inside look/history-policing-united-states-part-1.

4. See David Dorado Romo, "To Understand the El Paso Massacre, Look to the Long Legacy of Anti-Mexican Violence at the Border," *Texas Observer*, August 9, 2019, www.texasobserver.org/to-understand-the-el-paso-massacre-look-to-the-long -legacy-of-anti-mexican-violence-at-the-border/.

5. Catherine A. Paul, "Fugitive Slave Act of 1850," Social Welfare History Project, Virginia Commonwealth University Libraries, 2016, socialwelfare.library.vcu.edu /federal/fugitive-slave-act-of-1850/.

6. Nicholas Villanueva Jr., *The Lynching of Mexicans in the Texas Borderlands* (Albuquerque: University of New Mexico Press, 2017).

7. Douglas Harper, "Exclusion of Free Blacks in the North," Abbeville Institute, December 23, 2014, www.abbevilleinstitute.org/exclusion-of-free-blacks-in-the-north/.

8. Linton Weeks, "When the KKK Was Mainstream," National Public Radio, March 19, 2015.

9. See, e.g., Clay Risen, "The Ku Klux Klan's Surprising History," *New York Times*, December 4, 2017; Patrick Lacroix, "Lacroix on Richard, 'Not a Catholic Nation: The Ku Klux Klan Confronts New England in the 1920s,'" H-AmRel, March 2016, net works.h-net.org/node/15697/reviews/117687/lacroix-richard-not-catholic-nation-ku -klux-klan-confronts-new-england; Cecilia Rasmussen, "Klan's Tentacles Once Extended to Southland," *Los Angeles Times*, May 30, 1999.

10. Philip Bump, "For Decades, the Ku Klux Klan Openly Endorsed Candidates for Political Office," *Washington Post*, February 29, 2016.

11. Irene Hsu, "The Echoes of Chinese Exclusion," *New Republic*, June 28, 2018, newrepublic.com/article/149437/echoes-chinese-exclusion.

12. David A. Reed, "America of the Melting Pot Comes to End," *New York Times*, April 27, 1924.

13. "The Immigration Act of 1924 (The Johnson-Reed Act)," Office of the Historian, Department of State, history.state.gov/milestones/1921-1936/immigration-act.

14. Peter Dunphy, "The State of Native American Voting Rights," Brennan Center for Justice, March 13, 2019, www.brennancenter.org/our-work/analysis-opinion /state-native-american-voting-rights.

15. See, for example, Joseph Darda, "The Surprising Roots of Recent White Extremism," *Los Angeles Review of Books*, April 9, 2019, https://lareviewofbooks.org /article/the-surprising-roots-of-white-extremism/; Kirk Wallace Johnson, *The Fisherman and the Dragon: Fear, Greed, and a Fight for Justice on the Gulf Coast* (New York: Viking, 2022).

16. See, for example, "Old Smoke: The Death of Daniel Burros: A Jewish Klansman Who Did More than Just Hate Himself," Straus Media, February 16, 2015, www .nypress.com/news/old-smoke-the-death-of-daniel-burros-a-jewish-klansman-who -did-more-than-just-hate-himself-LVNP1020030225302259991; Bob Moser, "Hitler and the Sea Monkeys," Southern Poverty Law Center, April 20, 2004, www.splcenter .org/fighting-hate/intelligence-report/2004/hitler-and-sea-monkeys; Leo Oladimu, "I Was a Black Nazi Skinhead," Narratively, November 11, 2018, www.narratively.com /p/i-was-a-black-nazi-skinhead; Philip Bump, "Why Non-White People Might Advocate White Supremacy," *Washington Post*, May 8, 2023.

17. Kerry Flynn, "Vice Distances Itself—Again—from Co-Founder Who Started Proud Boys," *CNN Business*, October 1, 2020, www.cnn.com/2020/10/01/media/vice -gavin-mcinnes-proud-boys/index.html.

18. Adam Leith Gollner, "The Secret History of Gavin McInnes," *Vanity Fair*, June 29, 2021.

19. Gavin McInnes, "Introducing: The Proud Boys," *Taki's Magazine*, September 15, 2016, www.takimag.com/article/introducing_the_proud_boys_gavin_mcinnes/.

20. According to McInnes, obtaining the first degree requires declaring allegiance publicly by reciting the Proud Boys' pledge, "I am a Western chauvinist and I refuse to apologize for creating the modern world." The second degree requires an applicant to stand in a circle of Proud Boys who punch him until he can name five breakfast cereals. The applicant must also swear to abstain from masturbating and limit viewing pornography to once a month. The third degree requires obtaining a Proud Boys tattoo or brand.

21. Gollner, "The Secret History of Gavin McInnes"; Vic Berger, "I Started This Gang Called The Proud Boys," YouTube (October 16, 2018), www.youtube.com /watch?v=G95qjjQaNho.

22. LolAntonio44727287, "*Joe Rogan Experience* #920 Gavin McInnes," Daily Motion (2017), at 50:30, www.dailymotion.com/video/x5vlwan.

23. Jared Holt, "Proud Boys' Violence: A Pattern," Right Wing Watch, October 15, 2018, www.rightwingwatch.org/post/proud-boys-violence-a-pattern/.

24. "Patrick Buchanan: Unrepentant Bigot," Anti-Defamation League, February 27, 2012, www.adl.org/resources/profile/patrick-buchanan-unrepentant-bigot; Jake Tapper, "Who's Afraid of Pat Buchanan," Salon, September 4, 1999, www.salon.com/1999/09/04/pat/.

25. George Packer, "The Fall of Conservatism," *New Yorker*, May 19, 2008.

26. Rick Perlstein, "Exclusive: Lee Atwater's Infamous 1981 Interview on the Southern Strategy," *The Nation*, November 13, 2012, www.thenation.com/article/archive/exclusive-lee-atwaters-infamous-1981-interview-southern-strategy/.

27. Perry Bacon Jr., "Have Democrats Reached the Limit of White Appeasement Politics?," *Washington Post*, November 11, 2021.

28. Patrick Joseph Buchanan, "Culture War Speech: Address to the Republican National Convention," Voices of Democracy, August 17, 1992, voicesofdemocracy.umd.edu/buchanan-culture-war-speech-speech-text/.

29. Jonah Goldberg, "Killing Whitey," *National Review*, February 25, 2002, www.nationalreview.com/2002/02/killing-whitey-jonah-goldberg/.

30. Howard Kurtz, "Pat Buchanan: The Jewish Question," *Washington Post*, September 20, 1990; "Pat Buchanan's Greatest Hits," *Washington Post*, February 4, 1987.

31. Richard A. Serrano, "Militias See Buchanan as Their Kind of Candidate," *Los Angeles Times*, February 22, 1996.

32. Holger Marcks and Janina Pawelz, "From Myths of Victimhood to Fantasies of Violence: How Far-Right Narratives of Imperilment Work," *Terrorism and Political Violence*, July 24, 2020, doi.org/10.1080/09546553.2020.1788544.

33. McInnes, "Introducing: The Proud Boys."

34. Jason Wilson, "Gavin McInnes Is Latest Far-Right Figure to Sue Anti-Hate Watchdog," *Guardian*, February 4, 2019.

35. Ian Shapira, "Inside Jason Kessler's Hate-Fueled Rise," *Washington Post*, August 11, 2018.

36. Jemima McEvoy, "Who Are the Proud Boys, the Group Behind the Controversial Portland Rally?," *Forbes*, September 26, 2020, www.forbes.com/sites/jemimamcevoy/2020/09/26/who-are-the-proud-boys-the-group-planning-a-controversial-portland-rally/?sh=7ed075df654a.

37. Leighton Akio Woodhouse, "After Charlottesville, the American Far Right Is Tearing Itself Apart," *The Intercept*, September 21, 2017, theintercept.com/2017/09/21/gavin-mcinnes-alt-right-proud-boys-richard-spencer-charlottesville/.

38. William Bastone, "Repeat Felon Is Hero Alt-Right Deserves," The Smoking Gun, May 8, 2017, http://www.thesmokinggun.com/documents/crime/meet-the

-based-stickman-173908; Indictment, *State of Texas v. Kyle Sean Chapman*, 427th Judicial District Court of Travis County, July 26, 2018, ia803106.us.archive.org/28/items/6306574-Kyle-Chapman-charges/6306574-Kyle-Chapman-charges_djvu.txt (reflecting federal felon in possession charge).

39. Caroline Orr Bueno, Ph.D. (@RVAwonk), "Here's Rebel Media's Gavin McInnes talking about the 'military division' of Proud Boys that he founded w/violent felon Kyle Chapman," X (May 8, 2017), twitter.com/RVAwonk/status/861618156460273664.

40. Alyssa Pereira, "Far-Right Bay Area Figure Kyle 'Based Stickman' Chapman Posts Bail in Texas for Assault Charge," SFGate, July 11, 2018, www.sfgate.com/local-donotuse/article/Far-right-Bay-Area-figure-Kyle-Based-Stickman-13063731.php.

41. "Proud Boys' Bigotry Is on Full Display," Anti-Defamation League, December 24, 2020, www.adl.org/resources/blog/proud-boys-bigotry-full-display.

42. Alex Brizee, "White Nationalist Sentenced to 3 Months in Jail After Battering Health Care Worker," December 27, 2022, www.spokesman.com/stories/2022/dec/27/white-nationalist-sentenced-to-3-months-in-jail-af/.

43. Will Sommer, "Proud Boys Founder Gavin McInnes Claims He's Quitting Far-Right Group," *Daily Beast*, November 21, 2018, www.thedailybeast.com/proud-boys-founder-gavin-mcinnes-quits-far-right-group.

44. Colin Moynihan and Ali Winston, "Far-Right Proud Boys Reeling After Arrests and Scrutiny," *New York Times*, December 23, 2018.

45. Jason Wilson, "Proud Boys Founder Gavin McInnes Quits 'Extremist' Far-Right Group," *Guardian*, November 22, 2018.

46. Tess Owen, "Gavin McInnes Wears Proud Boys Colors Again, Throws Support Behind Jan. 6 Defendants," *Vice*, January 12, 2022, www.vice.com/en/article/k7w743/gavin-mcinnes-wears-proud-boy-colors-again-throws-support-behind-jan-6-defendants.

47. McInnes, "Introducing: The Proud Boys."

48. Andy Campbell, "Exclusive: Roger Stone Admits He's Been Advising the Proud Boys for Years," September 22, 2022, www.huffpost.com/entry/roger-stone-we-are-proud-boys_n_632c57ebe4b09d8701bd02e2.

49. Laura Italiano, "The January 6 Investigators Obtained a Video of Roger Stone Reciting the Proud Boys' 'Fraternity Creed,' the First Step for Initiation to the Extremist Group," *Business Insider*, July 12, 2022, www.businessinsider.com/roger-stone-proud-boys-fraternity-creed-video-january-6-committee-2022-7?op=1.

50. Jerry Iannelli and Meg O'Connor, "Roger Stone Admits Extensive Ties to Extremist Group Florida Proud Boys in Court," *Miami New Times*, February 21, 2019, www.miaminewtimes.com/news/roger-stone-admits-ties-to-florida-proud-boys-jacob-engels-enrique-tarrio-11093554.

51. Time Elfrink, "The Chairman of the Far-Right Proud Boys Sat Behind Trump

at His Latest Speech," *Washington Post*, February 19, 2019; Will Carless, "How a Trump Booster Group Helped the Head of Extremist Proud Boys Gain Access to the White House," *USA Today*, December 19, 2020, www.usatoday.com/story/news/na tion/2020/12/19/latinos-trump-group-tied-proud-boys-leader-enrique-tarrio /3931868001/.

52. Roger Sollenberger, "How Did a Proud Boys Leader with a Felony Record Get into the White House," *Salon*, December 15, 2020, www.salon.com/2020/12/15/how -did-a-proud-boys-leader-with-a-felony-record-get-into-the-white-house/; Tom Jackman, Paul Duggan, Ann E. Marimow, and Spencer S. Hsu, "Proud Boys Sparked Clashes During Pro-Trump Rally, D.C. Officials Say," *Washington Post*, December 14, 2020.

53. Ibid.

54. "A Proud Boy Leader Who Burned a Black Lives Matter Flag Gets 5 Months in Jail," Associated Press, August 23, 2021, www.npr.org/2021/08/23/1030430809 /proud-boys-enrique-tarrio-sentence.

55. Sophia Peel, "Multnomah County Republican Party Signed Agreement with Proud Boy–Affiliated Security Team at Portland Meeting," *Williamette Week*, May 10, 2021, www.wweek.com/news/city/2021/05/10/multnomah-county-republican-party -signed-agreement-with-proud-boy-affiliated-security-team-at-portland-meeting/.

56. Troy Brynelson and Sergio Olmos, "Far Right Protest Brawler Assists with Security at Clark County GOP Meeting," Oregon Public Broadcasting, February 24, 2021, www.opb.org/article/2021/02/25/clark-county-republicans-tusitala-tiny-toese/.

57. Patricia Mazzei and Alan Feuer, "How the Proud Boys Gripped the Miami -Dade Republican Party," *New York Times*, June 2, 2022, www.nytimes.com /2022/06/02/us/miami-republicans-proud-boys.html.

58. J. M. Berger, "How White Nationalists Learned to Love Donald Trump," Politico, October 25, 2016, www.politico.com/magazine/story/2016/10/donald-trump -2016-white-nationalists-alt-right-214388/.

59. See, for example, Ali Vitali, "Trump Preaches 'Law and Order' Amid Renewed Push to Reform Veterans Affairs," NBC News, July 11, 2016; "Full Text: Donald Trump 2016 RNC Draft Speech Transcript," Politico, July 21, 2016, www.politico .com/story/2016/07/full-transcript-donald-trump-nomination-acceptance-speech -at-rnc-225974.

60. David Griffith, "The 2016 POLICE Presidential Poll," PoliceMag.com, September 2, 2016, http://www.policemag.com/channel/patrol/articles/2016/09/the-2016 -police-presidential-poll.aspx.

61. Dara Lind, "Trump Just Delivered the Most Chilling Speech of His Presidency," Vox, July 28, 2017, www.vox.com/policy-and-politics/2017/7/28/16059486 /trump-speech-police-hand.

62. Fabiola Cineas, "Donald Trump Is the Accelerant," Vox, January 9, 2021, www.vox.com/21506029/trump-violence-tweets-racist-hate-speech.

63. Andy Campbell, "Leaked Proud Boy Chats Show Members Plotting Violence at Rallies," Huffington Post, May 22, 2019, www.huffpost.com/entry/proud-boys-chat-logs-premeditate-rally-violence-in-leaked-chats_n_5ce1e231e4b00e035b928683.

64. Arun Gupta, "Road to Jan. 6: How the Portland Police Grew to Love the Proud Boys and Paved the Way for Trump's Insurrection," Rawstory, January 14, 2022, www.rawstory.com/proud-boys-in-portland/.

65. Katie Shepherd, "Portland Police Saw Right-Wing Protesters as 'Much More Mainstream' than Leftist Ones," Williamette Week, June 27, 2018, www.wweek.com/news/courts/2018/06/27/portland-police-saw-right-wing-protesters-as-much-more-mainstream-than-leftist-ones/.

66. Katie Shepherd, "Texts Between Portland Police and Patriot Prayer Ringleader Joey Gibson Show Warm Exchange," Willamette Week, February 14, 2019, www.wweek.com/news/courts/2019/02/14/texts-between-portland-police-and-patriot-prayer-ringleader-joey-gibson-show-warm-exchange/.

67. Maxine Bernstein, "Portland Cop's Chatty Texts to Patriot Prayer Spur Outrage but Are Standard Police Strategy, Experts Say," The Oregonian, February 16, 2019, www.oregonlive.com/crime/2019/02/police-experts-weigh-in-on-portland-lieutenants-controversial-text-messages-with-patriot-prayer-leader.html.

68. Michael Kunzelman, "Connecticut Police Officer: I Quit Proud Boys over Fears of 'Far-Left' Attacks," Hartford Courant, November 13, 2019, apnews.com/article/c104d88974eb41ad92d3a691a78c912b.

69. David D. Kirkpatrick and Alan Feuer, "Police Shrugged Off the Proud Boys, Until They Attacked the Capitol," New York Times, March 14, 2021.

70. Rachel Kurzius, "D.C. Police Can't Determine Whether Officers Who Fist Bumped Proud Boy on July 4 Violated Policy," DCist, February 7, 2020, dcist.com/story/20/02/07/officers-who-fist-bumped-proud-boy-on-july-4-didnt-violate-policy-d-c-police-determine/.

71. Anna Orso, "Police Under Fire for 'Coddling' Violent Groups of White People in Fishtown, South Philly," Philadelphia Inquirer, June 26, 2020.

72. Jeremy Roebuck, Ellie Rushing, and Oona Goodin-Smith, "Philly's Police Union Says It Didn't Invite Proud Boys to a Pence After-Party. It Didn't Ask Them to Leave, Either," Philadelphia Inquirer, July 10, 2020.

73. Tom Schuba, "Watchdog: CPD Overlooked Incriminating Evidence While Investigating Cop's Ties to Far Right Proud Boys and Should Have Fired Him," Chicago Sun-Times, October 25, 2022, https://chicago.suntimes.com/crime/2022/10/25/23423522/watchdog-cpd-overlooked-evidence-investigating-cops-ties-to-proud-boys-fired-him.

74. See, for example, Natalie Orenstein, "Kyle 'Based Stickman' Back in Jail for Violating Bail Terms," Berkeleyside, Deember 22, 2017, www.berkeleyside .com/2017/12/22/kyle-based-stickman-chapman-back-jail-violating-bail- terms; Colin Moynihan, "2 Proud Boys Sentenced to 4 Years for Brawl with Anti-fascists at Republican Club," *New York Times*, October 22, 2019; Aaron Mesh, "Right-Wing Fighter Tusitala 'Tiny' Toese Arrested at Portland Airport for 2018 Sidewalk Assault," *Williamette Week*, October 5, 2019, www.wweek.com/news/courts/2019/10/05/right-wing-fighter-tusitala-tiny-toese-arrested-at-airport-for-2018-sidewalk-assault/; Jayati Ramakrishnan, "6 Indicted on Charges Related to May Day Brawl at Portland Bar," *Oregonian*, August 22, 2019, www.oregonlive.com/crime/2019/08/6-indict ed-on-charges-related-to-may-day-brawl-at-portland-bar.html; Aaron Mesh, "Right-Wing Fighter Tusitala 'Tiny' Toese Arrested at Portland Airport for 2018 Sidewalk Assault," *Williamette Week*, October 5, 2019, www.wweek.com/news/courts/2019 /10/05/right-wing-fighter-tusitala-tiny-toese-arrested-at-airport-for-2018-sidewalk -assault/; "Proud Boys Member, Who Pointed Gun, Arrested in Portland," Reuters, September 30, 2020, www.reuters.com/article/us-global-race-protests-portland /proud-boys-member-who-pointed-gun-arrested-in-portland-idUSKBN26L3TQ; Lois Beckett, "Enrique Tarrio, Leader of Right-Wing Proud Boys, Arrested Ahead of Rallies," *Guardian,* January 4, 2021.

75. Ramon Antonio Vargas, "Plaquemines Deputy Tied to Far-Right Group Proud Boys Has Been Fired by Sheriff's Office," *Advocate*, August 16, 2018, www.the advocate.com/new_orleans/news/crime_police/article_753dad6c-a1a2-11e8-9694-e3 4608514381.html.

76. Andy Matarrese, "Deputy Fired over Proud Boys Sweatshirt," *Columbian*, July 20, 2018, www.columbian.com/news/2018/jul/20/clark-county-sheriffs-deputy -fired-proud-boys-sweatshirt/#.W1Ijc3PGMPA.twitter.

77. Jason Wilson, "FBI Now Classifies Far-Right Proud Boys as 'Extremist Group,' Documents Say," *Guardian*, November 19, 2018.

78. Maxine Bernstein, "Head of Oregon's FBI: Bureau Doesn't Designate Proud Boys as Extremist Group," Oregon Live, December 5, 2018, www.oregonlive.com /crime/2018/12/head-of-oregons-fbi-bureau-doesnt-designate-proud-boys-as-ex tremist-group.html.

79. See Emily Berman, "Domestic Intelligence: New Powers, New Risks," Brennan Center for Justice, 2011, www.brennancenter.org/sites/default/files/legacy/AGG ReportFINALed.pdf.

80. Alan Feuer and Adam Goldman, "F.B.I. Had Informants in Proud Boys, Court Papers Suggest," *New York Times*, November 14, 2022.

81. Associated Press, "FBI Enlisted Proud Boys Leader to Inform on Antifa, Lawyer Says," NBC News, March 31, 2021; Aram Roston, "Exclusive: Before Jan. 6, FBI

Collected Information from at Least 4 Proud Boys," Reuters, April 26, 2021, www.reu ters.com/article/us-usa-proudboys-fbi-exclusive-idCAKBN2CD1WL.

82. Katelyn Polantz, "In Bid to Avoid Jail, Proud Boys Leader Claims He Was in Contact with FBI Years Before Capitol Riot," CNN, March 30, 2021, www.cnn .com/2021/03/30/politics/proud-boys-fbi-contacts/index.html; Claire Goforth, "En- rique Tarrio Says Proud Boys' Communications with D.C. Police on Jan. 6 Will Prove His Innocence," Daily Dot, August 4, 2022, www.dailydot.com/debug/enrique-tar rio-proud-boys-coordinated-police/.

83. George Zornick, "DC Cop Charged with Helping Proud Boys During Jan. 6 Insurrection," *HuffPost*, May 19, 2023, www.huffpost.com/entry/dc-cop-charged -proud-boys-insurrection_n_64678005e4b0bfd64481a18f.

84. Alan Feuer and Zach Montegue, "D.C. Police Lieutenant Charged with Leak- ing Information to Proud Boys Leader," *New York Times*, May 19, 2023.

85. Hannah Rabinowitz and Holmes Lybrand, "Video Released of Oath Keepers, Proud Boys Leaders Meeting 24 Hours Before January 6 Attack," CNN, May 24, 2022.

86. Associated Press, "A Proud Boys Leader Who Burned a Black Lives Matter Flag Gets 5 Months in Jail," National Public Radio, August 23, 2021.

87. Aram Roston, "Proud Boys Leader Enrique Tarrio Was an FBI Informant," *Guardian*, January 27, 2021.

3. Racism, White Supremacy, and Far-Right Militancy in Law Enforcement

1. Joseph Guzman, "California Police Stop Black Drivers at Higher Rates, Analy- sis Finds," *The Hill*, January 3, 2020, thehill.com/changing-america/respect/equality /476685-california-police-stop-black-drivers-at-higher-rates; Brad Heath, "Racial Gap in U.S. Arrest Rates: 'Staggering Disparity,'" *USA Today*, November 18, 2014, www.usatoday.com/story/news/nation/2014/11/18/ferguson-black-arrest-rates /19043207/; German Lopez and Javier Zarracina, "Study: Black People Are 7 Times More Likely than White People to Be Wrongly Convicted of Murder," Vox, March 7, 2017, www.vox.com/policy-and-politics/2017/3/7/14834454/exoneration-innocence -prison-racism; German Lopez, "There Are Huge Racial Disparities in How US Police Use Force," Vox, November 14, 2018, www.vox.com/identities/2016/8/13/17938186 /police-shootings-killings-racism-racial-disparities; Timothy Williams, "Black Peo- ple Are Charged at a Higher Rate than Whites. What If Prosecutors Didn't Know Their Race?," *New York Times*, June 12, 2019; Christopher Ingraham, "Black Men Sentenced to More Time for Committing the Exact Same Crime as a White Person, Study Finds," *Washington Post*, November 16, 2017.

2. Radley Balko, "There's Overwhelming Evidence That the Criminal Justice Sys- tem Is Racist. Here's the Proof," *Washington Post*, June 10, 2020.

3. Joe Davidson, "Implicit Bias Training Seeks to Counter Hidden Prejudice in Law Enforcement," *Washington Post*, August 16, 2016.

4. See, e.g., "Murder in Mississippi," *American Experience*, PBS, www.pbs.org /wgbh/americanexperience/features/freedomsummer-murder/; "Mississippi Burning," FBI, n.d., www.fbi.gov/history/famous-cases/mississippi-burning.

5. U.S. Department of Justice, Civil Rights Division, "Investigation of the 1964 Murders of Michael Schwerner, James Chaney, and Andrew Goodman," June 2016, www.justice.gov/crt/case-document/file/1041791/download.

6. *In Re the Courier-Journal and Louisville Times Company, Petitioners, v. Robert Marshall and Martha Marshall, Respondents*, 828 F.2d 361 (6th Cir. 1987); *Marshall v. Bramer*, 828 F.2d 325 (6th Cir. 1987).

7. Hector Tobar, "Deputies in 'Neo-Nazi' Gang, Judge Found: Sheriff's Department: Many at Lynwood Office Have Engaged in Racially Motivated Violence Against Blacks and Latinos, Jurist Wrote," *Los Angeles Times*, October 12, 1991.

8. Celeste Fremon, "The Downfall of Sheriff Baca," *Los Angeles Magazine*, May 14, 2015, www.lamag.com/longform/downfall/2/.

9. Fox 4 Staff, "2 Southlake Officers Fired over Swastika Drawing," Fox 4, July 28, 2023.

10. Associated Press, "Court Upholds Firing of Trooper with Klan Ties," NBC News, February 7, 2009, www.nbcnews.com/id/wbna29432935#.XjP0by 2ZN0s.

11. *State v. Henderson*, 277 Neb. 240 (Neb. 2009).

12. Associated Press, "Police Ties to Ku Klux Klan Shock Florida Town of Fruitland Park," *Guardian*, July 21, 2014.

13. Andy Campbell, "KKK Cop Fired After Nazi Salute Photo Surfaces," *HuffPost*, September 3, 2015, www.huffpost.com/entry/kkk-cop-fired-nazi-salute_n_55e885 d9e4b0c818f61b24c2.

14. Derek Hawkins, "Ex-Prison Guards in Ku Klux Klan Plotted to Kill a Black Inmate. An FBI Informant Caught Them," *Washington Post*, August 16, 2017.

15. Melanie Burney, "Former Bordentown Police Chief, Convicted of Lying to FBI, Will Be Released from Prison," *Philadelphia Inquirer*, June 1, 2023.

16. Lisa Rose, "This Is the First Police Officer Charged with a Federal Hate Crime in at Least 10 Years," CNN, December 21, 2018.

17. See, e.g., Isaac Avilucea, "Former Bordentown Police Chief Frank Nucera Wants Verdict Thrown Out Based Off White Juror Guilt," *Trentonian*, December 17, 2019, www.trentonian.com/news/former-bordentown-chief-frank-nucera-wants -verdict-thrown-out-based/article_83507f0e-210f-11ea-9e97-57fba72c1239.html; Melanie Burney, June 1, 2023.

18. Kelly Weill, "Cop Working at High School Revealed as White Nationalist Or-

ganizer," *Daily Beast*, March 18, 2019, www.thedailybeast.com/virginia-cop-daniel-morley-revealed-as-identity-evropa-member.

19. Hannah Gais and Creede Newton, "New York Fired Racist Prison Guard for Identity Evropa Membership," Southern Poverty Law Center, August 29, 2022, www.splcenter.org/hatewatch/2022/08/29/new-york-fired-racist-prison-guard-identity-evropa-membership.

20. "Oath Keepers," Southern Poverty Law Center, www.splcenter.org/fighting-hate/extremist-files/group/oath-keepers.

21. Mike Giglio, "A Pro-Trump Militant Group Has Recruited Thousands of Police, Soldiers, and Veterans," *Atlantic*, November 2020, www.theatlantic.com/magazine/archive/2020/11/right-wing-militias-civil-war/616473/.

22. Jonathan Levinson, "Dozens of Oregon Law Enforcement Officers Have Been Members of the Far-Right Oath Keepers Militia," Oregon Public Broadcasting, October 15, 2021, www.opb.org/article/2021/10/15/dozens-of-oregon-law-enforcement-officers-joined-far-right-oath-keepers-militia/.

23. "The Oath Keepers Data Leak: Unmasking Extremism in Public Life," Anti-Defamation League, September 6, 2022, www.adl.org/resources/report/oath-keepers-data-leak-unmasking-extremism-public-life.

24. Jordan Libowitz and Sara Wiatrak, "Emails Reveal Secret Service Contacts with Oath Keepers," CREW, August 23, 2023, www.citizensforethics.org/reports-investigations/crew-investigations/emails-reveal-secret-service-contacts-with-oath-keepers/.

25. Sara Cardine, "O.C. Sheriff's Officials Investigating Deputy Seen Wearing Extremist Insignia at Costa Mesa Protest," *Los Angeles Times,* June 3, 2020.

26. "CPD Investigating After Officer Wore Extremist Militia Logo to Downtown Protest Saturday," CBS Chicago, June 8, 2020, www.cbsnews.com/chicago/news/cpd-investigating-after-officer-wore-extremist-militia-logo-to-downtown-protest-saturday/.

27. Tom Schuba, "Under Pressure from City's Watchdog, CPD Reopens Probe of Cop Who Wore Extremist Symbol During Racial Justice Protest," *Chicago Sun-Times*, March 6, 2023, chicago.suntimes.com/crime/2023/3/6/23627776/three-percenter-cpd-chicago-police-department-cop-extremist-symbol-racial-justice-protest-proud-boy.

28. Ibid.

29. Tom Schuba and Dan Mihalopoulos, "Chicago Cops Tied to Oath Keepers Barred from Testifying in Court, Kim Foxx Decides," *Chicago Sun-Times*, November 17, 2023, https://chicago.suntimes.com/2023/11/17/23965413/oath-keepers-chicago-police-department-cook-county-states-attorney-kim-foxx.

30. Katherine Cook, "Salem Police Chief Apologizes in Response to Viral Video of Officer with Armed Group," KGW, June 6, 2020, www.kgw.com/article/news/lo

cal/protests/salem-police-chief-apologizes-in-response-to-viral-video-of-officer
/283-d7f4ce66-6f8d-4a25-a478-ae3999648d51.

31. Chuck Tanner and Devin Burghart, "Three Percenters Pose with Olympia Police Officer, Sparks Need for Thorough Investigation," Institute for Research and Education on Human Rights, June 18, 2020, www.irehr.org/2020/06/18/three-percenters-pose-with -olympia-police-officer-sparks-need-for-thorough-investigation/#_ftn3.

32. "Prohibiting Private Armies at Public Rallies: A Catalogue of Relevant State Constitutional and Statutory Provisions," Institute for Constitutional Advocacy and Protection, February 2018, www.law.georgetown.edu/icap/wp-content/uploads/sites /32/2018/04/Prohibiting-Private-Armies-at-Public-Rallies.pdf.

33. Kate Irby, "White Extremists Kill More Cops, but Black Extremists Tracked More Closely," SFGate, January 5, 2018, www.sfgate.com/nation/article/White -extremists-kill-more-cops-but-black-12525636.php.

34. Jay Barmann, "Santa Cruz Shooter Charged Along with 'Boogaloo Movement' Accomplice in Oakland Shooting of Federal Officers," SFist, June 16, 2020, sfist.com/2020/06/16/santa-cruz-cop-killer-charged-along-with-boogaloo/.

35. Tess Owen, "A Boogaloo Boi Leader Just Got Arrested for Allegedly Firing AK-47-Style Rifle During a George Floyd Protest," Vice News, October 23, 2020, www.vice.com/en/article/dy8zyw/a-boogaloo-boi-leader-just-got-arrested-for-al legedly-firing-ak-47-during-george-floyd-protest.

36. Jeff German, "Boogaloo Informant Reveals How He Helped FBI Infiltrate Las Vegas Group," Las Vegas Review-Journal, July 7, 2020, www.reviewjournal.com/in vestigations/boogaloo-informant-reveals-how-he-helped-fbi-infiltrate-las-vegas -group-2069071/. For a broader assessment of the Boogaloo movement, see "Assessing the Threat from Accelerationists and Militia Extremists: Hearing Before the Subcomm. on Intelligence and Counterterrorism of the H. Comm. on Homeland Security," 116th Congress, 2020 (statement of Heidi L. Beirich, cofounder and executive vice president, Global Project Against Hate and Extremism), 25.

37. Dakin Andone, "This Group Compiled Police Officer's Offensive Facebook Posts. Now Departments Are Taking Action," CNN, June 20, 2019.

38. Alicia Victoria Lozano, "13 Philadelphia Officers to Be Fired over Racist, Violent Facebook Posts," NBC10 Philadelphia, July 18, 2019, www.nbcphiladelphia.com /news/national-international/philadelphia-police-officers-facebook-posts/170494/; Chris Palmer, "2 More Philly Cops to Be Fired in Facebook Probe, Bringing Total to 15," Philadelphia Inquirer, September 11, 2019.

39. Cassandra Jaramillo, "Dallas Police Department Disciplines 13 Officers for Offensive Social Media Posts," Dallas Morning News, January 30, 2020, www.dallas news.com/news/crime/2020/01/31/dallas-police-department-disciplines-13-offi cers-for-offensive-social-media-posts/.

40. Associated Press, "2 St. Louis Police Officers Fired Over Facebook Posts," CBS News, December 10, 2019.

41. Alan Pyke, "Racist, Homophobic SF Cops Will Likely Be Fired, After Years-Long Court Saga," ThinkProgress, September 13, 2018, thinkprogress.org/sf-cops-who-exchanged-racist-homophobic-texts-will-likely-be-fired-after-years-long-court-saga-f94aa43ccc94/.

42. "DA: SFPD Officers Sent Recent Racist Texts Mocking the Racist Text Scandal," SFist, March 31, 2016, sfist.com/2016/03/31/da_sfpd_officers_sent_even_more_and/.

43. Community Oriented Policing Services (COPS), "Collaborative Reform Initiative: An Assessment of the San Francisco Police Department," Department of Justice, October 2016, xi, www.sfdph.org/dph/files/jrp/DOJ-Report.pdf.

44. Maura Dolan, "3,000 Cases Possibly Affected by S.F. Police Texting, D.A. Says," Los Angeles Times, May 7, 2015.

45. Michael Praats, "EXCLUSIVE: Racist Rants Released of Former WPD Officers Recorded on Police Cam," WECT News 6, November 10, 2022, www.wect.com/2022/11/11/exclusive-racist-rants-released-former-wpd-officers-recorded-police-cam-heart-1/; "Professional Standards Report of Internal Investigation," Wilmington Police Department, June 11, 2020.

46. Jason Green and Robert Salonga, "San Jose Police Officers' Racist Posts Exposed by Blogger," Mercury News, June 26, 2020, www.mercurynews.com/2020/06/26/san-jose-police-officers-racist-facebook-posts-exposed-by-blogger/.

47. Kevin Rector, "Bias, Far-Right Sympathies Among California Law Enforcement Going Unchecked," Los Angeles Times, April 28, 2022, www.latimes.com/california/story/2022-04-28/audit-of-california-law-enforcement-finds-extreme-bias-among-officers-goes-unchecked.

48. Michael S. Tilden, "Law Enforcement Departments Have Not Adequately Guarded Against Biased Conduct," Auditor of the State of California, April 26, 2022.

49. "Investigation into the City of Minneapolis and the Minneapolis Police Department," Minnesota Department of Human Rights, April 27, 2022.

50. Zolan Kanno-Youngs, "62 Border Agents Belonged to Offensive Facebook Group, Investigation Finds," New York Times, July 15, 2019; Ryan Devereaux, "Border Patrol Chief Carla Provost Was a Member of Secret Facebook Group," The Intercept, July 12, 2019, theintercept.com/2019/07/12/border-patrol-chief-carla-provost-was-a-member-of-secret-facebook-group/.

51. Ryan Devereaux, "The Bloody History of Border Militias Runs Deep—And Law Enforcement Is Part of It," The Intercept, April 23, 2019, theintercept.com/2019/04/23/border-militia-migrants/.

52. Jeff Stein, "Classified US Intelligence Chat Rooms a 'Dumpster Fire' of Hate

Speech, Says Ex-NSA Contractor," Spy Talk, March 11, 2022, www.spytalk.co/p/clas
sified-us-intelligence-chat-rooms.

53. "Report of Investigation, Case 21-0018-IN, Office of the Inspector General of
the Intelligence Community (Date Redacted)," Investigations Division, www.wash
ingtonpost.com/documents/2be1fd11-4c6d-435b-9cd8-3a74465499dd.pdf?itid=lk
_inline_manual_11.

54. Stein, "IG Report Confirms Hate Speech in Classified IC Chat Rooms."

55. Nick Schwellenbach, "Hundreds of Oath Keepers Have Worked for DHS,
Leaked List Shows," Project on Government Oversight, www.pogo.org/investiga
tion/2022/12/hundreds-of-oath-keepers-have-worked-for-dhs-leaked-list-shows.

56. Office of the Chief Security Officer, "Report to the Secretary of Homeland
Security Domestic Violent Extremism Internal Review: Observations, Findings, and
Recommendations," U.S. Department of Homeland Security, March 11, 2022.

57. Rebecca Beitsch, "Democrats Push DHS for Plan to Root Out Internal Extremists," The Hill, July 17, 2023, thehill.com/policy/national-security/4102252-dem
ocrats-push-dhs-for-plan-to-root-out-internal-extremists/.

58. Will Carless, "Federal Agencies Promised to Tackle Extremism. Years Later,
Experts See Efforts Sputtering Out," USA Today, September 18, 2023, www.usatoday
.com/story/news/investigations/2023/09/18/dhs-promised-to-combat-extremism
-now-it-wont-address-the-issue/70880213007/.

59. Maddy Crowell and Sylvia Varnham O'Regan, "Extremist Cops: How US Law
Enforcement Is Failing to Police Itself," Guardian, December 13, 2019.

60. Doggrell v. City of Anniston, 277 F. Supp. 3d 1239 (N.D. Ala. 2017).

61. Maddy Crowell and Sylvia Varnham O'Regan, Guardian, December 13,
2019.

62. William Thornton, "Anniston, Justice Dept. Partnership Aimed at Reducing
Tension," AL.com, June 26, 2015, www.al.com/news/anniston-gadsden/2015/06/an
niston_justice_dept_partners.html.

63. "Extremism in American Law Enforcement: Far Greater Transparency, Accountability Needed," Anti-Defamation League, June 3, 2021, www.adl.org/re
sources/report/extremism-american-law-enforcement-far-greater-transparency
-accountability-needed.

64. Timothy Williams, "Cast-Out Police Officers Are Often Hired in Other Cities," New York Times, September 10, 2016.

65. Rachel Knapp, "New Colbert Police Chief Linked to Neo-Nazi Websites
Claims Identity Theft," News12, August 26, 2017, www.kxii.com/content/news/New
-Colbert-police-chiefs-name-linked-to-neo-Nazi-websites-441804593.html.

66. Kelly Weill, "Oklahoma Police Chief Resigns over Neo-Nazi Ties, Gets Job in
Neighboring Police Force," Daily Beast, September 17, 2018, www.thedailybeast.com

/oklahoma-police-chief-resigns-over-neo-nazi-ties-gets-job-in-neighboring-police
-force; Michael Hutchins, "Former Colbert Police Chief with Neo-Nazi Background
Back in Law Enforcement," *Herald Democrat*, September 13, 2018, www.heralddemo
crat.com/news/20180913/former-colbert-police-chief-with-neo-nazi-background
-back-in-law-enforcement.

67. Glynis Kazanjian, "Eastern Shore Police Chief Gets Suspended 2-Year Sentence for Falsifying Cop's Hiring Papers," Maryland Matters, January 17, 2020, www
.marylandmatters.org/blog/eastern-shore-police-chief-gets-suspended-2-year-pris
on-sentence-for-falsifying-hiring-papers/.

68. Brandon Holveck, "Former Dover Officer Removed from Greensboro Police
Staff After Use of Force Reports Surface," Delaware Online, August 2, 2019, www
.delawareonline.com/story/news/2019/08/02/former-dover-officer-removed-greens
boro-police-staff/1903657001/.

69. William Terrill and Jason R. Ingram, "Citizen Complaints Against the Police:
An Eight City Examination," *Police Quarterly*, October 2015, 20, doi: 10.1177
/1098611115613320.

70. Ibid., 17.

71. James Queally and Ben Poston, "For Years, California Police Agencies Have
Rejected Almost Every Racial Profiling Complaint They Received," *Los Angeles
Times*, December 14, 2020, www.latimes.com/california/story/2020-12-14/california
-police-racial-profiling-complaints-rejected.

72. Steven Rafael et al., "Racial and Gender Disparities in Police Stops: What
Does the 2021 Racial Identity and Profiling Act Data Tell Us?," California Policy Lab
Committee on Revision of the Penal Code, May 2023, www.capolicylab.org/wp-con
tent/uploads/2023/05/California-Policy-Lab-Analysis-of-2021-RIPA-Data.pdf.

73. See John Kelly and Mark Nichols, "We Found 85,000 Cops Who've Been Investigated for Misconduct. Now You Can Read Their Records," *USA Today*, April 24, 2019,
www.usatoday.com/in-depth/news/investigations/2019/04/24/usa-today-reveal
ing-misconduct-records-police-cops/3223984002/; Claire Bushey and Christine
Zhang, "Small Share of US Police Draw Third of Complaints in Big Cities," *Financial
Times*, May 28, 2021.

74. Edika G. Quispe-Torreblanca and Neil Stewart, "Causal Peer Effects in Police
Misconduct," *Nature Human Behavior* 3 (August 2019), doi/10.1038/s41562-019
-0612-8.

75. Ibid.

4. Hidden in Plain Sight

1. Counterterrorism Division, *Counterterrorism Policy Directive and Policy
Guide*, FBI, March 7, 2019, 89.

2. Counterterrorism Division, *White Supremacist Infiltration of Law Enforcement*, FBI, October 17, 2006, 4.

3. Ibid., 6; Associated Press, "Ex-Md. Cop Pleads Guilty to Civil Rights Crimes," NBC News, August 8, 2006.

4. Ibid., 4.

5. "White Supremacist Extremism Poses Persistent Threat of Lethal Violence," FBI and Department of Homeland Security, May 10, 2017, 4.

6. See, e.g., Weiyi Cai et al., "White Extremist Ideology Drives Many Deadly Shootings," *New York Times*, August 5, 2019, www.nytimes.com/interactive /2019/08/04/us/white-extremist-active-shooter.html; David Ingram, Brandy Zadrozny, and Corky Siemaszko, "Gilroy Garlic Festival Gunman Referred to 'Might Is Right' Manifesto Before Shooting," NBC News, July 29, 2019; Jana Winter, "Texas Mass Shooter Posted Neo-Nazi Content, FBI Document Reveals," *Rolling Stone*, May 8, 2023, www.rollingstone.com/politics/politics-features/allen-texas-mass -shooter-motivated-by-white-supremacist-beliefs-feds-1234731085/; Sean Cotter, "Authorities Release Diary of Massachusetts Rampage Killer, Who Wrote 'Racism Is Healthy,' " *The Mercury News*, July 8, 2021, www.mercurynews.com/2021/07/08 /authorities-release-diary-of-winthrop-rampage-perp-who-wrote-racism-is -healthy/; Rina Torchinsky, "Details Emerge About the Suspect in the Buffalo Mass Shooting," NPR, May 16, 2022, www.npr.org/2022/05/16/1099053942/what-we -know-about-the-suspect-in-the-buffalo-mass-shooting; Nouran Salahieh, et al., "A Federal Hate Crime Probe Is Underway After 3 People Were Killed in a Racist Rampage in Jacksonville, Officials Say. Here's What We Know," August 28, 2023, www .cnn.com/2023/08/28/us/jacksonville-florida-shooting-what-we-know/index.html.

7. Counterterrorism Division, *White Supremacist Infiltration of Law Enforcement*, 3.

8. "Confronting Violent White Supremacy (Part II): Adequacy of the Federal Response: Hearing before the Subcommittee on Civil Rights and Civil Liberties of the Committee on Oversight and Reform, House of Representatives," 116th Congress, 2019, 22.

9. Counterterrorism Division, *White Supremacist Infiltration of Law Enforcement*, 6. See also *Pickering v. Board of Education*, 391 U.S. 563 (1968); *Garcetti v. Ceballos*, 547 U.S. 410, 417 (2006).

10. "Confronting Violent White Supremacy (Part II)."

11. Jordan Williams, "Raskin Requests FBI Briefing on Extremism in Law Enforcement," *The Hill*, March 10, 2021, thehill.com/homenews/house/542541-raskin -demands-briefing-on-white-supremacy-in-law-enforcement.

12. Jonathan Ben-Menachem, "The Cops at the Capitol," The Appeal, January 13, 2021, theappeal.org/the-cops-at-the-capitol/; Hannah Rabinowitz, "Ex-DEA Agent

Charged with Bringing Gun to Capitol Grounds on January 6 and Lying to FBI," CNN, July 20, 2021; Vida B. Johnson, "The Capitol Insurrection and White Supremacist Infiltration of US Police," *Yes Magazine*, January 19, 2021, www.yesmagazine.org /opinion/2021/01/19/capitol-insurrection-police-white-supremacy.

13. Michael S. Schmidt and Luke Broadwater, "Officers' Injuries, Including Concussions, Show Scope of Violence at Capitol Riot," *New York Times*, February 11, 2021.

14. Whitney Wild and Paul LeBlanc, "6 Capitol Police Officers Suspended, 29 Others Being Investigated for Alleged Roles in Riot," CNN, February 18, 2021.

15. Sonnet Swire, "US Capitol Police Announces Six Disciplinary Cases Against Officers from Jan. 6 Insurrection," CNN, September 12, 2021.

16. Luke Broadwater, "Capitol Police Officer Charged with Obstructing Justice in Jan. 6 Case," *New York Times*, October 15, 2021.

17. Ryan J. Reilly, "FBI Says Former Agent Arrested over Jan. 6 Called Officers Nazis and Encouraged Mob to 'Kill 'Em,' " NBC News, May 2, 2023; Justin Klawans, "1/6 Rioter Thomas Caldwell, Who Used to Work for FBI, Told Crowd to 'Hang the Traitors': DOJ," *Newsweek*, December 16, 2021, www.newsweek.com/1-6-rioter -thomas-caldwell-who-used-work-fbi-told-crowd-hang-traitors-doj-1660351.

18. Ken Dilanian and Ryan J. Reilly, "GOP Witnesses Undermined Jan. 6 Cases with Conspiracy Theories, FBI Says," NBC News, May 18, 2023.

19. Josh Margolin, "White Supremacists 'Seek Affiliation' with Law Enforcement to Further Their Goals, Internal FBI Report Warns," ABC News, March 8, 202. See Ben-Menachem, "Cops at the Capitol"; Lindsay Watts, "6 Capitol Police Officers Suspended, 35 Under Investigation After Capitol Riot, Spokesperson Says," Fox 5 DC, February 18, 2021, www.fox5dc.com/news/6-capitol-police-officers-suspended-35 -under-investigation-after-capitol-riot-spokesperson-says.

20. Representative Jamie Raskin, Letter to FBI Director Christopher Wray, March 9, 2021.

21. Ryan J. Reilly and Ken Dilanian, "FBI Official Was Warned After January 6 That Some in the Bureau Were 'Sympathetic' to the Capitol Rioters," NBC News, October 14, 2022.

22. Hannah Grabenstein, "What You Need to Know About Jeffrey Clark's 2020 Election Charges," *PBS NewsHour*, September 8, 2023, www.pbs.org/newshour/poli tics/what-you-need-to-know-about-jeffrey-clarks-2020-election-charges.

23. Michael Goldberg, "How 6 Mississippi Officers Tried to Cover Up Their Torture of 2 Black Men," Associated Press, August 4, 2023, apnews.com/article/missis sippi-deputies-guilty-pleas-civil-rights-e4937b4cd1d2ed2388b2fd1c3aeefcb9.

24. Michael Goldberg, "Deputies Accused of Shoving Guns in Mouths of 2 Black Men," Associated Press, March 27, 2023, apnews.com/article/mississippi-depu ties-black-violent-arrests-61acf712b13fc3c77dce76e508fa94c1.

25. Timothy Bella, "FBI Arrests Officers Who Allegedly Used Police Dogs to Attack People," *Washington Post*, August 18, 2023.

26. Katie Nielsen, "Antioch Police Racist Texts: Nearly Half of Department Now Involved in Scandal," CBS Bay Area, April 18, 2023, www.cbsnews.com/sanfrancisco /news/antioch-police-racist-texts-nearly-half-of-department-now-involved-in-scan dal/.

27. Taylor Romine, "Officers in Bay Area Police Department Are Charged with Civil Rights Violations as Part of FBI Investigation," CNN, August 18, 2023.

28. See Michael German and Sara Robinson, "Wrong Priorities on Fighting Terrorism," Brennan Center for Justice, October 31, 2018.

29. Brian Bowling and Andrew Conte, "Trib Investigation: Cops Often Let Off Hook for Civil Rights Complaints," *Tribune-Review*, March 12, 2016, archive.triblive .com/news/nation/trib-investigation-cops-often-let-off-hook-for-civil-rights-com plaints/.

30. "Justice Department Rejects 96% of Civil Rights Cases Against Police—Report," *Guardian*, March 14, 2016.

31. 18 U.S.C. § 242. See also Andrea J. Ritchie and Joey L. Mogul, "In the Shadows of the War on Terror: Persistent Police Brutality and Abuse of People of Color in the United States," *DePaul Journal for Social Science* 1, no. 2 (January 2016): 234–35; *Screws v. United States*, 325 U.S. 91, 101 (1945); *United States v. Guest*, 383 U.S. 745, 761 (1966).

32. See Aneri Shah, "Reinvigorating the Federal Government's Role in Civil Rights Enforcement Under 18 USC §242: The George Floyd Justice in Policing Act's Not So Reckless Proposal," *Seton Hall Law Review*, 2022; Taryn Merkl, "Protecting Against Police Brutality and Official Miscondut," Brennan Center for Justice, April 29, 2021, www.brennancenter.org/sites/default/files/2021-04/BCJ-12 6%20Civil Rights.pdf.

33. Erin Donaghue, "In a First, FBI to Begin Collecting National Data on Police Use of Force," CBS News, November 22, 2018.

34. "Addressing Police Misconduct Laws Enforced by the Department of Justice," United States Department of Justice, updated December 13, 2019, www.justice.gov /crt/addressing-police-misconduct-laws-enforced-department-justice.

35. Mike Levine, "Why the Justice Department's Review of Police Agreements Matters," ABC News, April 4, 2017.

36. Kimbriell Kelly, Sarah Childress, and Steven Rich, "Forced Reforms, Mixed Results," *Washington Post*, November 13, 2015.

37. Zachary A. Powell et al., "Police Consent Decrees and 1983 Civil Rights Litigation," *Criminology and Public Policy* (2017): 575–605.

38. Maxine Bernstein, "Portland Police Not Meeting Federal Requirements on

Use of Force, Training, Justice Department Finds," Oregon Live, February 11, 2021, www.oregonlive.com/crime/2021/02/portland-police-not-meeting-federal-require ments-on-use-of-force-training-justice-department-finds.html; Jonathan Levinson, "U.S. Justice Department Says Portland Police Continue to Violate Their Own Use-of-Force Policies," Oregon Public Broadcasting, July 27, 2022, www.opb.org/article /2022/07/27/us-justice-department-portland-police-use-of-force-settlement/.

39. Maxine Bernstein, "Federal Justice Department Wants Body-Worn Cameras on Portland Police, a Civilian to Oversee Police Training," Oregon Live, July 15, 2021, www.oregonlive.com/crime/2021/07/federal-justice-department-wants-body-worn -cameras-on-portland-police-a-civilian-to-oversee-police-training.html.

40. Katie Benner, "Sessions, in Last-Minute Act, Sharply Limits Use of Consent Decrees to Curb Police Abuses," *New York Times*, November 8, 2018, www.nytimes .com/2018/11/08/us/politics/sessions-limits-consent-decrees.html; Office of the U.S. Attorney General to Heads of Civil Litigating Components, United States Attorneys, "Principles and Procedures for Civil Consent Decrees and Settlement Agreements with State and Local Governmental Entities," November 7, 2018, www.justice.gov /opa/press-release/file/1109621/download.

41. Joshua Clark Davis, "William Barr's Police-Fueled War on Civil Rights," *Nation,* December 27, 2019, www.thenation.com/article/archive/barr-police-civil -rights/; U.S. Department of Justice, "Third Annual Attorney General's Award for Distinguished Service in Policing," video, December 3, 2019, www.justice.gov/opa /video/third-annual-attorney-general-s-award-distinguished-service-policing.

42. White House Briefing Room, "Fact Sheet: President Biden to Sign Historic Executive Order to Advance Effective, Accountable Policing and Strengthen Public Safety," May 25, 2022, www.whitehouse.gov/briefing-room/statements-releases/2022 /05/25/fact-sheet-president-biden-to-sign-historic-executive-order-to-advance-effec tive-accountable-policing-and-strengthen-public-safety/.

43. "Justice Department Launches National Law Enforcement Accountability Database," press release, December 18, 2023, www.justice.gov/opa/pr/justice-depart ment-launches-national-law-enforcement-accountability-database.

44. White House Briefing Room, "Executive Order on Advancing Effective, Accountable Policing and Criminal Justice Practices to Enhance Public Trust and Public Safety," May 25, 2022, sec. 3 (iv), www.whitehouse.gov/briefing-room/pres idential-actions/2022/05/25/executive-order-on-advancing-effective-account able-policing-and-criminal-justice-practices-to-enhance-public-trust-and-public -safety/.

45. See Ari Feldman, "Activists Want Bias Training for Cops. ADL Provides It. But Does It Work?," *The Forward*, June 17, 2020, forward.com/news/national/448948 /police-george-floyd-protest-implicit-bias/; Tomas Chamorro-Premuzic, "Implicit

Bias Training Doesn't Work," Bloomberg, January 4, 2020, www.bloomberg.com /opinion/articles/2020-01-04/implicit-bias-training-isn-t-improving-corporate-di versity?sref=LSnlJj5m; Michael Hobbes, " 'Implicit Bias' Trainings Don't Actually Change Police Behavior," *HuffPost*, June 12, 2020, www.huffpost.com/entry/implicit -bias-training-doesnt-actually-change-police-behavior_n_5ee28fc3c5b60b 32f010ed48; Jeremy Stahl, "The NYPD Paid $4.5 Million for a Bias Trainer. She Says She's Not the Solution," *Slate*, June 18, 2020.

46. Tom James, "Can Cops Unlearn Their Unconscious Biases?," *The Atlantic*, December 23, 2017.

47. Ari Feldman, June 17, 2020.

48. Candace Wang, "Can Implicit Bias Training Help Cops Overcome Racism?," *Popular Science*, June 16, 2020, www.popsci.com/story/science/implicit-bias-train ing-police-racism-black-lives-matter/.

49. Michelle M. Duguid and Melissa C. Thomas-Hunt, "Condoning Stereotyping? How Awareness of Stereotyping Prevalence Impacts Expression of Stereotypes," *Journal of Applied Psychology* 100 (2015): 343–59, pubmed.ncbi.nlm.nih.gov/2531 4368/; "Ironic Effects of Anti-Prejudice Messages," Association for Psychological Science, July 6, 2011.

50. "Confronting Violent White Supremacy (Part II)," 22–23.

51. *Brady v. Maryland*, 373 U.S. 83 (U.S. 1963).

52. *Giglio v. United States*, 405 U.S. 150, 153 (U.S. 1972).

53. Vida B. Johnson, "KKK in the PD: White Supremacist Police and What to Do About It," *Lewis & Clark Law Review* 27, no. 1 (April 1, 2019): 205, 234.

54. Associated Press, "Prosecutor Adds 22 St. Louis Officers to 'Exclusion List' over Racist Facebook Posts," CBS News, June 19, 2019.

55. Tom Schuba and Dan Mihalopoulos, "Chicago Cops Tied to Oath Keepers Barred from Testifying in Court, Kim Foxx Decides," *Chicago Sun-Times*, November 17, 2023, https://chicago.suntimes.com/2023/11/17/23965413/oath-keepers-chica go-police-department-cook-county-states-attorney-kim-foxx.

56. Anser Hassan, "Judge Issues Landmark Ruling Against Contra Costa County D.A.'s Office over Racial Bias," ABC 7 News, May 21, 2023, abc7news.com/contra-cos ta-county-district-attorney-office-superior-court-judge-ruling-racial-bias-rac ism-charging-decisions-das-antioch-police-investigation/13277527/.

57. Richard Luscombe, "Florida Prosecutor Sorry for Racist Memo That Singled Out Hispanic Residents," *Guardian*, April 21, 2023.

58. Jim Garamone, "Austin Orders Military Stand Down to Address Challenge of Extremism in the Ranks," U.S. Department of Defense, February 3, 2021, www.de fense.gov/News/News-Stories/Article/Article/2492530/austin-orders-military-stand -down-to-address-challenge-of-extremism-in-the-ranks/.

59. Ellen Mitchell, "Pentagon Takes Step Toward New Screening Procedures to Weed Out Extremists," *The Hill*, April 9, 2021, thehill.com/policy/defense/547447 -pentagon-takes-step-toward-new-screening-procedures-to-weed-out-extremists/.

60. See, for example, Hannah Allam, "A Police Chief Got Rid of a Neo-Nazi. Then Came the Hard Part," *Washington Post*, May 8, 2023.

61. Allison Pecorin, "Why Congress Has Failed to Pass Policing Reform in Recent Years," ABC News, January 27, 2023.

62. Denise Lavoie, Tatyana Monnay, and Juliette Rihl, "Some States Are Struggling to Implement Policing Reforms Passed After George Floyd's Murder," PBS, October 31, 2022.

63. Will Carless, "The Military Ordered Big Steps to Stop Extremism. Two Years Later, It Shows No Results," *USA Today*, July 21, 2023, www.usatoday.com/story /news/investigations/2023/07/21/defense-secretary-lloyd-austin-extremism-re forms/70429571007/.

64. Tess Owen, "All the Terrible Things Proud Boys Have Done Since Storming the Capitol," *Vice News*, June 23, 2021, www.vice.com/en/article/pkb377/all-the-ter rible-things-proud-boys-have-done-since-storming-the-capitol; Katie Shepherd, "Portland Police Stand Down as Proud Boys and Far-Right Militias Flash Guns and Brawl with Antifa Counterprotesters," *Washington Post*, August 22, 2022.

65. Hannah Knowles, "California Police Fire Officer Who Was a Proud Boy, Saying They Have No Tolerance for 'Hate Groups,' " *Washington Post*, April 11, 2021.

66. Alexandra Meeks, Natasha Chen, and Stephanie Becker, "Authorities in California Dismiss 90 Cases So Far Due to the Involvement of Torrance Officers Under Investigation for Racist Texts," CNN, December 9, 2021.

5. Resetting Federal Law Enforcement Priorities

1. Harsha Panduranga, "Why Biden's Strategy for Preventing Domestic Terrorism Could Do More Harm than Good," *Los Angeles Times*, June 21, 2021, www.la times.com/opinion/story/2021-06-21/domestic-terrorism-homeland-security -violence-prevention.

2. "150 Years of the Department of Justice," U.S. Department of Justice, August 17, 2022, www.justice.gov/history/timeline/150-years-department-justice#event -1388571.

3. Ibid.

4. William M. Carter Jr., "The Anti-Klan Act in the Twenty-First Century," *Harvard Law Review* 136, no. 4 (2023): 251–87.

5. Alan W. Clarke, "The Ku Klux Klan Act and the Civil Rights Revolution: How Civil Rights Litigation Came to Regulate Police and Correctional Officer Misconduct," *St. Mary's Law Review on Minority Issues* 7, no. 2 (Spring 2005): 151–82.

6. U.S. Department of Justice, "150 Years of the Department of Justice."

7. See, e.g., Matt Matthews, *The Posse Comitatus Act and the United States Army: A Historical Perspective* (Fort Leavenworth, KS: Combat Studies Institute Press, 2006), www.armyupress.army.mil/Portals/7/Hot-Spots/docs/Civil-Unrest/posse%20comitatus.pdf; James R. Weber, *The Posse Comitatus Act of 1878: An Historical Perspective and Implications for Homeland Defense* (Carlisle Barracks, PA: US Army War College, 2003).

8. "Lynching in America: Confronting the Legacy of Racial Terror," Equal Justice Initiative, 2017, https://eji.org/reports/lynching-in-america/. Report abstract.

9. Adam Clymer, "How Sept. 11 Changed Goals of the Justice Dept.," *New York Times*, February 28, 2002.

10. "Statement of Attorney General John Ashcroft before the United States Senate Committee on Appropriations Subcommittee on Commerce, Justice, and State, The Judiciary, and Related Agencies," Hearing on U.S. Federal Efforts to Combat Terrorism, May 9, 2001, www.justice.gov/archive/ag/testimony/2001/ag_statement_05_09_01.htm

11. See, e.g., Counterterrorism Section, "Counterterrorism White Paper," U.S. Department of Justice, June 22, 2006.

12. U.S. Department of Justice, Inspector General, "The External Effects of the Federal Bureau of Investigation's Reprioritization Efforts," Audit Report 05-37, 2005, iii.

13. U.S. Department of Justice, Inspector General, "Follow-Up Audit of Federal Bureau of Investigation Personnel Resource Management and Casework," Audit Report 10-24, 2010, 43.

14. "Confronting the Rise of Domestic Terrorism in the Homeland, Before the Committee on Homeland Security," 116th Congress, 2019, 36.

15. "Oversight of the Federal Bureau of Investigation: Hearing Before the Senate Judiciary Committee," 117th Congress, December 5, 2023 (Statement of Christopher Wray, Director, Federal Bureau of Investigation).

16. Faiza Patel and Meghan Koushik, "Countering Violent Extremism," Brennan Center for Justice, 2017.

17. Henry Schuster, "Domestic Terror: Who's the Most Dangerous," CNN, August 24, 2005.

18. See, e.g., Sam Levin, "Stabbed at a Neo-Nazi Rally, Called a Criminal: How Police Targeted a Black Activist," *Guardian*, May 25, 2018; Matt Coker, "7 Charged in Anaheim KKK Melee—But Stabby Klanner Not One of Them," *O.C. Weekly*, July 1, 2016, www.ocweekly.com/7-charged-in-anaheim-kkk-melee-but-stabby-klanner-not-one-of-them-7305812-2/; James Queally, "Ku Klux Klan Rally in Anaheim Erupts in Violence; 3 Are Stabbed and 13 Arrested," *Los Angeles Times*, February 27, 2016; Frank

John Tristan, "Huntington Beach Pro-Trump March Turns into Attack on Anti-Trump Protesters," *O.C. Weekly*, March 26, 2017, www.ocweekly.com/huntington-beach-pro -trump-march-turns-into-attack-on-anti-trump-protesters-press-7991623/; Mike Carter and Steve Miletich, "Couple Charged with Assault in Shooting, Melee During UW Speech by Milo Yiannopoulos," *Seattle Times*, April 24, 2017, www.seattletimes.com /seattle-news/crime/couple-charged-with-assault-in-shooting-melee-during-uw -speech-by-milo-yiannopoulos/; Frances Robles, "As White Nationalist in Charlottes- ville Fired, Police 'Never Moved,'" *New York Times*, August 25, 2017, www.nytimes .com/2017/08/25/us/charlottesville-protest-police.html.

19. Federal Bureau of Investigation and Department of Homeland Security, "Stra- tegic Intelligence Assessment and Data on Domestic Terrorism," 2021, 21.

20. Arie Perliger, "Challengers from the Sidelines: Understanding America's Vio- lent Far-Right," Combating Terrorism Center at West Point, 2013, 86, 100. https://ctc .westpoint.edu/challengers-from-the-sidelines-understanding-americas-vio lent-far-right/.

21. Joshua D. Freilich and Steven M. Chermak. "Preventing Deadly Encounters Between Law Enforcement and American Far-Rightists," *Crime Prevention Studies* 25 (2009): 141–72.

22. NPR, "Dylann Roof Said He Wanted to Start a Race War, Friends Say," June 19, 2005, www.npr.org/2015/06/19/415809511/dylann-roof-said-he-wanted-to-start-a-race -war-friends-say; NBC News, "Church Gunman Reportedly Said, 'I have to do it,' " June 18, 2015, www.nbcnews.com/video/church-gunman-reportedly-said-i-have-to -do-it-467402819802.

23. Ryan J. Reilly, "FBI Director James Comey Still Unsure if White Supremacist's Attack in Charleston Was Terrorism," *HuffPost*, July 9, 2015, www.huffpost.com/en try/james-comey-charleston-terrorism_n_7764614.

24. Shane Harris, "White House Won't Back FBI Chief on Charleston 'Terror,' " *Daily Beast*, April 14, 2017, www.thedailybeast.com/white-house-wont-back-fbi -chief-on-charleston-terror.

25. Jelani Cobb, "Terrorism in Charleston," *New Yorker*, June 20, 2015.

26. See, e.g., DaNeen L. Brown, "Red Summer: When Racist Moms Ruled," *Amer- ican Experience*, PBS, February 4, 2021, www.pbs.org/wgbh/americanexperience/fea tures/t-town-red-summer-racist-mobs/; Mark Ellis, "J. Edgar Hoover and the Red Summer of 1919," *Journal of American Studies*, April 1994, www.jstor.org/stable /27555783?saml_data=eyJzYW1sVG9rZW4iOiI5OTU4ZDk4Mi01ZTZjLTQ 4NzgtYmRmZi0zMTY2MTk$Y2M2MzQiLCJlbWFpbCI6Im1pY2hhZWwuZ2Vyb WFuQG55dS5lZHUiLCJpbnN0aXR1dGlvbklkcyI6WyJhZmJhYzkxNi0yYTEx LTQ5ZjAtOTg3Ny0zM2IzNTJiYTk5NTIiXX0.

27. Bureau of Justice Statistics, "Hate Crime Victimization, 2004–2015," U.S.

Department of Justice, June 2017; "Justice Department Releases Update on Hate Crimes Prosecutions and Announces Launch of New Hate Crimes Website," press release, Department of Justice, October 29, 2018, www.justice.gov/opa/pr/justice-de partment-releases-update-hate-crimes-prosecutions-and-announces-launch-new -hate; "Justice Department Releases Update on Hate Crimes Prosecutions and An nounces Launch of New Hate Crimes Website," press release, Department of Justice, 2018, www.justice.gov/opa/pr/justice-department-releases-update-hate-crimes-pros ecutions-and-announces-launch-new-hate.

28. TRAC, "Few Federal Hate Crime Referrals Result in Prosecution," Syracuse University, August 12, 2019.

29. U.S. Department of Justice, "Fact Sheet: Justice Department Efforts to Combat Hate Crimes," updated August 7, 2023, www.justice.gov/hatecrimes/spotlight/com bating-hate-crimes.

30. In 2019, 15,588 law enforcement agencies participated in UCR hate crime re porting, out of approximately 18,000 law enforcement agencies nationwide. The vast majority of those participating reported zero hate crimes (86.1 percent). See Uni form Crime Reporting Program, "2019 Hate Crime Statistics," FBI, 2019. The FBI changed the way it collected this data in 2020, making comparisons to later years difficult.

31. Jeffrey Collins, "South Carolina Democrats Frustrated over No Hate Crime Law," Associated Press, May 2, 2023.

32. Nick Gass, "Dylann Roof Charged with Federal Hate Crime," Politico, July 22, 2015, www.politico.com/story/2015/07/dylann-roof-federal-hate-crime -120473.

33. "Dylann Roof Is First to Get Death Sentence for Federal Hate Crime," *PBS NewsHour*, January 10, 2017, www.pbs.org/newshour/show/news-wrap-dylann-roof -first-get-death-sentence-federal-hate-crime.

34. Amarnath Amarasingam, et al., "The Buffalo Attack: The Cumulative Mo mentum of Far-Right Terror," CTC Sentinel, July 2022, p. 1, https://ctc.westpoint.edu /wp-content/uploads/2022/07/CTC-SENTINEL-072022.pdf.

35. "Video, Attorney Lynch's Statement Following the Federal Grand Jury Indict ment Against Dylann Storm Roof," U.S. Department of Justice, July 22, 2015, www .justice.gov/opa/video/attorney-general-lynchs-statement-following-federal -grand-jury-indictment-against-dylann.

36. Mary B. McCord, "Criminal Law Should Treat Domestic Terrorism as the Moral Equivalent of International Terrorism," Lawfare, August 21, 2017, www.law faremedia.org/article/criminal-law-should-treat-domestic-terrorism-moral-equiva lent-international-terrorism.

37. Angie Gad, "Domestic Terrorism Conference Series: Combatting Domestic

Terrorism with Thomas Brzozowski," State of New Jersey Offfice of Homeland Security and Preparedness, August 7, 2017, www.njohsp.gov/media/podcast-combating-domestic-terrorism-with-thomas-brzozowski.

38. Landon Schroder, "Domestic Terrorism: Inside the FBI's Joint Terrorism Task Force," *RVA Magazine*, August 1, 2018, rvamag.com/news/domestic-terrorism-inside-the-fbis-joint-terrorism-task-force-in-richmond.html/.

39. There are more than twenty-two different definitions or descriptions of terrorism written into federal law. See Nicholas J. Perry, "The Numerous Federal Legal Definitions of Terrorism: The Problem of Too Many Grails," *Notre Dame Law School Journal of Legislation* (2004): 249, https://scholarship.law.nd.edu/cgi/viewcontent.cgi?article=1127&context=jleg.

40. 18 U.S.C. § 2332b(g)(5).

41. 18 U.S.C. § 113B.

42. 18 U.S.C § 2331(5) (2012).

43. 18 U.S.C § 2331(1) (2012).

44. Schroder, "Domestic Terrorism."

45. 18 U.S.C. § 2332b.

46. 18 U.S.C. § 2332b(g) (2012).

47. See, for example, *United States v. Reumayr*, No. No. 1:99-cr-01338 (D.N.M. Nov. 19, 1999) (Alfreid Heinz Reumayr, a Canadian national, plotted to blow up the Trans-Alaska oil pipeline); *United States v. Nesgoda*, No. 1:03-cr-00019 (M.D. Pa. Jan. 22, 2003) (Edward Nesgoda threatened to blow up a courthouse and was found with a stockpile of weapons including nineteen hand grenades in his house).

48. 18 U.S.C. § 2339B.

49. For an explanation of the designation process, see Michael German and Faiza Patel, "What Does It Mean to Designate the Muslim Brotherhood a Foreign Terrorist Organization?," Just Security, January 26, 2017, www.justsecurity.org/36826/designate-muslim-brotherhood-foreign-terrorist-organization/.

50. Faiza Patel, ed., *Domestic Intelligence: Our Rights and Safety* (New York: Brennan Center for Justice, 2013).

51. Ibid.

52. See, e.g., Antiterrorism and Foreign Mercenary Act, H.R. 5211, 97th Cong. (1982); S. 2255, 97th Cong. (1982); Prohibition Against the Training or Support of Terrorist Organizations, S. 2626, 98th Cong. (1984); H.R. 5613, 98th Cong. (1984); S. 266, 102d Cong. § 2 (1991); H.R. 769, 102d Cong. § 2 (1991). For a further discussion of this history, see Robert M. Chesney, "The Sleeper Scenario: Terrorism-Support Laws and the Demands of Prevention," *Harvard Journal on Legislation* 42, no.1 (2005): 5–18.

53. Chesney, "Sleeper Scenario," 9–10n35.

54. Ibid., 10–11.

55. Ibid., 5–18.

56. Violent Crime Control and Law Enforcement Act of 1994, Pub. L. No. 103-322, sec. 120005, 108 State. 1796, 2022-23 (codified at 18 U.S.C. § 2339A (2012)).

57. Antiterrorism and Effective Death Penalty Act of 1996, Pub. L. No. 104-132, sec. 303, 110 State. 1214, 1250–53 (codified at 18 U.S.C. § 2339B (2012)).

58. See Nancy Hollander, "The Holy Land Foundation: The Collapse of American Justice," *Washington and Lee Journal of Civil Rights and Social Justice* 20, no. 1 (Fall 2013): 45–61.

59. Ibid.

60. *United States v. El-Mezain*, 664 F.3d 467 (5th Cir. 2011), cert. denied, 133 S. Ct. 525 (2012); "Federal Judge Hands Down Sentences in Holy Land Foundation Case," press release, U.S. Department of Justice, May 27, 2010, www.justice.gov/opa/pr/fed eral-judge-hands-downs-sentences-holy-land-foundation-case.

61. Rachel Weiner, "Former Metro Police Officer Sentence to 15 Years in Prison for Supporting ISIS," *Washington Post*, February 23, 2018.

62. Karen Greenberg, ed., *The American Exception—Terrorism Prosecutions in the United States: The ISIS Cases, March 2014—August 2017* (New York: Center on National Security at Fordham Law, 2017), 24, 28.

63. Ibid.

64. Ryan J. Reilly, Ariel Edwards-Levy, and Christopher Mathias, "Americans Are Surprised Domestic Terrorism Isn't a Federal Crime. Most Think It Should Be," *HuffPost*, April 12, 2018, www.huffingtonpost.com/entry/domestic-terrorism-feder al-law-poll-doj-fbi_us_5acd1c78e4b09212968c8907.

65. "Threats to the Homeland: Hearing Before the S. Comm. on Homeland Sec. & Governmental Affairs," 115th Congress, September 27, 2017 (testimony of Christopher Wray, Director, Federal Bureau of Investigation).

66. "What We Investigate: Terrorism," FBI, www.fbi.gov/investigate/terrorism.

67. See "Domestic Terrorism in the Post-9/11 Era," FBI, September 7, 2009, ar chives.fbi.gov/archives/news/stories/2009/september/domterror_090709.

68. FBI, "What We Investigate: Terrorism."

69. Jerome P. Bjelopera, "Domestic Terrorism: An Overview," Congressional Research Service, R44921, August 21, 2017, sgp.fas.org/crs/terror/R44921.pdf.

70. See, e.g., George Michael, "David Lane and the Fourteen Words," *Totalitarian Movements and Political Religions* 3, no. 1 (March 2009): 43–61.

71. Ben Makuch, et al., "Accused Canadian Neo-Nazi Soldier Offered U.S. Terror Group Paramilitary Training," Vice, November 16, 2020, www.vice.com/en/article /xgzdaj/accused-canadian-neo-nazi-soldier-offered-us-terror-group-paramilitary -training.

72. Rick Noack, "Did a U.S. Neo-Nazi Group Inspire the Slaying of British Lawmaker Jo Cox?," *Washington Post*, June 17, 2016.

73. Alexander Clap, "Why American Right-Wingers Are Going to War in Ukraine," Vice, June 19, 2016, www.vice.com/en_us/article/exk4dj/nationalist-interest-v23n4.

74. Department of National Intelligence, "National Strategy for Counterterrorism," The White House, October 2018, 9.

75. "Foreign Terrorist Organizations," U.S. Department of State, n.d., www.state.gov/foreign-terrorist-organizations/.

76. "United States Designates Russian Imperial Movement and Leaders as Global Terrorists," press statement, U.S. Department of State, April 7, 2020, https://2017-2021.state.gov/united-states-designates-russian-imperial-movement-and-leaders-as-global-terrorists/.

77. "The U.S. Labeled a White Supremacist Group as 'Terrorists' for the First Time. It's Less Significant than You Think," *Washington Post*, April 30, 2020.

78. Kristina Sgueglia, "Chattanooga Shootings Inspired by Terrorists, FBI Chief Says," CNN, December 16, 2015, www.cnn.com/2015/12/16/us/chattanooga-shooting-terrorist-inspiration/index.html.

79. Ibid.

80. "Threats to the Homeland: Hearing Before the Senate Committee on Homeland Security andGovernmental Affairs," 115th Congress, October 10, 2018 (testimony of Christopher Wray, Director, Federal Bureau of Investigation), www.hsgac.senate.gov/wp-content/uploads/imo/media/doc/Testimony-Wray-2018-10-10.pdf.

81. U.S. Department of Homeland Security and U.S. Department of Justice, "Executive Order 13780: Protecting the Nation from Foreign Terrorist Entry into the United States, Initial Section 11 Report," 2018, 2.

82. Ellen Nakashima, "Justice Dept. Admits Error but Won't Correct Report Linking Terrorism to Immigration," *Washington Post*, January 3, 2019.

83. This data is derived from the Transactional Records Access Clearinghouse (TRAC), a data gathering and research organization at Syracuse University. TRAC's data is collected through its "systematic and informed use of the Freedom of Information Act (FOIA)." This particular data is based on the results of FOIA requests to the Executive Office of United States Attorneys, which is part of the Department of Justice, including data from FY 2009 through the end of FY 2018. See "About Us," Transactional Records Access Clearinghouse, n.d., https://trac.syr.edu/aboutTRACgeneral.html. See also "Domestic Terrorism Prosecutions Outnumber International," Transactional Records Access Clearinghouse Reports, September 21, 2017, https://trac.syr.edu/tracreports/crim/481/. It must be noted that government auditors have repeatedly

criticized the Justice Department for publishing inaccurate terrorism prosecution data, particularly for overstating terrorism statistics. But the data is useful for comparison purposes because it represents the Justice Department's claimed successes in these categories. See generally U.S. General Accounting Office, "Better Management Oversight and Internal Controls Needed to Ensure Accuracy of Terrorism-Related Statistics," GAO-03-266, 2003; U.S. Department of Justice, Inspector General, "Follow-up Audit of the Department of Justice's Internal Controls Over Reporting of Terrorism-Related Statistics," 12-37, 2012; Michael German and Sara Robinson, "Wrong Priorities on Terror," Brennan Center for Justice, October 31, 2018, 9.

84. Will Carless, "After Jan. 6 Riot, Hundreds of Identifiable People Remain Free. FBI Arrests Could Take Years," *USA Today*, March 2, 2023, www.usatoday.com/story /news/nation/2023/03/02/sedition-hunters-hundreds-jan-6-rioters-pending-fbi-ar rests/11283885002/.

85. Clare Hymes and Cassidy McDonald, "Two Proud Boys Committed 'Crimes of Terrorism' During Capitol Riot, Prosecutors Say," CBS News, February 19, 2021, www.cbsnews.com/news/proud-boys-capitol-riot-terrorism-crimes/; Clare Hymes and Cassidy McDonald, "Oath Keepers Member Committed 'Crime of Terrorism' in Capitol Riot, Prosecutors Say," CBS News, February 24, 2021, www.cbsnews.com /news/oath-keepers-jessica-watkins-crime-of-terrorism/.

86. *United States v. Harpham*, No. 2:11-cr-00042 (E.D. Wash. Mar. 22, 2011).

87. These statutes are 18 U.S.C. § 956 (conspiracy to kill, kidnap, or injure persons or damage property in a foreign country), 18 U.S.C. § 2332 (killing or violence against a U.S. national outside of the United States), 18 U.S.C. § 2339D (receiving military-type training from a foreign terrorist organization), 18 U.S.C. § 2340A (torture committed outside the United States), 18 U.S.C. § 2442 (recruitment or use of child soldiers during active hostilities), and 21 U.S.C. § 960a (drug-related conduct that provides value to foreign terrorist organizations or terrorist persons and groups).

88. *USA v. Wilson*, Docket No. 4:18-cr-03005 (D. Neb. Jan. 17, 2018).

89. See Jessica Robinson, "Man Admits He Attempted to Bomb MLK Parade Because of Race," NPR, September 7, 2011, www.npr.org/templates/story/story.php?story Id=140272486; River Donaghey, "Armed Neo-Nazi Attempted Terror Attack on Amtrak Train, FBI Says," Vice, January 5, 2018, www.vice.com/en_us/article/7xewbg /armed-neo-nazi-attempted-terror-attack-on-amtrak-train-fbi-says-vgtrn.

90. *United States v. Nesgoda*, No. 1:03-cr-00019 (M.D. Pa. Jan. 22, 2003).

91. David Slade, "Rush Man's Bail Doubled in Police Assault," *Morning Call*, April 2, 2002, articles.mcall.com/2002-04-02/news/3413495_1_troopers-bail-judge -lectures.

92. These offenses are 18 U.S.C. § 175, 18 U.S.C. § 175b, 18 U.S.C. § 175c, 18 U.S.C.

§ 229, 18 U.S.C. § 831, 18 U.S.C. § 832, 18 U.S.C. § 2281a, 18 U.S.C. § 2332a, 18 U.S.C. § 2332h, 18 U.S.C. § 2332i, 42 U.S.C. § 2122, 42 U.S.C. § 2283, and 42 U.S.C. § 2284.

93. Peter Bergen, Bruce Hoffman, Michael Hurley, and Erroll Southers, *Jihadist Terrorism: A Threat Assessment*, Bipartisan Police Center, September 2013.

94. Walter Griffin, "Report: 'Dirty Bomb' Parts Found in Slain Man's Home," *Bangor Daily News*, February 10, 2009, www.bangordailynews.com/2009/02/10 /news/state/report-dirty-bomb-parts-found-in-slain-mans-home/.

95. A.C. Thompson, "An Atomwaffen Member Sketched a Map to Take the Neo-Nazis Down. What Path Officials Took Is a Mystery," ProPublica, November 20, 2018, www.propublica.org/article/an-atomwaffen-member-sketched-a-map-to-take -the-neo-nazis-down-what-path-officials-took-is-a-mystery.

96. Paul Harris, "They Seemed Normal But Plotted to Kill Thousands," *Guardian*, March 20, 2004.

97. Trevor Aaronson, "Homegrown Material Support: The Domestic Terrorism Law the Justice Department Forgot," *The Intercept*, March 23, 2019, theintercept .com/2019/03/23/domestic-terrorism-material-support-law/.

98. Criminal Complaint, *United States v. Feight*, No. 1:14-cr-00012 (N.D.N.Y. Jun. 18, 2023), https://storage.courtlistener.com/recap/gov.uscourts.nynd.97017/gov .uscourts.nynd.97017.1.0.pdf.

99. Aaronson, "Homegrown Material Support."

100. Ibid.

101. *United States v. Feight*, No. 1:14-cr-00012 (N.D.N.Y. Jan. 22, 2014); *United States v. Crawford*, No. 1:14-cr-00030 (N.D.N.Y. Jan. 16, 2014); "New York Man Sentenced to 30 Years for Plot to Kill Muslims," press release, U.S. Department of Justice, December 19, 2016, www.justice.gov/opa/pr/new-york-man-sentenced-30-years-plot -kill-muslims.

102. Reilly, Edwards-Levy, and Mathias, "Americans Are Surprised Domestic Terrorism Isn't a Federal Crime."

103. *United States v. Looker*, 168 F.3d 484 (4th Cir. 1998); *United States v. Looker*, No. 1:96-mj-00033 (N.D.W. Va. Oct. 9, 1996); *United States v. Rogers*, No. 1:96-mj-00031 (N.D.W. Va. Oct. 9, 1996); *United States v. Beauregard*, No. 8:99-cr-00410 (M.D. Fla. Dec. 2, 1999); "Militia Head Jailed on Bomb Plot Charges," *Los Angeles Times*, December 9, 1999; *United States v. Cash*, No. 2:01-cr-00169 (E.D.N.Y. Feb. 14, 2001), Robert E. Kessler, "Acquittal in Environmental Terrorism Case," *Newsday*, May 21, 2004, www.brewingtonlaw.com/sites/default/files/pressclips2004/Acquittal-in-Ter rorism-Case-Newsday-052104.pdf; Al Baker, "A Federal Case in Suffolk: Eco-Terrorism or Adolescence in Bloom?," *New York Times*, 2001; *United States v. Feight*, No. 1:14-cr-00012 (N.D.N.Y. Jan. 22, 2014); *United States v. Crawford*, No. 1:14-cr-00030 (N.D.N.Y. Jan. 16, 2014).

104. See *United States v. Looker*, 168 F.3d 484 (4th Cir. 1998); *United States v. Looker*, No. 1:96-mj-00033 (N.D.W. Va. Oct. 9, 1996); *United States v. Rogers*, No. 1:96-mj-00031 (N.D.W. Va. Oct. 9, 1996); Richard A. Serrano, "7 Militiamen Held in Plot to Blow Up FBI Facility," *Los Angeles Times*, October 12, 1996; Dennis Cauchon, "Militiaman Convicted Under Anti-Terrorism Law," *USA Today*, August 26, 1997, www .fpparchive.org/media/documents/war_on_terrorism/Militiaman%20Convicted%20 Under%20Anti-Terrorism%20Law_Dennis%20Cauchon_Aug.%2026,%201997 _USA%20Today.pdf.

105. Matt Zapotosky, "Ohio Woman Who Corresponded with Dylann Roof and Plotted Mass Violence Pleads Guilty to Terror Charge," *Washington Post*, August 29, 2019.

106. Cleve R. Wootson, Jr. and Mark Berman, "A Woman Wanted to Commit a Mass Murder—So She Contacted Dylann Roof, Authorities Say," *Washington Post*, December 11, 2018.

107. Alex Amend and the Network Contagion Research institute, "On GAB, Domestic Terrorist Robert Bowers Engaged with Several Influential Alt-Right Figures," Southern Poverty Law Center, November 1, 2018, www.splcenter.org/hatewatch /2018/11/01/gab-domestic-terrorist-robert-bowers-engaged-several-influen tial-alt-right-figures; A.C. Thompson, "Once Defiant, All Four White Supremacists Charged in Charlottesville Violence Plead Guilty," ProPublica, May 6, 2019, www .propublica.org/article/all-four-white-supremacists-charged-in-charlottesville-vi olence-plead-guilty.

108. Ben Collins, "Pittsburgh Synagogue Shooting Suspect Threatened Jewish Groups, Pushed Migrant Caravan Conspiracies," NBC News, October 27, 2018; Michael Hill, "Synagogue Shooter Was Obsessed with Jewish Refugee Agency," AP, October 30, 2018.

109. "Hate Crime Laws," U.S. Department of Justice, www.justice.gov/crt/hate -crime-laws.

110. "Hate Crime Laws, Explained," Southern Poverty Law Center, September 7, 2022, www.splcenter.org/news/2022/09/07/hate-crime-laws-timeline?gclid=CjwK CAjwq4imBhBQEiwA9Nx1BsDLBpcyWLB1MYbn0GEPYFg5qodlLKP-NE7U 1U4EUHqM29KEb6NTsxoCpY8QAvD_BwE.

111. "Counterterrorism Policy Directive and Policy Guide," Federal Bureau of Investigation, Counterterrorism Division, April 1, 2015, updated November 18, 2015), 15, https://assets.documentcloud.org/documents/3423189/CT-Excerpt.pdf.

112. Alan Neuhauser, "Sessions Calls Charlottesville Attack Domestic Terrorism," *US News and World Report*, August 14, 2017, www.usnews.com/news/national -news/articles/2017-08-14/jeff-sessions-calls-charlottesville-attack-domestic -terrorism.

113. See, e.g., John Sepulvado and Bert Johnson, "Californian Who Helped Lead Charlottesville Used Berkeley as a Test Run," KQED News, August 14, 2017, www .kqed.org/news/11611600/californian-who-helped-organize-charlottesville-protests -used-berkeley-as-a-test-run; Justin Carissimo, "1 Dead, 19 Injured After Car Plows into Protesters in Charlottesville," CBS News, August 12, 2017; Hal Bernton, "Bracing for a Fight, Patriot Prayer's Right-Wing Faithful Head to Portland for Saturday Rally," *Seattle Times*, August 3, 2018, www.seattletimes.com/seattle-news/northwest/brac ing-for-a-fight-patriot-prayers-right-wing-faithful-head-to-portland-for-saturday -rally/; Kelly Weill, "White Supremacist Arrested Days After Dodging a Murder Charge," *Daily Beast*, April 19, 2018, www.thedailybeast.com/white-suprema cist-let-off-for-attempted-murder-arrested-for-domestic-violence.

114. A.C. Thompson, Ali Winston, and Darwin BondGraham, October 19, 2017.

115. 18 U.S.C. § 2101 (2012).

116. Rahima Nasa, "Four Men Arrested Over Unrest During 2017 'Unite the Right' Rally," *Frontline*, PBS, October 2, 2018, www.pbs.org/wgbh/frontline/article /four-men-arrested-over-unrest-during-2017-unite-the-right-rally/.

117. Debra Cassens Weiss, "4th Circuit Strikes Down Part of Federal Anti- Rioting Law But Upholds its Use in Charlottesville Case," *ABA Journal*, August 25, 2020, www.abajournal.com/news/article/4th-circuit-strikes-down-part-of-federal -anti-rioting-law-but-upholds-its-use-in-charlottesville-case.

118. A.C. Thompson, Ali Winston, and Darwin BondGraham, October 19, 2017.

119. A.C. Thompson, "Member of White Supremacist Group Pleads Guilty to As- saulting Protesters at 2017 Rally," ProPublica, November 21, 2018, www.propublica .org/article/member-of-white-supremacist-group-pleads-guilty-to-assaults-at-2017 -rally.

120. A.C. Thompson, "Federal Judge Dismisses Charges Against 3 White Su- premacists," ProPublica, June 4, 2019, www.pbs.org/wgbh/frontline/article/federal -judge-dismisses-charges-against-3-white-supremacists/.

121. Ali Winston, "Jailed, Released, Jailed Again: Whiplash in a Leading Neo- Nazi's Legal Case," *Guardian*, March 2, 2024.

122. *United States v. Robert Boman*, Status Hearing Transcript, United States Dist. Ct. for the Central Dist. Of CA, p. 30, February 21, 2024, https://s3.document cloud.org/documents/24439352/boman-change-of-plea-transcript.pdf.

123. *United States v. Robert Rundo and Robert Boman*, Order Regarding Motions to Dismiss, U.S. Dist. Ct. for the Central Dist. Of CA, p. 2, February 21, 2024, https:// s3.documentcloud.org/documents/24436350/judge-cormac-carney-dismisses-run do-indictment.pdf.

124. Meghann Cuniff, "9th Circuit Stays Future Release Orders for Neo-Nazi Robert Rundo Amid Dismissal Appeal," Legal Affairs and Trials with Meghann Cuniff, March 14, 2024, www.legalaffairsandtrials.com/p/9th-circuit-stays-future-re lease.

125. See, e.g., Antonio J. Califa, "RICO Threatens Civil Liberties," *Vanderbilt Law Review* 43 (1990): 805–46; David B. Filvaroff, "Conspiracy and the First Amendment," *University of Pennsylvania Law Review* 121, no. 2 (1972): 189–253.

126. 18 U.S.C. § 1961 (2012).

127. Tori Richards, "Trials Seek to Crush Aryan Brotherhood," *San Francisco Chronicle*, March 14, 2006, www.sfgate.com/news/article/trials-seek-to-crush-aryan -brotherhood-2502116.php.

128. "Aryan Brotherhood," Southern Poverty Law Center, www.splcenter.org /fighting-hate/extremist-files/group/aryan-brotherhood.

129. Richards, "Trials Seek to Crush Aryan Brotherhood."

130. Amy Clark, "4 Aryan Brotherhood Leaders Convicted," CBS News, July 28, 2006, www.cbsnews.com/news/4-aryan-brotherhood-leaders-convicted/.

131. Associated Press, "Prison Aryans Are Sentenced to Life Terms," *New York Times*, November 22, 2006, www.nytimes.com/2006/11/22/us/22aryan.html

132. "34 Alleged Aryan Brotherhood of Texas Gang Members Indicted on Federal Racketeering Charges," press release, Department of Justice, November 9, 2012, www.justice.gov/opa/pr/34-alleged-aryan-brotherhood-texas-gang-members-indict ed-federal-racketeering-charges.

133. "Eight Individuals with Alleged Ties to the Aryan Circle Arrested and Charged in Connection with Murder," press release, Department of Justice, March 20, 2018, www.justice.gov/opa/pr/eight-individuals-alleged-ties-aryan-circle-arrested -and-charged-connection-murder-0.

134. Juan A. Lozano, "24 Indicted in Probe of White Supremacist Prison Gang," Associated Press, October 15, 2020, www.apnews.com/article/race-and-ethnicity -shootings-indictments-crime-conspiracy-5142d34dfbf08646f4c984acf78e9a01.

135. Will Sommer, "Drug Dealing White Supremacist Gang Ordered Hits on Suspected Informants: Feds," *Daily Beast*, February 12, 2019, www.thedailybeast.com /drug-dealing-arkansas-white-supremacist-gang-ordered-hits-on-suspected-infor mants-feds.

6. A Strategy for Change

1. Committee on Homeland Security and Governmental Affairs, "Planned in Plain Sight: A Review of the Intelligence Failures in Advance of January 6th, 2021," 117th Congress, 2023, 44, www.hsgac.senate.gov/wp-content/uploads/230627_HS GAC-Majority-Report_Jan-6-Intel.pdf.

2. Devlin Barrett and Matt Zapotosky, "FBI Report Warned of 'War' at Capitol, Contradicting Claims There Was No Indication of Looming Violence," *Washington Post*, January 12, 2021.

3. Committee on Homeland Security and Governmental Affairs, "Planned in Plain Sight: A Review of the Intelligence Failures in Advance of January 6th, 2021," 58.

4. Ibid., 29.

5. Ibid., 31.

6. Ibid., 32; Jamelle Bouie, "The Most Frightening Part of the Trump Indictment," *New York Times*, August 4, 2023.

7. Devlin Barrett, "Senate Panel Finds More Pre–Jan. 6 Intelligence Failures by FBI, DHS," *Washington Post*, June 27, 2023.

8. Committee on Homeland Security and Governmental Affairs, "Planned in Plain Sight: A Review of the Intelligence Failures in Advance of January 6th, 2021," 104.

9. Meg Anderson and Nick McMillan, "1,000 People Have Been Charged for the Capitol Riot. Here's Where Their Cases Stand," National Public Radio, March 25, 2023.

10. See Katie Shepherd, "The Feds Say He Is an Extremist Leader Who Directed Rioters. He Also Had Top Secret Clearance and Worked for the FBI, His Lawyer Says," *Washington Post,* February 9, 2021; Mike Giglio, "A Pro-Trump Militant Group Has Recruited Thousands of Police, Soldiers, and Veterans," *Atlantic*, November 2020.

11. Ryan J. Reilly and Ken Dilanian, "FBI Official Was Warned After Jan. 6 That Some in the Bureau Were 'Sympathetic' to the Capitol Rioters," NBC News, October 14, 2022.

12. Paul Abbate, "Internal Concerns," FBI, January 13, 2021, vault.fbi.gov/@@dvpdffiles/f/4/f4d8fa57ba274002a3a5548d7742ec15/normal/dump_7.png.

13. Phillip Bump, "The Other Problem with Having Proud Boys Sympathizers in the D.C. Police," *Washington Post*, May 19, 2023.

14. Jana Winter and Sharon Weinberger, "The FBI's New U.S. Terrorist Threat: 'Black Identity Extremists,'" Yahoo News, October 10, 2017, news.yahoo.com /fbi-identified-domestic-terrorist-threat-154236979.html.

15 "Black Identity Extremists Likely Motivated to Target Law Enforcement Officers," FBI, August 3, 2017, available at www.documentcloud.org/documents/40677 11-BIE-Redacted.html.

16. Domestic Terrorism Prevention Act of 2017, S. 2148, 115th Congress, § 123 (2017).

17. See, for example, Kahron Spearman, "Yes, Of Course the Proud Boys Are White Nationalists, Here's Why," Daily Dot, October 9, 2020. www.dailydot.com/de bug/proud-boys-white-nationalists/; Will Carless, "Proud Boys Splintering After Capitol Riot, Will More Radical Factions Emerge?," *USA Today*, February 12, 2021, www.usatoday.com/story/news/nation/2021/02/12/proud-boys-splintering-after -capitol-riot-revelations-leader/6709017002/.

18. Sen. Richard J. Durbin et al., Letter to Attorney General William P. Barr and

FBI Director Christopher Wray, May 2, 2019, www.durbin.senate.gov/imo/media/doc/Letter%20to%20AG%20Barr%20and%20Director%20Wray%20on%20vio lent%20white%20supremacist%20threat,%205-2-19.pdf.

19. "The Rising Threat of Domestic Terrorism: A Review of the Federal Response to Domestic Terrorism and the Spread of Extremist Content on Social Media," United States Senate Committee on Homeland Security and Government Affairs, 2022.

20. "Strategic Intelligence Assessment and Data on Domestic Terrorism," 2021, report submitted by the FBI and the Department of Homeland Security, 116th Congress, May 2021, 20, www.fbi.gov/file-repository/fbi-dhs-domestic-terrorism-strate gic-report.pdf/view.

21. Ibid.

22. Ibid., 22.

23. *Threats to the Homeland*, 117th Cong. (2022).

24. Ken Klippenstein, "The FBI Is Hunting a New Domestic Terror Threat: Abortion Rights Activists," *The Intercept*, June 15, 2023, https://theintercept.com/2023/06/15/fbi-abortion-domestic-terrorism.

25. Michael German and Emily Hockett, "Standards for Opening an FBI Investigation So Low They Make the Statistic Meaningless," Just Security, May 2, 2017, www.justsecurity.org/40451/standards-opening-fbi-investigation-statistic-mean ingless/.

26. "National Abortion Federation Releases 2021 Violence and Disruption Report," National Abortion Federation, May 19, 2022, prochoice.org/national-abor tion-federation-releases-2021-violence-disruption-report/.

27. "Strategic Intelligence Assessment and Data on Domestic Terrorism," May 2021, 21.

28. "Murder and Extremism in the United States in 2017," Anti-Defamation League, January 12, 2018, www.adl.org/resources/report/murder-and-extremism -united-states-2017.

29. "Murder and Extremism in the United States in 2018," Anti-Defamation League, January 18, 2019, www.adl.org/resources/report/murder-and-extremism -united-states-2018#the-perpetrators.

30. "Murder and Extremism in the United States in 2019," Anti-Defamation League, February 26, 2020, www.adl.org/resources/report/murder-and-extremism -united-states-2019.

31. Federal Bureau of Investigation & Dept. of Homeland Security, *Strategic Intelligence Assessment and Data on Domestic Terrorism*, October 2022, 6, www.fbi.gov /file-repository/fbi-dhs-domestic-terrorism-strategic-report-2022.pdf/view.

32. "Murder and Extremism in the United States in 2020," Anti-Defamation

League, February 1, 2021, www.adl.org/resources/report/murder-and-extremism
-united-states-2020.

33. "Strategic Intelligence Assessment and Data on Domestic Terrorism," Federal
Bureau of Investigation and Department of Homeland Security, June 2023, 10, www
.dni.gov/files/NCTC/documents/news_documents/2023-7-19_FBI-DHS-Strate
gic-Intelligence-Assessment-and-Data-on-Domestic-Terrorism.pdf.

34. "Murder and Extremism in the United States in 2022," Anti-Defamation
League, February 22, 2023, www.adl.org/resources/report/murder-and-extremism
-united-states-2022.

35. *Brennan Center for Justice at New York University Law School v. United States
Department of Justice*, 613 F. Supp. 3d 387 (D.D.C. 2020).

36. *Brennan Center for Justice at New York University Law School v. United States
Department of Justice*, 613 F. Supp. 3d 387, Memorandum Opinion and Order (D.D.C.
2021).

37. Faiza Patel and Charles Kurzman, "The Reality Behind Inflated Domestic Terrorism Prosecution Numbers," Brennan Center for Justice, May 10, 2023, www.bren
nancenter.org/our-work/analysis-opinion/reality-behind-inflated-domestic
-terrorism-prosecution-numbers.

38. Gowri Ramachandran, "How Congress Can Help Protect Election Workers,"
Brennan Center for Justice, March 25, 2022; Sheera Frenkel, "Proud Boys Regroup,
Focusing on School Boards and Town Councils," *New York Times*, December 14,
2021; Sarah D. Wire, "Threats Against Members of Congress Are Skyrocketing. It's
Changing the Job," *Los Angeles Times,* September 20, 2021.

39. Alexander Burns, "Joe Biden's Campaign Announcement Video, Annotated,"
New York Times, April 25, 2019.

40. The White House, "FACT SHEET: National Strategy for Countering Domestic
Terrorism," June 15, 2021, www.whitehouse.gov/briefing-room/statements-re
leases/2021/06/15/fact-sheet-national-strategy-for-countering-domestic-terrorism/.

41. Department of National Intelligence, "National Strategy for Counterterrorism," The White House, October 2018, 9.

42. Ibid., 10.

43. Ibid., 9.

44. Lynn Langton and Madeline Masucci, Bureau of Justice Statistics, "Special
Report: Hate Crime Victimization, 2004–2015," U.S. Department of Justice, June
2017; "Fact Sheet: Justice Department Efforts to Combat Hate Crimes," press release,
U.S. Department of Justice, updated August 7, 2023, www.justice.gov/hatecrimes
/spotlight/combating-hate-crimes.

45. "Confronting Violent White Supremacy (Part II): Adequacy of the Federal
Response, Before the H. Comm. On Oversight and Reform, Subcommittee on Civil

Rights and Civil Liberties," 116th Congress, 2019, 22 (statement of Michael Mc-Garrity, Assistant Director, Counterterrorism Division, FBI, and Calvin Shivers, Deputy Assistant Director, Criminal Investigative Division, FBI).

46. "Guidance Regarding Investigations and Cases Related to Domestic Violent Extremism," Office of the Deputy Attorney General, Department of Justice, March 8, 2021, www.scribd.com/document/507550668/DVE-Guidance#fullscreen&from _embed.

47. Sean Emery, "Blaze Bernstein Murder Case: Samuel Woodward Charged with a Hate Crime, DA Says," *O.C. Register*, August 2, 2018, www.ocregister .com/2018/08/02/samuel-woodward-will-face-a-hate-crime-enhancement-in-the -blaze-bernstein-murder-case/; David K. Li, "White Supremacist Pleads Guilty to Race-Hate Murder of Black Man in New York," NBC News, January 23, 2019; Aimee Green, "Russell Couterier: Racial Bias Murder Conviction Could Be the First in 30 Years in Oregon," *Oregonian*, March 19, 2019, www.oregonlive.com/news/2019/03 /jury-finds-russell-courtier-guilty-of-murdering-black-teen-with-jeep.html.

48. Juan A. Lozano, "24 Indicted in Probe of White Supremacist Prison Gang," ABC News, October 15, 2020; Will Sommer, "Drug Dealing White Supremacist Gang Ordered Hits on Suspected Informants: Feds," *Daily Beast*, February 12, 2019, www .thedailybeast.com/drug-dealing-arkansas-white-supremacist-gang-ordered-hits -on-suspected-informants-feds.

49. Isabel Rosales, "39 Suspected Gang Members Charged in Major Drug, Gun Trafficking Investigation in Pascoe," ABC Action News, November 15, 2018, www .abcactionnews.com/news/region-pasco/39-suspected-gang-members-charged-in -major-drug-gun-trafficking-investigation-in-pasco.

50. "Bank Crime Statistics," FBI, n.d., www.fbi.gov/investigate/violent-crime /bank-robbery/bank-crime-reports.

51. 18 U.S.C. § 2113.

52. 18 U.S.C. § 1951.

53. "Bank Crime Statistics, January 1, 2016—December 31, 2016," FBI, 2017, www .fbi.gov/file-repository/bank-crime-statistics-2016.pdf/view.

7. Focusing the FBI

1. "The Capitol Insurrection: Unexplained Delays and Unanswered Questions (Part II)," Hearing Before the Committee on Oversight and Reform, U.S. House of Reps., 117th Congress, 2021.

2. "Hearing on U.S. Capitol Attack, Day 2 Part 1, Hearing Before the Senate Rules Committee and Homeland Security Committee," 117th Congress, 2021.

3. "The Capitol Insurrection: Unexplained Delays and Unanswered Questions (Part II)."

4. "Capitol Attack: Federal Agencies' Use of Open Source Data and Related Threat Products Prior to January 6, 2021," Government Accountability Office, May 2022.

5. Rachael Levy, "Domestic Terrorism Law Is Debated Anew," *Wall Street Journal*, February 13, 2021; Rachel Oswald, "Lawmakers Divided over Need for New Domestic Terrorism Law," Roll Call, April 19, 2019, rollcall.com/2021/04/19/lawmakers-divided-over-need-for-new-domestic-terrorism-law/; Lucy Tu, "Defining Domestic Terrorism: Does the U.S. Need Criminal Penalties for Domestic Terrorism Events?," *Harvard Political Review*, June 4, 2021, https://harvardpolitics.com/united-states-domestic-terrorism/.

6. Ryan J. Reilly, "U.S. Capitol Attack Is Reshaping the Federal Counterterrorism Budget," *HuffPost*, June 5, 2021, www.huffpost.com/entry/justice-department-fbi-budget-capitol-attack_n_60b7e6c5e4b0169ca9709229.

7. House Select Committee on Appropriations, "Report of the Select Committee on Appropriations for Employees Engaged in the Detection and Prevention of Fraud," H.R. Rep. No. 2320 at 482-491 (1909).

8. "Marcus Garvey," *American Experience*, PBS, n.d., www.pbs.org/wgbh/americanexperience/features/garvey-biography/.

9. Michel duCille, "Black Moses, Red Scare," *Washington Post*, February 12, 1997.

10. "Final Report of the Senate Select Committee to Study Government Operations: Intelligence Activities and the Rights of Americans, Book III," S. Rep. No. 94-755 (1976), 180.

11. Ibid.

12. Tim Weiner, *Enemies: A History of the FBI* (New York: Random House, 2012), 123, 241–48.

13. "Final Report of the Senate Select Committee to Study Government Operations: Intelligence Activities and the Rights of Americans, Book III," 180.

14. "The Federal Bureau of Investigation's Compliance with the Attorney General's Investigative Guidelines," U.S. Department of Justice, Inspector General, 2005, 36.

15. "Hearing on FBI Charter Act of 1979, S. 1612, Before the Select Committee on the Judiciary," 96th Congress, 1980, 14 (statement of Benjamin Civiletti, Attorney General of the United States).

16. Emily Berman, "Domestic Intelligence: New Powers, New Risks," Brennan Center for Justice, January 18, 2011, 21.

17. John Ashcroft, "The Attorney General's Guidelines on General Crimes, Racketeering Enterprise, and Terrorism Enterprise Investigations," Department of Justice, 2002, 22. The Ashcroft guidelines also doubled the duration of "preliminary inquiries"—which could be opened based on an "allegation or information"—to 180 days, with two possible renewals, for an eighteen-month maximum.

18. "FBI Chief: 9/11 Surveillance Taxing Bureau," *Washington Post*, June 6, 2002.

19. "Unleashed and Unaccountable: The FBI's Unchecked Abuse of Authority," ACLU, September 17, 2013, 10. See Trevor Aaronson, "The Informants," *Mother Jones*, September–October, 2011, www.motherjones.com/politics/2011/07/fbi-terrorist-in formants/.

20. Michael B. Mukasey, "The Attorney General Guidelines for Domestic FBI Operations," U.S. Department of Justice, 2008; Berman, "Domestic Intelligence."

21. "ACLU EYE on the FBI: The FBI Is Engaged in Unconstitutional Racial Profiling and Racial 'Mapping,' " ACLU, October 20, 2011, www.aclu.org/documents/aclu -eye-fbi-fbi-engaged-unconstitutional-racial-profiling-and-racial-mapping?redi rect=national-security%2Faclu-eye-fbi-fbi-engaged-unconstitutional-racial-profil ing-and-racial-mapping.

22. Ibid.

23. George Joseph and Murtaza Hussain, "FBI Tracked an Activist Involved with Black Lives Matter as They Traveled Across the U.S., Documents Show," *The Intercept*, March 19, 2018, theintercept.com/2018/03/19/black-lives-matter-fbi-surveillance/.

24. Charlie Savage, "F.B.I. Agents Get Leeway to Push Privacy Bounds," *New York Times*, June 12, 2011; "Letter to Senate Judiciary Committee on New FBI Rules," Brennan Center for Justice, July 27, 2011.

25. Office of the Inspector General, "A Review of the FBI's Investigations of Certain Domestic Advocacy Groups," Department of Justice, 2010, 187. "We also found that FBI case agents sometimes did a poor job of documenting the predication for opening investigations. . . . As a result, in the absence of clear contemporaneous documentation, FBI agents and supervisors sometimes provided the OIG with speculative, after-the-fact rationalizations for their prior decisions to open investigations that we did not find persuasive."

26. Jeremy Scahill and Ryan Deveraux, "Blacklisted: The Secret Government Rulebook for Labelling You a Terrorist," *The Intercept*, July 23, 2014.

27. *Elhady et al. v. Kable et al.*, 993 F.3d 208 (2021), 10 ("Plaintiffs . . . have been forcibly arrested (often at gunpoint) and detained for long hours in front of their family"); Gregory Hoyt, "Busted: Sheriff's Deputy Detains FBI Agent After Being Unable to Confirm His Identity," Law Enforcement Today, March 14, 2020, www.lawenforce menttoday.com/sheriffs-deputy-detains-fbi-agent-after-being-unable-to-confirm -his-identity/.

28. *Terry v. Ohio*, 392 U.S. 1 (1968).

29. Office of the Inspector General, "FBI's Compliance with the Attorney General's Investigative Guidelines," Department of Justice, September 2005, 56.

30. "Guidance for Federal Law Enforcement Agencies Regarding the Use of Race, Ethnicity, Gender, National Origin, Religion, Sexual Orientation, Gender Identity, and Disability," U.S. Department of Justice, May 2023, 2.

31. Ibid., 3. The 2023 guidance updated and improved the Justice Department's racial profiling limits originally issued in 2003 and revised in 2014.

32. "Domestic Investigations and Operations Guide" (henceforth DIOG), FBI, § 4.1.2 ("If a well-founded basis to conduct investigative activity exists, however, and that basis is not solely activity that is protected by the First Amendment or on the race, ethnicity, gender, national origin or religion, sexual orientation, or gender identity of the participants—FBI employees may assess or investigate these activities, subject to other limitations in the AGG-Dom and the DIOG"). See also DIOG § 4.3.2.

33. Michael German, "The FBI Targets a New Generation of Black Activists," Brennan Center for Justice, June 26, 2020, www.brennancenter.org/our-work/analysis-opinion/fbi-targets-new-generation-black-activists; "Leaked FBI Documents Show FBI Developed 'Iron Fist' to Counter 'Black Identity Extremists,' " Rights and Dissent, September 5, 2019, www.rightsanddissent.org/news/leaked-fbi-documents-show-fbi-developed-iron-fist-to-counter-black-identity-extremists/.

34. Christopher Wray, "The Threat Posed by the Chinese Government and the Chinese Communist Party to the Economic and National Security of the United States," Hudson Institute, July 7, 2020, www.hudson.org/national-security-defense/transcript-the-threat-posed-by-the-chinese-government-and-the-chinese-communist-party-to-the-economic-and-national-security-of-the-united-states; "Advocacy Groups, Community Organizations, and Science Associations Urge President-Elect Joe Biden to End Justin Department's 'China Initiative,' " Brennan Center for Justice, January 5, 2021, www.brennancenter.org/our-work/analysis-opinion/advocacy-groups-community-organizations-and-science-associations-urge; Patrick Toomey and Ashley Gorski, "A Chinese American Scientist and His Family Are Battling the FBI's Profiling in Court," American Civil Liberties Union, April 2, 2021, www.aclu.org/news/national-security/a-chinese-american-scientist-and-his-family-are-battling-the-fbis-profiling-in-court/; "Anti-Racial Profiling Project," Asian Americans Advancing Justice, www.advancingjustice-aajc.org/anti-profiling-civil-rights-national-security.

35. Michael German and Alex Liang, "End of Justice Department's 'China Initiative' Brings Little Relief to U.S. Academics," Brennan Center for Justice, March 25, 2022, www.brennancenter.org/our-work/analysis-opinion/end-justice-departments-china-initiative-brings-little-relief-us.

36. Sam Levin, "Revealed: FBI Investigated Civil Rights Group as 'Terrorism' Threat and Viewed KKK as Victims," *Guardian*, February 1, 2019.

37. Ryan Lovelace, "Audit Reveals FBI Rule-Breaking in Probes Involving Politicians, Religious Groups, Media," *Washington Times*, March 11, 2022, www.washingtontimes.com/news/2022/mar/11/fbi-audit-reveals-agents-rule-breaking-investigati/.

38. DIOG § 18.5.5.3 ("The doctrine of misplaced confidence provides that a

person assumes the risk when dealing with a third party that the third party might be a government agent and might breach the person's confidence.").

39. Federal law requires only one party to a conversation to consent to government monitoring of the communication. 18 U.S.C. § 2511(2)(c) (1986).

40. Rachel Levinson-Waldman and Jesus A. Rodriguez, "Guardrails Needed for FBI Access to Social Media Monitoring," Just Security, January 26, 2021, www.justse curity.org/74313/guardrails-needed-for-fbi-access-to-social-media-monitoring/.

41. "A Review of the FBI's Investigations of Certain Domestic Advocacy Groups," U.S. Department of Justice, Inspector General, E2006006, 2010, 186 ("The applicable standard in the Guidelines for predication was low, especially for preliminary inquiries, which required only the 'possibility' of a federal crime. In part as a result of this standard, we found in most cases that the FBI did not violate the Guidelines in opening these investigations").

42. Bruce Schneier, "Why Data Mining Won't Stop Terror," Wired, March 9, 2006, www.wired.com/2006/03/why-data-mining-wont-stop-terror-2/?tw=wn_in dex_2. "Total information awareness" refers to an eponymous government tracking system, first reported by the New York Times in 2002, that was "envisioned to give law enforcement access to private data without suspicion of wrongdoing or a warrant." Congress cut funding to the program in 2003. See, "Total 'Terrorism' Information Awareness (TIA)," Electronic Privacy Information Center, n.d., archive.epic.org/pri vacy/profiling/tia/.

43. Lee Fang, "FBI Expands Ability to Collect Cellphone Location, Monitor Social Media, Recent Contracts Show," The Intercept, June 24, 2020, theintercept .com/2020/06/24/fbi-surveillance-social-media-cellphone-dataminr-venntel; Ken Dilanian, "Why Did the FBI Miss the Threats About Jan. 6 on Social Media?," NBC News, March 8, 2021.

44. Alex Young, "Too Much Information: Ineffective Intelligence Collection," Harvard International Review, August 18, 2019.

45. Nancy Bilyeau, " 'You Can't Solve Domestic Terrorism with an Algorithm,' " The Crime Report, January 20, 2021, thecrimereport.org/2021/01/20/you-cant-solve -domestic-terrorism-with-an-algorithm/; Jenna McLaughlin, "The White House Asked Social Media Companies to Look for Terrorists. Here's Why They'd #Fail," The Intercept, January 20, 2016, theintercept.com/2016/01/20/the-white-house-asked-so cial-media-companies-to-look-for-terrorists-heres-why-theyd-fail; Timme Bisgaard Munk, "100,000 False Positives for Every Real Terrorist: Why Anti-Terror Algorithms Don't Work," First Monday, September 4, 2017, firstmonday.org/ojs/index.php/fm /article/download/7126/6522.

46. Devlin Barrett and Matt Zapotosky, "FBI Report Warned of 'War' at Capitol,

Contradicting Claims There Was No Indication of Looming Violence," *Washington Post*, January 12, 2021.

47. See, e.g., Nathan Bernard, "Maine Spy Agency Spread Far-Right Rumors of BLM Protest Violence," Mainer, July 7, 2020, mainernews.com/maine-spy-agency -spread-far-right-rumors-of-blm-protest-violence/; Adam Goldman, Katie Benner, and Zolan Kanno-Youngs, "How Trump's Focus on Antifa Distracted Attention from the Far-Right Threat," *New York Times*, February 1, 2021.

48. See, e.g., "Examining the January 6 Attack on the U.S. Capitol, Hearing Before the Senate Comittee on Homeland Sec. and Goverment Affairs and Senate Committee on Rules and Administration," 117th Cong., 2021 (testimony of Melissa Smislova, Acting Under Secretary for the Office of Intelligence and Analysis: "Actual intent to carry out violence can be difficult to discern from the angry, hyperbolic— and constitutionally protected—speech and information commonly found on social media and other online platforms"); Internal Review Team, "Report on DHS Administrative Review into I&A Open Source Collection and Dissemination Activities During Civil Unrest, January 6, 2021," Department of Homeland Security, October 2021, 22–24, http://cdn.cnn.com/cnn/2021/images/10/01/internal.review.report.2021 0930.pdf.

49. Matt Mathers, "Four Stabbed and One Shot as Violence Erupts at Pro-Trump Rallies Attended by Far-Right," *Independent*, December 13, 2020, www.independent .co.uk/news/world/americas/trump-protest-stabbing-shooting-election-b1772169 .html; Craig Timberg, "Man Arrested in Olympia, Wash., After Pro-Trump Demonstrations Turn Violent," *Washington Post*, December 13, 2020; Jason Wilson, "Portland Suffers Serious Street Violence as Far Right Return 'Prepared to Fight,' " *Guardian*, August 28, 2020.

50. Sergio Olmos and Conrad Wilson, "At Least 3 Men from Oregon Protest Appear to Have Joined Insurrection at U.S. Capitol," Oregon Public Broadcasting, January 10, 2021, www.opb.org/article/2021/01/10/oregonwashington-protest-insur rection-david-anthony-medina-tim-davis/.

51. Faiza Patel, Rachel Levinson-Waldman, Raya Koreh, and Sophia DenUyl, "Social Media Monitoring," Brennan Center for Justice, May 22, 2019, www.brennancen ter.org/our-work/research-reports/social-media-monitoring.

52. Lee Fang, "Why Was an FBI Joint Terrorism Task Force Tracking a Black Lives Matter Protest?," *The Intercept*, March 12, 2015, theintercept.com/2015/03/12 /fbi-appeared-use-informant-track-black-lives-matter-protest/.

53. Inspector General, "FBI's Compliance with the Attorney General's Investigative Guidelines," Department of Justice, September 2005, 2 ("We found that the FBI's compliance with each of the four Investigative Guidelines differed considerably by Guideline and field office. The most significant problems were failures to comply with

the Confidential Informant Guidelines. For example, we identified one or more Guidelines violations in 87 percent of the confidential informant files we examined"); Inspector General, "Audit of the Federal Bureau of Investigation's Management of Its Confidential Human Source Validation Processes," U.S. Department of Justice, November 2019.

54. Adam Gabbatt, "FBI Agents Caught Cheating on Key Exam," *Guardian*, September 28, 2010.

55. Charlie Savage, "F.B.I. Focusing on Security Over Ordinary Crime," *New York Times*, August 23, 2011.

56. Mukasey, "The Attorney General Guidelines for Domestic FBI Operations," 21.

57. See, generally, "Unleashed and Unaccountable: The FBI's Unchecked Abuse of Authority," ACLU, September 17, 2013 (noting, for instance, that FBI agents have "mapped" the demographic information of Black, Chinese, Muslim, and Russian communities, among others, through their assessment authority and have surveilled Native American environmental protesters participating in nonviolent civil disobedience).

58. See, e.g., Will Arkin, "This Shadow Government Agency Is Scarier than the NSA," Gawker Phase Zero, June 1, 2015, http://phasezero.gawker.com/this-shadow -government-agency-is-scarier-than-the-nsa-1707179377; Justin Elliot and Theodoric Meyer, "Claim on 'Attacks Thwarted' by NSA Spreads Despite Lack of Evidence," ProPublica, October 23, 2013, www.propublica.org/article/claim-on-attacks-thwarted -by-nsa-spreads-despite-lack-of-evidence; McLaughlin, "The White House Asked Social Media Companies to Look for Terrorists."

59. See, e.g., Colleen Rowley, "Inspector General Criticism Doesn't Faze FBI Raids on Midwestern Anti-War Activists," *HuffPost*, September 25, 2010, www.huffpost .com/entry/inspector-general-critici_b_738932; Karen Greenberg, "Liberty Is Security: The Lesson Not Drawn from the Post-9/11 Government Overreach," *HuffPost*, October 2, 2016, www.huffpost.com/entry/liberty-is-security_b_12302898; Jake Laperruque, "Secrets, Surveillance, and Scandals: The War on Terror's Unending Impact on Americans' Private Lives," Project on Government Oversight, September 7, 2021, www.pogo.org/analysis/2021/09/secrets-surveillance-and-scandals-the-war-on -terrors-unending-impact-on-americans-private-lives/.

60. Luke Barr et al., "Missed Signals in 4 Mass Shootings: What Went Wrong?," ABC News, May 20, 2022, https://abcnews.go.com/Politics/missed-signals-mass -shootings-wrong/story?id=84846610.

61. Joseph I. Lieberman and Susan M. Collins, "A Ticking Time Bomb: Counterterrorism Lessons from the U.S. Government's Failure to Prevent the Fort Hood Attack," U.S. Senate Committee on Homeland Security and Governmental Affairs, 2011, 2.

62. William H. Webster, "Final Report of the William H. Webster Commission on the Federal Bureau of Investigation, Counterterrorism Intelligence, and the Events at Fort Hood, Texas, on November 5, 2009," 112th Congress, 2012, 35, 87–88; Mariah Blake, "Internal Documents Reveal How the FBI Blew Fort Hood," *Mother Jones*, August 27, 2013, www.motherjones.com/politics/2013/08/nidal-hasan-anwar-awlaki -emails-fbi-fort-hood/.

63. "Unclassified Summary of Information Handling and Sharing Prior to the April 15, 2013, Boston Marathon Bombings," Offices of the Inspector General, Central Intelligence Agency, Department of Justice, and Department of Homeland Security, April 10, 2014, 7–8.

64. See Josh Gerstein, "FBI Knew Earlier of Boston Bombing Suspect," Politico, June 15, 2013; Deborah Sontag, David M. Herszenhorn, and Serge F. Kovaleski, "A Battered Dream, Then a Violent Path," *New York Times*, April 27, 2013.

65. "Unclassified Summary of Information Handling and Sharing," 9–10.

66. "Statement by Special Agent in Charge Richard DesLauriers Regarding Information Sharing," press release, FBI, May 9, 2013, archives.fbi.gov/archives/boston /press-releases/2013/statement-by-special-agent-in-charge-richard-deslauriers-re garding-information-sharing.

67. "Russia Warned U.S. About Boston Marathon Bomb Suspect Tsarnaev: Report," Reuters, March 25, 2014, www.reuters.com/article/us-usa-explosions-bos ton-congress/russia-warned-u-s-about-boston-marathon-bomb-suspect-tsarnaev -report-idUSBREA2P02Q20140326.

68. Susan Zalkind, "The Murders Before the Marathon," February 25, 2014, *Boston Magazine*, www.bostonmagazine.com/news/2014/02/25/waltham-murders-bos ton-marathon/.

69. Rachel Treisman, "Prosecutors: Proud Boys Gave Leader 'War Powers,' Planned Ahead for Capitol Riot," NPR, March 2, 2021, https:// www.npr.org/2021 /03/02/972895521/prosecutors-proud-boys-gave-leader-war-powers-planned-ahead -for-capitol-riot; David D. Kirkpatrick and Alan Feuer, "Police Shrugged Off the Proud Boys, Until They Attacked the Capitol," *New York Times*, March 14, 2021, updated August 23, 2021, www.nytimes.com/2021/03/14/us/proud-boys-law-enforce ment.html.

70. S. 2355, 116th Congress (2019–2020).

71. "Strengthening Intelligence Oversight," Brennan Center for Justice, May 27– 28, 2015, 9, www.brennancenter.org/sites/default/files/analysis/Strengthening_Intel ligence_Oversight_Conference_Report.pdf.

72. See, e.g., Adam Gabat, "Close to Home: How U.S. Far-Right Terror Flourished in Post-9/11 Focus on Islam," *Guardian*, September 26, 2021; Will Potter, "If Right-Wing Violence Is Up 400%, Why Is the FBI Targeting Environmentalists?," Truthout,

January, 21, 2013, truthout.org/articles/if-right-wing-violence-is-up-400-why-is-the
-fbi-targeting-environmentalists/; Sam Levin, February 1, 2019; Goldman, Benner,
and Kanno-Youngs, "How Trump's Focus on Antifa Distracted Attention from the
Far-Right Threat."

8. A New Approach to Policing Hate Crimes

1. Abené Clayton, " 'Far from Justice': Why Are Nearly Half of US Murders Going
Unsolved?," *Guardian*, February 27, 2023.

2. Jack McDevitt et al., "Improving the Quality and Accuracy of Bias Crime Statistics Nationally: An Assessment of the First Ten Years of Bias Crime Data Collection," Center for Criminal Justice Policy Research and Justice Research and Statistics
Association, July 2000; Bureau of Justice Statistics, "Hate Crime Victimization,
2004–2015," Office of Justice Programs, U.S. Department of Justice, June 2017.

3. Civil Rights Division, "Hate Crime Laws," U.S. Department of Justice, March 7,
2019, www.justice.gov/crt/hate-crime-laws.

4. 28 U.S.C. § 534 (1990).

5. Conn. Gen. Stat. §§ 53a-181j–53a-181j.

6. N.H. Rev. Stat. Ann. § 651:6 (f).

7. Fla. Stat. Ann. §§ 876.17, 876.18.

8. These statutes may be divided into several types, including "penalty enhancement statutes, statutes that define bias crime as new and separate crime, civil rights
statutes that penalize for violating an individual's civil rights, and statutes that allo-
cate resources to the collection and release of hate crime statistics." See Harbani
Ahuja, "The Vicious Cycle of Hate: Systemic Flaws in Hate Crime Documentation in
the United States and the Impact on Minority Communities," *Cardozo Law Review*
37 (2016): 1887–88 (discussing the variation within statutes).

9. N.J. Rev. Stat. 2C:16-1(a)(3).

10. *State v. Pomianek*, 429 N.J. Super. 339, 343, 358-59 (App. Div. 2013).

11. *State v. Pomianek*, 221 N.J. 66 (N.J. 2015).

12. Ariel Hart, "Georgia Court Strikes Down Law on Hate," *New York Times*,
October 26, 2004.

13. Erin Donahue, "Prosecutors in Spa Shootings Could Be First to Weigh Georgia's New Hate Crimes Law," CBS News, March 24, 2021, www.cbsnews.com/news
/atlanta-spa-shootings-prosecutors-georgia-new-hate-crime-law/.

14. Jeffrey Collins, "South Carolina's Push to Be Next-to-Last State with Hate
Crimes Law Stalls Again," Associated Press, February 28, 2024, https://apnews.com
/article/hate-crimes-south-carolina-wyoming-a680e606857286045edb63fea8
9d9a3c.

15. Russell Contreras, "DOJ: More Police Departments Are Declining to Report

Hate Crimes," *Axios*, March 19, 2022, www.axios.com/2022/03/19/doj-police-depart-ments-decline-report-hate-crimes.

16. Civil Rights Program, "Policy Implementation Guide," FBI, October 18, 2010, www.aclu.org/sites/default/files/field_document/ACLURM003541.pdf.

17. "Crime/Law Enforcement Stats (Uniform Crime Reporting Program)," FBI, n.d., www.fbi.gov/how-we-can-help-you/more-fbi-services-and-information/ucr.

18. In 2019, 15,588 law enforcement agencies participated in UCR hate crime reporting, out of approximately 18,000 law enforcement agencies nationwide. The vast majority of those participating reported zero hate crimes (86.1 percent). See Criminal Justice Information Services Division, "Hate Crimes by Jurisdiction, 2019," FBI Uniform Crime Report, https://ucr.fbi.gov/hate-crime/2019/topic-pages/jurisdiction.

19. McDevitt et al., "Improving the Quality and Accuracy of Bias Crime Statistics Nationally," 13; Criminal Justice Information Services Division, "Hate Crimes by Jurisdiction, 2019," FBI: Uniform Crime Report, https://ucr.fbi.gov/hate-crime/2019/topic-pages/jurisdiction; Ibid.

20. See "Table 2: Incidents, Offenses, Victims, and Known Offenders 2019," FBI Uniform Crime Report, n.d., https://ucr.fbi.gov/hate-crime/2019/topic-pages/tables/table-2.xls.

21. Ibid.

22. Grace Kena and Alexandra Thompson, "Hate Crime Victimization, 2005–2019," U.S. Department of Justice, September 2021, 3, https://bjs.ojp.gov/sites/g/files/xyckuh236/files/media/document/hcv0519_1.pdf.

23. Ibid., 4.

24. "FBI Updates the Hate Crime Training Manual," U.S. Department of Justice, www.justice.gov/hatecrimes/spotlight/FBI-Hate-Crimes-Training.

25. Criminal Justice Information Services Division, "Supplemental Hate Crime Statistics, 2021," FBI, U.S. Department of Justice, March 2023, le.fbi.gov/file-reposi tory/supplemental-hate-crime-statistics-2021.pdf/view.

26. Gloria Oladipo, "FBI Report Shows Stark Increase in U.S. Hate Crimes and Drop in Violent Crime," *Guardian*, October 16, 2023.

27. McDevitt et al., "Improving the Quality and Accuracy of Bias Crime Statistics Nationally," 5, 9–11.

28. "Deputy Attorney General Rod J. Rosenstein Delivers Remarks at a Law Enforcement Roundtable Regarding Improving Identification and Reporting of Hate Crimes," U.S. Department of Justice, October 29, 2018, www.justice.gov/opa/speech/deputy-attorney-general-rod-j-rosenstein-delivers-remarks-law-enforcement-roundtable.

29. See, generally, German Lopez, "Why It's So Hard to Prosecute a Hate Crime,"

Vox, May 23, 2017, www.vox.com/identities/2017/4/10/15183902/hate-crime-trump-law (highlighting law enforcement reticence to label crimes "hate crimes").

30. Ryan Katz, "Hate Crime Law Results in Few Convictions and Lots of Disappointment," ProPublica, April 10, 2017, www.propublica.org/article/hate-crime-law-results-in-few-convictions-and-lots-of-disappointment.

31. See McDevitt et al., "Improving the Quality of Bias Crime Statistics," 108–9.

32. Ibid., 37.

33. See William B. Rubenstein, "The Real Story of U.S. Hate Crime Statistics: An Empirical Analysis," *Tulane Law Review* 78 (2004): 1213, 1219.

34. "Police Violence Report 2017," Mapping Police Violence, 2022.

35. Frank Edwards et al., "Risk of Police-Involved Death by Race/Ethnicity and Place, United States, 2012–2018," *American Journal of Public Health* 108 (2018): 1241, 1243–44. See also Scottie Andrew, "Police Are Three Times More Likely to Kill Black Men, Study Finds: 'Not a Problem Confined to a Single Region,'" *Newsweek*, July 23, 2018, www.newsweek.com/black-men-three-times-likely-be-killed-police-1037922.

36. Jon Swaine et al., "Black Americans Killed by Police Twice as Likely to Be Unarmed as White People," *Guardian*, June 1, 2015.

37. International Human Rights Clinic, "Lack of Accountability for Police Killings of Minorities and Other Vulnerable Populations in the United States, Before the Inter-American Commission on Human Rights," Santa Clara University, December 7, 2017.

38. Sam Levin, " 'It Never Stops': Killings by US Police Reach Record High in 2022," *Guardian*, January 6, 20203, www.theguardian.com/us-news/2023/jan/06/us-police-killings-record-number-2022.

39. 959 F. Supp. 2d 540 (2013). See also Editorial Board, "Racial Discrimination in Stop and Frisk," *New York Times*, August 12, 2013.

40. Editorial Board, "Racial Discrimination in Stop and Frisk."

41. Ibid.

42. See, generally, Aziz Z. Huq, "The Consequences of Disparate Policing: Evaluating Stop and Frisk as a Modality of Urban Policing," *Minnesota Law Review* 101 (2017): 2397.

43. Suhail Bhat, "NYPD Quality-of-Life Crackdown Sends Thousands to Criminal Court, Undoing Landmark Reforms," *The City*, September 12, 2023.

44. Elizabeth Davis et al., "Special Report: Contacts Between Police and the Public, 2015," Bureau of Justice Statistics, October 2018, 16–17.

45. See, for example, Jonathan Mummolo, "Militarization Fails to Enhance Police Safety or Reduce Crime but May Harm Police Reputation," *Proceedings of the National Academy of Sciences* 115 (2018): 9181.

46. See Jasmine Sankofa, "Mapping the Blank: Centering Black Women's Vulnerability to Police Sexual Violence to Upend Mainstream Police Reform," *Howard Law Journal* 59 (2016): 651, 665, 668–69; see also Mary S. Jacobs, "The Violent State: Black Women's Invisible Struggle Against Police Violence," *William & Mary Journal of Women and Law* 24 (2017): 39.

47. See Tom Jackman, "When Cops Are Suspects, Feds Often Take Years to File Charges," *Washington Post*, October 23, 2018.

48. See Alice Speri, "The FBI Has Quietly Investigated White Supremacist Infiltration of Law Enforcement," *The Intercept*, January 31, 2017, theintercept.com /2017/01/31/the-fbi-has-quietly-investigated-white-supremacist-infiltration-of -law-enforcement/.

49. Brian Bowling and Andrew Conte, "Trib. Investigation: Cops Often Let Off Hook for Civil Rights Complaints," TribLive, March 12, 2016, archive.triblive.com /news/nation/trib-investigation-cops-often-let-off-hook-for-civil-rights-complaints/.

50. See Lisa Rose, "This Is the First Police Officer Charged with a Federal Hate Crime in at Least 10 Years," CNN, December 21, 2018.

51. Alexia Cooper and Erica L. Smith, "Homicide Trends in the United States, 1980–2008, Annual Rates for 2009 and 2010," Bureau of Justice Statistics, November 2011.

52. Ibid., 31.

53. Aamer Madhani, "Unsolved Murders: Chicago, Other Big Cities Struggle; Murder Rate a 'National Disaster,' " *USA Today*, August 10, 2018, www.usatoday.com /story/news/2018/08/10/u-s-homicide-clearance-rate-crisis/951681002/.

54. "Table 25: Percent of Offenses Cleared by Arrest or Exceptional Means by Population Group 2017," on file with FBI: Uniform Crime Report, 2017, ucr.fbi.gov /crime-in-the.u.s/2017/crime-in-the-u.s.-2017/topic-pages/tables/table-25.

55. Weihua Li and Jamiles Lartey, "As Murders Spiked, Police Solved About Half in 2020," Marshall Project, January 12, 2022, www.themarshallproject.org/2022 /01/12/as-murders-spiked-police-solved-about-half-in-2020.

56. Washington Post Investigative Team, "Murder with Impunity," *Washington Post*, January 7, 2019.

57. Ibid.

58. Sarah Ryley et al., "Tale of Two Cities: As Murders Hit Record Low in NYC, a Mountain of Cases Languishes in Outer Boroughs as Cops Focus More Manpower," New York *Daily News*, January 5, 2014, www.nydailynews.com/new-york/nyc-crime /forgotten-record-murder-rate-cases-unsolved-article-1.1566572.

59. Ibid.

60. Washington Post Investigative Team, "Murder with Impunity."

61. "Past Summary Ledgers," Gun Violence Archives, n.d., www.gunviolencear chive.org/past-tolls. (these numbers exclude the roughly 22,000 annual gun suicides).

62. Sarah Ryley et al., "Shoot Someone in a Major US City, and Odds Are You'll Get Away with It," BuzzFeed News, January 24, 2019, www.buzzfeednews.com/arti cle/sarahryley/police-unsolved-shootings.

63. Criminal Justice Information Services Division, "Uniform Crime Report, 2017 Crime in the United States: Rape," FBI Uniform Crime Report, 2018, 1, ucr.fbi .gov/crime-in-the-u.s/2017/crime-in-the.s.-2017/topic-pages/rape#:~:text=Over view,See%20Tables%201%20and%201A); Criminal Justice Information Services Di vision, "Table 7: Offense Analysis United States, 2013–2017," FBI Uniform Crime Re port, 2018, ucr.fbi.gov/crime-in-the-u.s/2017/crime-in-the-u.s.-2017/tables/table-7.

64. Criminal Justice Information Services Division, "Table 25: Percent of Of fenses Cleared by Arrest or Exceptional Means by Population Group, 2017," FBI Uni form Crime Report, June 7, 2019, ucr.fbi.gov/crime-in-the-u.s/2017/crime-in-the -u.s.-2017/topic-pages/tables/table-25.

65. Alexandra Svokos, "Massive Backlog of Untested Rape Kits Is 'A Public Safety Issue' That May Be Letting Offenders Slip Away, Experts Warn," ABC News, Janu ary 26, 2019.

66. See, for example, Dawn Beichner and Cassia Spohn, "Modeling the Effects of Victim Behavior and Moral Character on Prosecutors' Charging Decisions in Sexual Assault Cases," *Violence and Victims* 27 (2012): 3, 12; Cassia Spohn and David Holle ran, "Prosecuting Sexual Assault: A Comparison of Charging Decisions in Sexual Assault Cases Involving Strangers, Acquaintances, and Intimate Partners," *Justice Quarterly* 18: (2001), 651, 673.

67. U.S. Government Accounting Office, "Declinations of Indian Country Crim inal Matters," U.S. Department of Justice, 2012, 3–4. See also "Gender Based Violence and Intersecting Challenges Impacting Native American and Alaskan Village Com munities," VAW Net, September 1, 2016, vawnet.org/sc/gender-based-violence-and -intersecting-challenges-impacting-native-american-alaskan-village.

68. John Saul, "Untested Rape Kits Hid 817 Serial Predators in Detroit, Tens of Thousands More Concealed in Backlog Across U.S.," *Newsweek*, December 19, 2017, www.newsweek.com/rape-kit-untested-sexual-assault-serial-rapist-detroit-prosecu tor-nation-752440.

69. Scott Simon, "Detroit Kit Tests Indicate Hundreds of Serial Rapists," *Weekend Edition*, National Public Radio, January 13, 2018.

70. Lynn Langton and Madeline Masucci, "Special Report: Hate Crime Victim ization, 2004–2015," U.S. Department of Justice, June 2017, 5.

71. National Institute of Justice, "Five Things About Deterrence," Department of

Justice, 2016. See also Valerie Wright, "Deterrence in Criminal Justice," Sentencing Project (2010).

72. Langton and Masucci, "Hate Crime Victimization," 2 (charting approximately 250,000 annual victim reports of hate crimes between 2004–2015); McDevitt et al., "Improving the Quality of Bias Crime Statistics," 38–40 (describing hate crime reporting from 1991 to 1998); Kena and Thompson, "Hate Crime Victimization, 2005–2019" (describing victim reporting from 2005 to 2019).

73. See, for example, Ryan Katz, "Hate Crime Law Results in Few Convictions and Lots of Disappointment," ProPublica, April 10, 2017, www.propublica.org/article /hate-crime-law-results-in-few-convictions-and-lots-of-disappointment.

74. Neil Chakraborti, "Mind the Gap! Making Stronger Connections Between Hate Crime Policy and Scholarship," *Criminal Justice and Policy Review* 27 (2016): 577, 583. See also "White Supremacist Prison Gangs in the United States," Anti-Defamation League, 2016 (documenting the rise and presence of white supremacist gangs in prisons and jails across all fifty states); Alex Tatusian, "Prison Is a Real-Life Example of the World White Supremacists Want," Marshall Project, August 24, 2017, www.themarshallproject.org/2017/08/24/prison-is-a-real-life-example-of-the-world -white-supremacists-want.

75. Adam Neufeld et al., "White Supremacist Prison Gangs: 2022 Assessment," Center for Extremism, Anti-Defamation League, October 2022.

76. See Michael German and Emmanuel Mauleón, "Fighting Far-Right Violence and Hate Crimes," Brennan Center for Justice, July 1, 2019, 42, www.brennancenter .org/our-work/research-reports/fighting-far-right-violence-and-hate-crimes.

77. Criminal Justice Information Services Division, "Table 1: Incidents, Offenses, Victims, and Known Offenders by Bias Motivation, 2019," FBI Uniform Crime Report, https://ucr.fbi.gov/hate-crime/2019/topic-pages/tables/table-1.xls.

78. Ibid.

79. Criminal Justice Information Services Division, "Hate Crime in the United States Incident Analysis, 2021 and 2022," Federal Bureau of Investigation Crime Data Explorer, https://cde.ucr.cjis.gov/LATEST/webapp/#/pages/explorer/crime/hate-crime.

80. Eric Jensen et al., "The Chance That Two People Chosen at Random Are of Different Race and Ethnicity Has Increased Since 2010," U.S. Census Bureau, August 12, 2021, www.census.gov/library/stories/2021/08/2020-united-states-popula tion-more-racially-ethnically-diverse-than-2010.html; Criminal Justice Information Services Division, "Hate Crime in the United States Incident Analysis."

81. Compare Caroline Wolf Harlow, "Hate Crime Reported by Victims and Police," NCJ 209911, U.S. Department of Justice, November 2005, 11 (finding that between the years 2000 and 2003, youth aged seventeen and under accounted for approximately 21 percent of all offenders, with offenders between the ages of eighteen

and twenty constituting another 6.2 percent). See also Dr. James J. Nolan III et al., "NIBRS Hate Crimes 1995–2000: Juvenile Victims and Offenders," West Virginia University, 2004.

82. Criminal Justice Information Services Division, "Table 9: Known Offenders, 2022," Federal Bureau of Investigation Crime Data Explorer, 2023, https://cde.ucr.cjis.gov/LATEST/webapp/#.

83. Jordan Blair Woods, "Addressing Youth Bias Crime," *UCLA Law Review* 56 (2009): 1899, 1902.

84. See, for example, Kathy Dobie, "Investing Hate: Inside New York City's Task Force on Bias," *Harper's Magazine*, December 2010, harpers.org/archive/2018/12/new-york-city-police-department-hate-crimes-task-force/; Nickie D. Phillips, "The Prosecution of Hate Crimes: The Limitations of the Hate Crimes Typology," *Journal of Interpersonal Violence* 24 (2009): 883, 897, 900, 902.

85. William K. Raschbaum and Ali Winston, "Ilana Glazer Event at Synagogue Is Cancelled After Anti-Semitic Graffiti Is Found," *New York Times*, November 2, 2018, www.nytimes.com/2018/11/02/nyregion/broad-city-jewish-synagogue-anti-semitism.html.

86. Jeffrey C. Mays, "Man's Struggles with Mental Illness and Addiction Preceded Hate Crime Charges, Friends Say," *New York Times*, November 3, 2018, www.nytimes.com/2018/11/03/nyregion/anti-semitic-hate-crime-vandalism.html.

87. Emily Palmer, "After Years in Foster Care, Intern 'Adopted' by City Hall Catches a Break," *New York Times*, December 17, 2017, www.nytimes.com/2017/12/14/nyregion/after-years-in-foster-care-intern-adopted-by-city-hall-catches-a-break.html.

88. Ibid.

89. Ibid.

90. Mays, "Man's Struggles with Mental Illness."

91. Ruth Weissmann and Laura Italiano, " 'Kill All Jews' Graffiti Suspect Had a Dark Online Alter-Ego," *New York Post*, November 3, 2018, nypost.com/2018/11/03/kill-all-jews-graffiti-suspect-had-a-dark-online-alter-ego/.

92. Larry Celona, "Suspect Arrested for Scrawling 'Kill All Jews' in Synagogue," *New York Post*, November 2, 2018, nypost.com/2018/11/02/suspect-arrested-for-scrawling-kill-all-jews-in-synagogue/.

93. Rob Frehse and Augusta Anthony, "Brooklyn Man Faces 4 Hate Crime Charges After Synagogue Is Defaced with Anti-Semitic Messages, Fires Set," CNN, November 5, 2018.

94. "Learn About Hate Crimes," U.S. Department of Justice, n.d., www.justice.gov/hatecrimes/learn-about-hate-crimes.

95. Chakraborti, "Mind the Gap!," 581.

96. In a 2019 Brennan Center review of statutes addressing hate crimes in all fifty states, U.S. territories, and the District of Columbia, three states—Colorado, Illinois, and New Jersey—were identified to have hate crime statutes that included varying alternatives to address communal harms or restorative justice recommendations, including mediated victim/offender counseling, community service within the communities affected by the hate crimes, or establishing educational programs, and training on diversity and inclusion. See Colo. Rev. Stat. § 18-9-121 (2013) (including restorative justice counseling if requested by the victim); Ill. Comp. Stat. 4070/1-99 (2007) (establishing a commission on hate crimes and discrimination with the purpose of eradicating hate violence through education and community engagement); N.J. Rev. Stat. §52-9DD-9 (2013) (tasking the New Jersey Human Relations Counsel with addressing community harms from hate crimes).

97. Ill. Comp. Stat. 20 § 4070 et seq.; Ill. Comp. Stat. 20 § 4070/15 (1).

98. Ill. Comp. Stat. 20 §§ 4070/15 (2)–(4). See Neil Chakraborti, "Responding to Hate Crime: Escalating Problems, Continued Failings," *Criminology and Criminal Justice* 18 (2017): 387, 393.

99. See "Attorney General Madigan Urges Governor to Restore State Hate Crimes Commission," press release, Illinois Attorney General, March 8, 2017, ag.state.il.us /pressroom/2017_03/20170308b.html (quoting Madigan as saying "appointing members to this commission is a critical responsibility that the governor has ignored for too long").

100. "Report of Recommendations of the Illinois Commission on Discrimination and Hate Crimes," Illinois Commission on Discrimination and Hate Crimes, 2022, https://cdhc.illinois.gov/content/dam/soi/en/web/cdhc/documents/8.5.2022-%20Re port%20of%20Recommendations%20of%20the%20Illinois%20Commission%20 on%20Discrimination%20and%20Hate%20Crimes.pdf.

101. "Xenophobia, Islamophobia, and Anti-Semitism in NYC Leading Up to and Following the 2016 Presidential Election," New York City Commission on Human Rights, 2018, 16–18, www.nyc.gov/assets/cchr/downloads/pdf/publications/MASAJS _Report.pdf.

102. Ibid., 12.

103. Ibid., 17.

104. See, e.g., Chakraborti, "Mind the Gap!," 538 (finding that these preferences are shared by victims of violent and nonviolent attacks, as well as victims from different communities, ages, and backgrounds).

105. Lode Walgrave, "Restorative Justice for Juveniles: Just a Technique or a Fully Fledged Alternative?," *Howard Journal of Crime and Justice* 34 (1995): 228, 230.

106. Jenny Paterson et al., "The Sussex Hate Crime Project," University of Sussex, January 2018, 10, www.sussex.ac.uk/webteam/gateway/file.php?name=sussex-hate -crime-project-report.pdf&site=430.

107. Ibid., 37.

108. Pete Wallis, *Understanding Restorative Justice: How Empathy Can Close the Gap Created by Crime* (Bristol: Policy Press, 2014), 4.

9. Policing the Police

1. "Report of the Independent Commission on the Los Angeles Police Department," Christopher Independent Commission, July 1991, i.

2. Anjuli Sastry Krbechek and Karen Grigsby Bates, "When LA Erupted in Anger: A Look Back at the Rodney King Riots," National Public Radio, April 26, 2017, www.npr.org/2017/04/26/524744989/when-la-erupted-in-anger-a-look-back-at-the-rodney-king-riots.

3. See, for example, Jim Newton, "Church Thanks Agents Who Thwarted Attack," *Los Angeles Times*, January 17, 1994.

4. "Report of the Independent Commission on the Los Angeles Police Department," x.

5. Ibid., 99.

6. Ibid., 73.

7. Ibid., iv.

8. Lauren-Brooke Eisen, "The 1994 Crime Bill and Beyond: How Federal Funding Shapes the Criminal Justice System," Brennan Center for Justice, September 9, 2019, www.brennancenter.org/our-work/analysis-opinion/1994-crime-bill-and-beyond-how-federal-funding-shapes-criminal-justice.

9. Ibid.; Ranya Shannon, "3 Ways the 1994 Crime Bill Continues to Hurt Communities of Color," Center for American Progress, May 10, 2019, www.amer icanprogress.org/article/3-ways-1994-crime-bill-continues-hurt-communities -color/.

10. Seth Stoughton, "Law Enforcement's 'Warrior' Problem," *Harvard Law Review* 128, no. 6 (April 2015).

11. Civil Rights Division, "Investigation of the Ferguson Police Department," U.S. Department of Justice, March 4, 2015.

12. Christopher E. Smooth, "Blue Lives Matter Versus Black Lives Matter: Beneficial Social Policies as the Path Away from Punitive Rhetoric and Harm," *Vermont Law Review* 44, no. 3 (2020).

13. See, for example, Josh Koehn, "Blue Lives Matter, Police Union Miss Key Moment for Change by Attacking Black Lives Matter," San Jose Inside, July 25, 2016, www.sanjoseinside.com/opinion/blue-lives-matter-sj-police-union-miss-key-mo ment-for-change-by-attacking-black-lives-matter/; Matthew Guariglia, " 'Blue Lives' Do Matter—That's the Problem," *Washington Post*, November 30, 2017.

14. "Executive Order—Establishment of the President's Task Force on 21st

Century Policing," press release, Office of the Press Secretary, the Obama White House, December 18, 2014, obamawhitehouse.archives.gov/the-press-office/2014/12 /18/executive-order-establishment-presidents-task-force-21st-century-policin.

15. "Final Report of the President's Task Force on 21st Century Policing," Office of Community Oriented Policing Services, May 2015.

16. Ibid.

17. Taimi Castle, " 'Cops and the Klan': Police Disavowal of Risk and Minimization of Threat from the Far-Right," *Critical Criminology* 29 (February 15, 2020): 215–35.

18. Michael German written testimony, "Hearing: The Right of the People Peaceably to Assemble: Protecting Speech by Stopping Anarchist Violence Before the U.S. Senate Committee on the Judiciary, Subcommittee on the Constitution," August 4, 2020, www.brennancenter.org/our-work/research-reports/testimony-us-senate-com mittee-judiciary-subcommittee-constitution.

19. Yacob Reyes, "U.S. Rep. Jim Jordan's List of Cities That 'Defunded' Police Doesn't Account for Reversals," Politifact, February 1, 2023, www.politifact.com/fact checks/2023/feb/01/jim-jordan/us-rep-jim-jordans-list-cities-defunded-police-doe/.

20. Grace Manthey, Frank Esposito, and Amanda Hernandez, "Despite 'Defunding' Claims, Police Funding Has Increased in Many US Cities," ABC News, October 16, 2022; Fola Akinnibi, Sarah Holder, and Christopher Cannon, "Cities Say They Want to Defund the Police. Their Budgets Say Otherwise," Bloomberg, January 12, 2021, www.bloomberg.com/graphics/2021-city-budget-police-funding/.

21. Weihua Li and Jamiles Lartey, "As Murders Spiked, Police Solved About Half in 2020," Marshall Project, January 12, 2022, www.themarshallproject.org/2022 /01/12/as-murders-spiked-police-solved-about-half-in-2020.

22. Shima Baughman, "Police Solve Just 2% of All Major Crimes," The Conversation, August 20, 2020, theconversation.com/police-solve-just-2-of-all-major-crimes -143878; Hassan Kanu, "Police Are Not Primarily Crime Fighters, According to the Data," Reuters, November 2, 2022, www.reuters.com/legal/government/police-are -not-primarily-crime-fighters-according-data-2022-11-02/.

23. Christopher M. Sullivan and Zachary P. O'Keeffe, "Evidence that Curtailing Proactive Policing Can Reduce Major Crime," *Nature Human Behavior* 1 (September 25, 2017): 730–37.

24. Theo Keith, "Minneapolis, St. Paul End Tumultuous 2021 by Increasing Police Spending," Fox 9, December 10, 2021, www.fox9.com/news/minneapolis-st-paul -end-tumultuous-2021-by-increasing-police-spending.

25. Shaila Dewan, " 'Re-Fund the Police'? Why It Might Not Reduce Crime," *New York Times*, November 8, 2021.

26. Jacqueline Alemany, Josh Dawsey, and Carol D. Leonnig, "Jan. 6 Panel

Staffers Angry at Cheney for Focusing So Much of Report on Trump," *Washington Post*, November 23, 2022.

27. Jon Ward, "FBI Director Wray Calls Republican Charges of FBI Bias 'Insane,' " Yahoo News, July 12, 2023, news.yahoo.com/fbi-director-wray-calls-republican -charges-of-fbi-bias-insane-221708155.html.

28. Adam Goldman and Alan Feuer, "Republicans Step Up Attacks on F.B.I. as It Investigates Trump," *New York Times*, December 28, 2022.

29. Tom Dreisbach, "An Attempted Attack on an FBI Office Raises Concerns About Violent Far-Right Rhetoric," NPR, August 12, 2022, www.npr.org /2022/08/12/1117275044/an-attempted-attack-on-an-fbi-office-raises-concerns -about-violent-far-right-rhe.

30. Neil MacFarquhar, "Efforts to Weed Out Extremists in Law Enforcement Meet Resistance," *New York Times*, May 11, 2021, www.nytimes.com/2021/05/11/us /police-extremists-state-laws.html.

31. Janelle Griffith, " 'He Choked Me Out': Others Detail Allegations of Abuse by Officer Who Knelt on George Floyd," NBC News, March 3, 2021, www.nbcnews.com/news /us-news/he-choked-me-out-others-detail-allegations-abuse-officer-who-n1259207.

32. Dakin Andone, "The Minneapolis Police Officer Who Knelt on George Floyd's Neck Had 18 Previous Complaints Against Him, Police Department Says," CNN, May 29, 2020, www.cnn.com/2020/05/28/us/minneapolis-officer-complaints-george -floyd/index.html.

33. Jonah E. Bromwich, "Court Vindicates Black Officer for Stopping Colleague's Chokehold," *New York Times*, April 13, 2021, www.nytimes.com/2021/04/13/nyre gion/cariol-horne-police-chokehold.html.

34. Mike Desmond et al., "A Month After Passage, Mayor Brown Signs Cariol's Law," WBFO-FM, October 28, 2020, www.wbfo.org/local/2020-10-28/a-month-after -passage-mayor-brown-signs-cariols-law.

35. Neil MacFarquhar, "Police Forces Have Long Tried to Weed Out Extremists in the Ranks. Then Came the Capitol Riot," *New York Times*, February 16, 2021, www .nytimes.com/2021/02/16/us/police-extremists-capitol-riot.html.

36. Vida B. Johnson, "KKK in the PD: White Supremacist Police and What to Do About It," *Lewis & Clark Law Review* 23, no. 2 (April 1, 2019): 205, 234, https://law .lclark.edu/live/files/28080-lcb231article2johnsonpdf.

37. Ibid., 226.

38. Law Enforcement Policy Center, "Standards of Conduct," International Association of Chiefs of Police, July 2019, 4, www.theiacp.org/sites/default/files/2020-06 /Standards%20of%20Conduct%20June%202020.pdf.

39. Criminal Justice Information Services, "National Use-of-Force Data Collec-

tion," FBI, www.fbi.gov/how-we-can-help-you/more-fbi-services-and-information /ucr/use-of-force.

40. Amir Vera, "There Is a Database Whose Mission Is to Stop Problematic Police Officers from Hopping Between Departments. But Many Agencies Don't Know It Exists," CNN, May 16, 2021, https://edition.cnn.com/2021/05/16/us/police-national-de certification-index-database/index.html&mkt=en-us.

41. See Taryn Merkl, "Protecting Against Police Brutality and Official Miscondut," Brennan Center for Justice, April 29, 2021, www.brennancenter.org/sites/de fault/files/2021-04/BCJ-12 6%20CivilRights.pdf.

42. David Shultz, "The $2 Billion-Plus Price of Injustice: A Methodological Map for Police Reform in the George Floyd Era," *Minnesota Journal of Law and Inequality,* May 2021, https://lawandinequality.org/wp-content/uploads/2021/05/The-2-Billion -Plus-Price-of-Injustice_-A-Methodological-Map-for.pdf.

43. Joshua Correll et al., "The Police Officer's Dilemma: Using Ethnicity to Disambiguate Potentially Threatening Individuals," Journal of Personality and Social Psychology 83, no. 6 (2002): 9, doi:10.1037//0022-3514.83.6.1314; Devon Carbado and L. Song Richardson, "Book Review, The Black Police: Policing Our Own," University of California Irvine Law School, April 1, 2018, 1992, https://scholarship.law.uci.edu /cgi/viewcontent.cgi?article=1691&=&context=faculty_scholarship&=&sei-redir =1&referer=https%253A%252F%252Fscholar.google.com%252Fscholar%253Fhl %253Den%2526as_sdt%253D0%25252C5%2526q%253Dare%252Bblack%252Bpolice %252Bofficers%252Bracist%2526btnG%253D#search=%22black%20police%20offi cers%20racist%22.

44. Bocar A. Ba et al., "The Role of Officer Race and Gender in Police-Civilian Interactions in Chicago," *Science,* February 12, 2021, https://policingresearch.org /wp-content/uploads/2022/01/Role-of-Officer-Race-and-Gender.pdf.

45. Katelyn E. Stauffer et al., "Would Having More Female Officers Improve Policing?," *Washington Post,* June 15, 2021.

46. Cori Pryor et al., "A National Study of Sustained Use of Force Complaints in Law Enforcement Agencies," *Journal of Criminal Justice* 64 (September–October 2019), www.sciencedirect.com/science/article/abs/pii/S0047235219302272.

47. Kyle Rozema and Max Schanzenbach, "Good Cop, Bad Cop: Using Civilian Allegations to Predict Police Misconduct," *American Economic Journal,* 2019, https:// pubs.aeaweb.org/doi/pdfplus/10.1257/pol.20160573.

48. Steven M. Chermak et al., "Law Enforcement Training and the Domestic Far Right," *Crime Prevention Studies,* December 2009.

49. Spencer Ackerman, "Obama Orders Government to Clean Up Terrorism Training," *Wired,* November 28, 2011, www.wired.com/2011/11/obama-islamophobia-review/.

50. Julia Harte and Alexandra Ulmer, "U.S. Police Trainers with Far-Right Ties

Are Teaching Hundreds of Cops," Reuters, May 6, 2022, www.reuters.com/investi gates/special-report/usa-police-extremism.

51. TJ L'Heureux et al., "A Right-Wing Sheriffs Group That Challenges Federal Law Enforcement Is Gaining Acceptance Around the Country," Associated Press, August 21, 2023, https://apnews.com/article/constitutional-sheriffs-5568cd0b6b276 80a28de8a098ed14210.

52. New Jersey Office of the State Comptroller, "The High Price of Unregulated Private Police Training to New Jersey," December 6, 2023, www.nj.gov/comptroller /reports/2023/20231206.shtml.

53. Cami Mondeaux, "Gaetz Demands Answers on FBI Agents Seen Kneeling at Black Lives Matter Protests," *Washington Examiner*, June 29, 2023, www.washington examiner.com/news/house/gaetz-demands-answers-fbi-agents-kneeling-black-lives -matter-protests.

54. Janelle Griffith, "NYPD Lieutenant Apologizes to Colleagues for Kneeling During George Floyd Protest," NBC News, June 12, 2020.

55. Bryan Pietsch, "Massachusetts Detective Is Fired over Black Lives Matter Post," *New York Times*, July 5, 2020.

56. Henry K. Lee, "Richmond Union Criticizes Chief for Wearing Uniform to Protest," *San Francisco Chronicle*, December 12, 2014, www.sfchronicle.com/crime /article/Richmond-cops-slam-chief-for-holding-Black-lives-5953636.php#/0.

57. Elizabeth Weise, " 'All Lives Matter' a Creed for Richmond, Calif. Police," *USA Today*, September 23, 2015, www.usatoday.com/story/news/nation/2015/09/23 /richmond-community-policing/72563038/.

58. Ephrat Livni, "How to Reimagine Policing and Public Safety that Works for Everyone," *New York Times*, December 17, 2020, www.nytimes.com/2020/12/17/busi ness/dealbook/police-reform-debate.html.

59. See Ari Feldman, "Activists Want Bias Training for Cops. ADL Provides It. But Does It Work?," *The Forward*, June 17, 2020, https://forward.com/news/na tional/448948/police-george-floyd-protest-implicit-bias/; Tomas Chamorro-Premuzic, "Implicit Bias Training Doesn't Work," Bloomberg, January 4, 2020, www.bloomberg .com/opinion/articles/2020-01-04/implicit-bias-training-isn-t-improving-corpo rate-diversity?sref=LSnlJj5m; Michael Hobbes, " 'Implicit Bias' Trainings Don't Actu- ally Change Police Behavior," *HuffPost*, June 12, 2020, www.huffpost.com/entry /implicit-bias-training-doesnt-actually-change-police-behavior_n_5ee28fc3c5b60b 32f010ed48; Jeremy Stahl, "The NYPD Paid $4.5 Million for a Bias Trainer. She Says She's Not the Solution," *Slate*, June 18, 2020.

60. Rick Trinkner, Erin M. Kerrison, and Phillip Atiba Goff, "The Force of Fear: Police Stereotype Threat, Self-Legitimacy, and Support for Excessive Force," *Law and Human Behavior* 43, no. 5 (2019): 421–35.

Conclusion: Law Enforcement's Role in Resisting White Supremacy

1. Jane Bowdler and Benjamin Harris, "Racial Inequality in the United States," U.S. Department of Treasury, July 21, 2022, home.treasury.gov/news/featured-sto ries/racial-inequality-in-the-united-states.

2. See, for example, Alleen Brown et al., "Leaked Documents Reveal Counterterrorism Tactics Used at Standing Rock to 'Defeat Pipeline Insurgencies,' " *The Intercept*, May 27, 2017; Colin Moynihan, "Officials Cast a Wide Net in Monitoring Occupy Movement," *New York Times*, May 22, 2014; George Joseph and Murtaza Hussein, "FBI Tracked an Activist Involved with Black Lives Matter as They Travelled Across the U.S., Documents Show," *The Intercept*, March 19, 2018.

3. Ruth Igielnik, "70% of Americans Say U.S. Economic System Unfairly Favors the Powerful," Pew Research Center, January 9, 2020.

4. Noah Baustin and Michael Barba, "San Francisco Used Force on Homeless People More than 1,300 Times in 5 Years," *San Francisco Standard*, August 24, 2023, sfstandard.com/2023/08/24/san-francisco-police-use-of-force-homeless-people/.

5. Jerome P. Bjelopera, "Domestic Terrorism: An Overview," Congressional Rsearch Service, R44921, available at sgp.fas.org/crs/terror/R44921.pdf.

6. Ibid., 59.

7. Adam Gabbatt, "Republicans 'Glorify Political Violence' by Embracing Extreme Gun Culture," *Guardian*, April 24, 2023; Michael S. Schmidt, Alan Feuer, Maggie Haberman, and Adam Goldman, "Trump Supporters' Violent Rhetoric in His Defense Disturbs Experts," *New York Times*, June 10, 2023; Paul Waldman, "Apocalyptic Rhetoric Is Just as Dangerous as the Violent Kind," *Washington Post*, August 16, 2023.

8. Ryan J. Reilly, "The Feds Say They're in for the Long Haul in the Jan. 6 Investigation. There Is a Time Limit," NBC News, January 6, 2023.

9. Melissa Quinn and Graham Kates, "Trump's 4 Indictments in Detail: A Quick-Look Guide to Charges, Trial Dates and Key Players for Each Case," CBS News, August 29, 2023.

10. Chanell Chandler and David Knowles, "Trump Found Guilty on all 34 Counts of Falsifying Business Records. Here's a Breakdown," Yahoo! News, May 30, 2024, www.yahoo.com/news/trump-found-guilty-on-all-34-counts-of-falsifying-business -records-heres-a-breakdown-211334652.html.

11. Zachary B. Wolf, "The Supreme Court Just Gave Presidents a Superpower," CNN, July 2, 2024.

12. Steve Benen, "In His Latest Pitch, Trump Wants to 'Indemnify All Police Officers,'" MSNBC, December 18, 2023, www.msnbc.com/rachel-maddow-show/mad dowblog/latest-pitch-trump-wants-indemnify-police-officers-rcna130283.

INDEX

ABOUT THE AUTHORS

Mike German is a fellow with the Liberty and National Security program at the Brennan Center for Justice at NYU Law School. He previously worked at the ACLU Washington Legislative Office and served sixteen years as an FBI special agent. He is the author of *Thinking Like a Terrorist: Insights of a Former FBI Undercover Agent* and *Disrupt, Discredit, and Divide: How the New FBI Damages Our Democracy* (The New Press).

Beth Zasloff is the author of *Hold Fast to Dreams: A College Guidance Counselor, His Students, and the Vision of a Life Beyond Poverty* (The New Press), winner of the Studs and Ida Terkel award. Her work has been featured in the *New York Times* and *The Atlantic* and on NPR. She is a graduate of the Johns Hopkins University Writing Seminars and has taught writing at New York University, at Johns Hopkins, and in New York City public schools. Read about her editing and co-author work at bethzasloff.com.

PUBLISHING IN THE PUBLIC INTEREST

Thank you for reading this book published by The New Press; we hope you enjoyed it. New Press books and authors play a crucial role in sparking conversations about the key political and social issues of our day.

We hope that you will stay in touch with us. Here are a few ways to keep up to date with our books, events, and the issues we cover:

- Sign up at www.thenewpress.com/subscribe to receive updates on New Press authors and issues and to be notified about local events
- www.facebook.com/newpressbooks
- www.twitter.com/thenewpress
- www.instagram.com/thenewpress

Please consider buying New Press books not only for yourself, but also for friends and family and to donate to schools, libraries, community centers, prison libraries, and other organizations involved with the issues our authors write about.

The New Press is a 501(c)(3) nonprofit organization; if you wish to support our work with a tax-deductible gift please visit www.thenewpress.com/donate or use the QR code below.